Foundation in Accountancy/ACCA

Business Technology (BT/FBT)

Practice & Revision Kit

For exams from 1 September 2022 to 31 August 2023

First edition 2011

Eleventh edition 2022

ISBN: 9781509745593

Previous ISBN: 9781509737116

e-ISBN: 9781509744558

British Library Cataloguing-in-Publication Data

A catalogue record for this book is available from the British Library

Published by

BPP Learning Media Ltd

BPP House, Aldine Place

142–144 Uxbridge Road

London W12 8AA

www.bpp.com/learningmedia

Printed in the United Kingdom

Note. Your learning materials, published by BPP Learning Media Ltd, are printed on paper obtained from traceable sustainable sources.

The contents of this course material are intended as a guide and not professional advice. Although every effort has been made to ensure that the contents of this course material are correct at the time of going to press, BPP Learning Media makes no warranty that the information in this course material is accurate or complete and accept no liability for any loss or damage suffered by any person acting or refraining from acting as a result of the material in this course material.

Contains public sector information licensed under the Open Government Licence v3.0

We are grateful to the Association of Chartered Certified Accountants for permission to reproduce past examination questions and extracts from the syllabus. The suggested solutions in the further question practice bank have been prepared by BPP Learning Media Ltd, except where otherwise stated.

Contents

Question index

	Marks	Time allocation (mins)	Page number	
			Questions	Answers
Part E: Personal effectiveness and communication in business				
23 Personal effectiveness and communication	31	37	81	185
24 Section E MTQs	24	29	84	187
Part F: Professional ethics in accounting and business				
25 Ethical considerations	34	41	89	189
26 Section F MTQs	24	29	93	191
Mixed banks				
27 Mixed Bank 1	38	46	98	194
28 Mixed Bank 2	40	48	103	196
29 Mixed Bank 3	40	48	109	199
30 Mixed Bank 4	40	48	114	200
31 Mixed Bank 5	40	48	118	202
32 Mixed Bank 6	38	46	123	205
33 Mixed Bank 7	42	50	129	208
Mock Exams				
Mock exam 1 (Specimen Exam)			215	233
Mock exam 2			245	263
Mock exam 3			275	291

Helping you with your revision

BPP Learning Media – ACCA Approved Content Provider

As an ACCA Approved Content Provider, BPP Learning Media gives you the **opportunity** to use revision materials reviewed by the ACCA examining team. By incorporating the ACCA examining team's comments and suggestions regarding the depth and breadth of syllabus coverage, the BPP Learning Media Practice & Revision Kit provides excellent, **ACCA-approved** support for your revision.

These materials are reviewed by the ACCA examining team. The objective of the review is to ensure that the material properly covers the syllabus and study guide outcomes, used by the examining team in setting the exams, in the appropriate breadth and depth. The review does not ensure that every eventuality, combination or application of examinable topics is addressed by the ACCA Approved Content. Nor does the review comprise a detailed technical check of the content as the Approved Content Provider has its own quality assurance processes in place in this respect.

BPP Learning Media do everything possible to ensure the material is accurate and up to date when sending to print. In the event that any errors are found after the print date, they are uploaded to the following website: www.bpp.com/learningmedia/Errata.

Selecting questions

We provide signposts to help you plan your revision, including a full **question index**.

Attempting mock exams

There are three mock exams that provide practice at coping with the pressures of the exam day. We strongly recommend that you attempt them under exam conditions. **Mock exam 1** is the ACCA Specimen Exam. **Mock exam 2** and **Mock exam 3** reflect the question styles and syllabus coverage of the exam.

Using your BPP Practice & Revision Kit

Aim of this Practice & Revision Kit

To provide the practice to help you succeed in the examination for FBT/BT Business and Technology.

To pass the examination you need a thorough understanding in all areas covered by the syllabus and teaching guide.

Recommended approach

- Make sure you are able to answer questions on **everything** specified by the syllabus and teaching guide. You cannot make any assumptions about what questions may come up in your exam. The examining team aims to discourage 'question spotting'.

- All sections have a selection of **OBJECTIVE QUESTIONS** (including Multiple Choice Questions). Make good use of the **HELPING HANDS** provided to help you answer the questions.

- There is a mark allocation for each question. Each mark carries with it a time allocation of 1.2 minutes. A 2-mark question should therefore be completed in 2.4 minutes.

- 76% of the exam consists of individual **objective test questions**. You should attempt each bank of objective test questions to ensure you are familiar with their styles and to practise your technique. Skills checkpoint 1 Approach to Objective Test Questions will provide useful guidance on how best to approach these questions.

- The remaining 24% of the exam consists of six multi-task questions, which are essentially a range of related objective test questions. Skills checkpoint 2 Approach to Multi-Task Questions will provide guidance on how to tackle these.

- Once you have completed all of the questions in the body of this Practice & Revision Kit, you should attempt the **MOCK EXAMS** under examination conditions. Check your answers against our answers to find out how well you did.

Passing the FBT/BT exam

FBT/BT Business and Technology introduces students (who may not have a business background) to the business entity made up of people and systems which interact with each other. There is a lot to learn, but none of it is particularly difficult and a good grasp of these topics will help you in higher-level business exams.

To access Foundations in Accountancy syllabi, visit the ACCA website: www.accaglobal.com

Computer-based exams

The Business and Technology exam is a computer-based exam (CBE).

Computer-based examinations (CBEs) are available for the Foundations In Accountancy exams. The CBE exams for the first seven modules can be taken at any time, these are referred to as 'exams on demand'. The Option exams can be sat in June and December of each year, these are referred to as 'exams on sitting'. Business and Technology is an 'exam on demand'. Computer-based examinations must be taken at an ACCA CBE Licensed Centre.

How do CBEs work?

- Questions are displayed on a monitor.
- Candidates enter their answer directly onto the computer.
- Candidates have two hours to complete the examination.
- Candidates are provided with a Provisional Result Notification showing their results before leaving the examination room.
- The CBE Licensed Centre uploads the results to the ACCA (as proof of the candidate's performance) within 72 hours.
- Candidates sitting the Option exams will receive their results approximately five weeks after the exams sitting once they have been marked by an expert.
- Candidates can check their exam status on the ACCA website by logging into myACCA.

Benefits

- Flexibility as the first seven modules, exams on demand, can be sat at any time.
- Resits for the first seven modules can also be taken at any time and there is no restriction on the number of times a candidate can sit a CBE.
- Instant feedback for the exams on demand as the computer displays the results at the end of the CBE.
- Results are notified to ACCA within 72 hours.

For more information on computer-based exams, visit the ACCA website:

www.accaglobal.com/gb/en/student/exam-support-resources/fundamentals-exams-study-resources/f1/technical-articles/cbe.html

Approach to examining the syllabus

The exam is structured as follows:

	No. of marks
Section A:	
30 compulsory objective questions of 2 marks each	60
16 compulsory objective questions of 1 mark each	16
Section B:	
6 compulsory multi-task questions of 4 marks each	24
	100

Note: The difference between the 2 mark and 1 mark objective test questions is that the 1 mark questions will be easier - for example, multiple choice questions will have only three possible choices instead of four.

Revision

This Practice and Revision kit has been reviewed by the BT/FBT examining team and contains the ACCA Specimen Exam, so if you just work through it to the end you would be very well prepared for the exam. You must also visit the ACCA website (www.accaglobal.com) to familiarise yourself with the CBE software. It is important to tackle questions under exam conditions. Allow yourself just the number of minutes shown next to the questions in the index and don't look at the answers until you have finished. Then correct your answer and go back to the Workbook for any topic you are having trouble with. Try the same questions again a week later – you will be surprised how much better you are getting. Doing the questions like this will really show you what you know, and will make the exam experience less worrying.

Doing the exam

If you have diligently done your revision you can pass this exam. There are a couple of points to bear in mind:

- Read the question properly.
- Don't spend more than the allotted time on each question. If you are having trouble with a question, use the 'flag for review' function in the exam software and carry on. You can come back to it at the end.

Essential skills areas to be successful in the Business and Technology exam

We think there are three areas you should develop in order to achieve exam success in FBT/BT:

(a) Knowledge application

(b) Specific FBT/BT skills

(c) Exam success skills

These are shown in the diagram below:

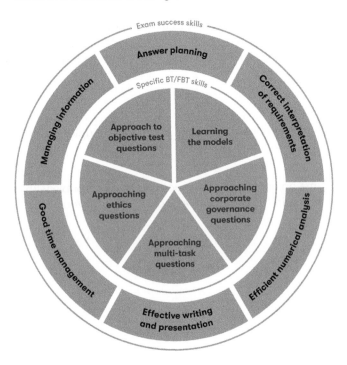

Specific BT/FBT skills

These are the skills specific to BT/FBT that we think you need to develop in order to pass the exam.

In the Workbook, there are five **Skills Checkpoints** which define each skill and show how it is applied in answering a question. A brief summary of each skill is given below.

Skill 1: Approaching objective test questions

All questions in the BT/FBT exam are OT questions, using a number of different formats.

BPP recommends a step-by-step technique for approaching objective test questions:

Step 1	Answer the easier questions first.
Step 2	Answer all questions.
Step 3	Start each question by reading the requirement.
Step 4	Apply your technical knowledge to the data in the question.

Skills checkpoint 1 covers this technique in detail through application to an exam-standard question.

BPP LEARNING MEDIA

Skill 2: Learning the models

There are many models in the BT/FBT syllabus that you need to know for the exam. This Skills Checkpoint provides you with advice on how to learn the models.

BPP recommends a step-by-step technique for learning the models:

Step 1	Look at the chapter overview to see the context in which the model belongs.
Step 2	Read through the technical section on the model quickly.
Step 3	Read the technical section again more slowly reflecting on what the model is saying and understanding it.
Step 4	Close your book and write a summary of as much of the model as you can remember.
Step 5	Write some notes, using the memory techniques detailed in the Skill.
Step 6	Attempt the questions in the further question practice to test your knowledge.

Skills checkpoint 2 covers this technique in detail through application to an exam-standard question.

Skill 3: Approaching corporate governance questions

Corporate governance questions involving application of knowledge are not done well according to the examiner's reports. Some techniques are introduced in this Skills Checkpoint to help you succeed better. While the skills are focussed at corporate governance questions, they can be applied to many other application questions in the BT/FBT exam.

BPP recommends a step-by-step technique for approaching corporate governance questions:

Step 1	Read the requirement of the question carefully.
Step 2	Read the scenario, think about: • Why does the situation present a threat to good corporate governance? • What should/could be done to reduce the threat?
Step 3	Read the options provided in the question. Eliminate those options which are obviously incorrect. Rank the remaining options and choose the most relevant/ likely option (s).

Skills checkpoint 4 covers this technique in detail through application to an exam-standard question.

Skills checkpoint 3 covers this technique in detail through application to an exam-standard question.

Skill 4: Approaching multi-task questions

The questions can be challenging because they tend to contain longer scenarios than the Section A questions, so you need to manage more information.

Section B of the exam contains six multi-task questions of four marks each. In this section you have to answer many different types of OT question, and details of the different types of question are given in this skills point.

BPP recommends a step-by-step technique for approaching multi-task questions:

Step 1	Read the requirements of all tasks.
Step 2	Recall any relevant technical theory.
Step 3	Read the scenario.
Step 4	Answer each task in turn, doing the easiest task first.

Skills Checkpoint 4 covers this technique in detail through application to an exam-standard question.

Skill 5: Approaching ethics questions

Questions on ethics are likely to feature highly in your exam. Ethics questions are difficult as they often require some judgement rather than being black and white.

A step-by-step technique for attempting these questions is outlined below. It is similar to the structure we have seen for our other Skills.

A step-by-step technique for attempting these questions is outlined below. It is similar to the structure we have seen for our other Skills.

| Step 1 | Read through the scenario, think about:

 • Whose ethics are under discussion (the company, and employee etc.)

 • What should they do/what should they have done if they are behaving ethically? |
| Step 2 | Read the options in the question:

 • Eliminate any options that are obviously not correct.

 • Choose from the remaining options based on which are most likely/most relevant. |

Skills checkpoint 5 covers this technique in detail through application to an exam-standard question.

Exam success skills

Passing the FBT/BT exam requires more than applying syllabus knowledge and demonstrating the specific FBT/BT skills; it also requires the development of excellent exam technique through question practice.

We consider the following six skills to be vital for exam success. The Skills Checkpoints show how each of these skills can be applied specifically to the FBT/BT exam.

Exam success skill 1

Managing information

You will not have to deal with large amounts of information in each individual question in FBT. Some of the questions in the exam will present you with a short scenario, particularly in the Section B questions. The skill is how you handle this information while working under time pressure.

You must take an active approach to reading each scenario. Focus on the requirement first, noting instructions, including words like "NOT". Then think about any technical knowledge that is relevant before reading the scenario for the question. Doing this means that your mind will be focussed as you read the scenario, which means you will take in the information better.

Exam success skill 2

Correct interpretation of the requirements

It is important to note the requirement carefully. Look out for the number of options you have to choose, as not all questions require only one option. Also, beware of tricks, such as the information being presented in one particular order in the scenario, but being presented in a different order in the options.

Exam success skill 3

Answer planning

Answer planning is a skill that you will need when you study higher level exams. It is not quite as relevant for the style of question in the FBT/BT exam.

Exam success skill 4

Efficient numerical analysis

While there could be a small number of numerical questions on topics such as elasticity of demand, the majority of questions in BT/ FBT are qualitative in nature so this skills is not as important as in some of the other ACCA exams.

An important tip in numerical questions is not to look at the options until you have completed the calculation as you think it should be done. The reason for this is that the "wrong answers" are chosen carefully to look very realistic, and you may be tempted to choose one of these if you don't do the calculation first.

Exam success skill 5

Effective writing and presentation

This skill is not relevant for BT/FBT as all the questions are objective test questions so you will not have to write.

Exam success skill 6

Good time management

The exam is 2 hours long. You should therefore spend 1.2 minutes per mark. It is best to work through Section A first, which should take you 91 minutes, before spending the remaining 29 minutes on Section B.

Don't get stuck on difficult questions - if a particular question does appear difficult, move on, and come back to it after you have answered all the easier questions.

Don't time yourself for each question, but do check every half hour that you have answered 25 marks worth of questions.

Two minutes before the end of your time for Section A, go back and answer all outstanding questions, even if you have to guess. There is no harm in guessing as there is no negative marking in ACCA exams, so the worst that can happen is you don't gain two marks for the question. If you find that this approach doesn't work for you, don't worry – you can develop your own technique.

Tackling multiple choice questions

MCQs are part of all Foundations in Accountancy exams.

The MCQs in your exam contain four possible answers. You have to **choose the option that best answers the question**. The incorrect options are called distracters. There is a skill in answering MCQs quickly and correctly. By practising MCQs you can develop this skill, giving you a better chance of passing the exam.

You may wish to follow the approach outlined below, or you may prefer to adapt it.

Step 1 Skim read all the MCQs and identify what appear to be the easier questions.

Step 2 Attempt each question – **starting with the easier questions** identified in Step 1. Read the question **thoroughly**. You may prefer to work out the answer before looking at the options, or you may prefer to look at the options at the beginning. Adopt the method that works best for you.

Step 3 Read the options and see if one matches your own answer. Be careful with numerical questions as the distracters are designed to match answers that incorporate common errors. Check that your calculation is correct. Have you followed the requirement exactly? Have you included every stage of the calculation?

Step 4 You may find that none of the options match your answer.

- Re-read the question to ensure that you understand it and are answering the requirement.

- Eliminate any obviously wrong answers.

- Consider which of the remaining answers is the most likely to be correct and select the option.

Step 5 If you are still unsure make a note and continue to the next question.

Step 6 Revisit unanswered questions. When you come back to a question after a break you often find you are able to answer it correctly straight away. If you are still unsure have a guess. You are not penalised for incorrect answers, so **never leave a question unanswered**!

A note of caution

After extensive practice and revision of MCQs, you may find that you recognise a question when you sit the exam. Be aware that the detail and/or requirement may be different. If the question seems familiar read the requirement and options carefully – **do not** assume that it is identical.

Using your BPP products

This Practice & Revision Kit gives you the question practice and guidance you need in the exam. Our other products can also help you pass:

- **Workbook** introduces and explains the knowledge required for your exam

You can purchase this product by visiting.www.bpp.com/learning-media.

Questions

> Part A: The business organisation, its stakeholders and the external environment

1 Business organisations and their stakeholders (16 mins)

1.1 Which of the following words completes this sentence appropriately?

'An organisation is a social arrangement which pursues collective [▼], which

controls its own performance and has a boundary separating it from its environment.'

Pull down list

- Goals
- Profits
- Stakeholders
- Tactics

(2 marks)

1.2 What is the term given to the idea that the combined output of a number of individuals working together will exceed that of the same individuals working separately?

○ Sympathy

○ Specialisation

○ Synergy

○ Systems thinking

(2 marks)

1.3 Which of the following statements is true?

○ Limited company status means that a company is only allowed to trade up to a predetermined turnover level in any one year.

○ For organisations that have limited company status, ownership and control are legally separate.

○ The benefit of being a sole trader is that you have no personal liability for the debts of your business.

○ Ordinary partnerships offer the same benefits as limited companies but are usually formed by professionals such as doctors and solicitors.

(2 marks)

1.4 An organisation is owned and run by central government agencies.

The organisation should be described as which of the following statements?

○ A voluntary sector organisation

○ A private sector organisation

○ A public sector organisation

(1 mark)

1.5   Which of the following groups may be considered to be stakeholders in the activities of a nuclear power station?

(1) The government

(2) Environmental pressure groups

(3) Employees

(4) Local residents

O   (1), (3) and (4)

O   (1), (2), (3) and (4)

O   (3) only

O   (1) and (3) only

(2 marks)

1.6   The term secondary stakeholders describes which group of stakeholders?

O   Stakeholders who conduct transactions with the organisation

O   Stakeholders who have a contractual relationship with the organisation

O   Stakeholders who do not have a contractual relationship with the organisation

(1 mark)

1.7   Which of the following organisations would rely most heavily on value for money indicators and efficiency rather than information on performance and profitability?

O   A private accountancy college

O   A local authority

O   A small retailer

(1 mark)

1.8   ADB is a business which is owned by its workers. The workers share the profits and they each have a vote on how the business is run.

Required

Which of the following should be used to describe ADB?

O   Public sector

O   Private sector

O   Not-for-profit

O   Co-operative

(2 marks)

(Total = 13 marks)

2 Business environment and legal framework   (36 mins)

2.1   What is an acronym used to describe the key elements of an organisation's external environment?

O   SWOT

O   SMART

O   PEST

(1 mark)

2.2 Which of the following is **NOT** a legitimate method of influencing government policy in the interests of a business?

   ○ Employing lobbyists to put the organisation's case to ministers or civil servants

   ○ Giving lawmakers non-executive directorships

   ○ Offering financial incentives to public officials to use their influence on the organisation's behalf

   ○ Attempting to influence public opinion, to put pressure on the legislative agenda

(2 marks)

2.3 Which word correctly completes the sentence?

   [▼] is an analysis of statistics on birth and death rates, age structures of people and ethnic groups within a community.

Pull down list

   • Demographics

   • Economics

   • Ergonomics

   • Psychographics

(2 marks)

2.4 A recent trend in organisation and management is the rise in 'virtual organisation' and 'virtual teamworking'.

To which of the following environmental (PEST) factors is this most directly attributed?

   ○ Economic

   ○ Socio-cultural

   ○ Technological

   ○ Political

(2 marks)

2.5 Which of the following rights of data subjects is also known as the right 'to be forgotten'?

   ○ Rectification

   ○ Portability

   ○ Erasure

(1 mark)

2.6 In the context of 'best practice' employment protection law, in which of the following circumstances is dismissal of an employee automatically considered unfair?

   ○ Selection for redundancy on the basis of age

   ○ Misconduct

   ○ Marriage to an employee of a key competitor

   ○ Incompetence

(2 marks)

2.7 Which of the following socio-cultural trends will have a direct impact on most business organisations?

(1) Increasing ethnic and religious diversity in populations

(2) Falling birthrates

(3) Focus on 'green' issues

(4) Increase in single-member households

O (3) only

O (1) and (3) only

O (1), (2) and (3) only

O (1), (2), (3) and (4)

(2 marks)

2.8 Porter's five forces model identifies factors which determine the nature and strength of competition in an industry.

Which of the following is **NOT** one of the five forces identified in Porter's model?

O Substitute products or services

O New entrants to the industry

O Bargaining power of customers

O Government regulation of the industry

(2 marks)

2.9 For what function in an organisation would demographic information about social class be most relevant?

O Human Resources

O Marketing

O Purchasing

(1 mark)

2.10 Which of the following is a support activity in Porter's value chain model?

O Procurement

O Operations

O Marketing and sales

O Inbound logistics

(2 marks)

2.11 Which of the following statements about the impact of technological developments on the role of accountants is **NOT** true?

O Automation and artificial intelligence allow the accountant to focus their time on verifying low-level transactions.

O Distributed ledger technology reduces the need for auditors to audit all transactions.

O Cloud accounting allows accountants to work collaboratively and with their clients.

O Big data and data analytics assist auditors to target key business risks

(2 marks)

2.12 BCD Co is a large trading company. Steve is the administration manager and is also responsible for legal and compliance functions. Sheila is responsible for after sales service and has responsibility for ensuring that customers who have purchased goods from BCD Co are fully satisfied. Sunny deals with suppliers and negotiates on the price and quality of inventory. He is also responsible for identifying the most appropriate suppliers of plant and machinery for the factory. Sam is the information technology manager and is responsible for all information systems within the company.

Required

According to Porter's value chain, which of the managers is involved in a primary activity as opposed to a support activity?

○ Steve

○ Sheila

○ Sunny

○ Sam

(2 marks)

2.13 What is the latest stage at which a new recruit to a company should first be issued with a copy of the company's health and safety policy statement?

○ When a position with the company is offered

○ As early as possible after employment

○ After the first few weeks of employment

○ During the final selection interview

(2 marks)

2.14 In Porter's five forces model, which of the following would **NOT** constitute a 'barrier to entry'?

○ Scale economies available to existing competitors

○ High capital investment requirements

○ Low switching costs in the market

(1 mark)

2.15 Three of the following strategies are closely related. Which is the exception?

○ Downsizing

○ Delegating

○ Delayering

○ Outsourcing

(2 marks)

2.16 Which of the following would be identified as a cultural trend?

○ Health and safety legislation

○ Concern with health and diet

○ Increasing age of the population

(1 mark)

2.17 For demographic purposes, which of the following is **NOT** a variable in the identification of social class?

○ Income level

○ Lifestyle

○ Occupation

○ Education

(2 marks)

2.18 Technological developments (automation and AI) mean that the role of the accountant and auditor to record and verify day-to-day transactions has become more important.

○ True

○ False

(1 mark)

(Total = 30 marks)

3 The macro-economic environment (28 mins)

3.1 Which of the following is **NOT** an element of fiscal policy?

○ Government spending

○ Government borrowing

○ Taxation

○ Exchange rates

(2 marks)

3.2 Which of the following is associated with a negative Public Sector Net Cash Requirement?

○ The government is running a budget deficit.

○ The government's expenditure exceeds its income.

○ The government is running a budget surplus.

○ Public Sector Debt Repayment (PSDR) is high.

(2 marks)

3.3 Which word correctly completes this statement?

[▼] taxes are collected by the Revenue authority from a business, which

attempts to pass on the tax to consumers in the price of goods.

Pull down list

• Direct

• Indirect

• Progressive

(1 mark)

3.4   If a government has a macro-economic policy objective of expanding the overall level of economic activity, which of the following would **NOT** be consistent with such an objective?

   ○ Increasing public expenditure

   ○ Lowering interest rates

   ○ Increasing taxation

(1 mark)

3.5   The currency in country X is the Krone while country Y uses the Euro. Country Y has recently experienced an increase in its exchange rate with Country X.

   Which of the following effects would result in Country Y?

   ○ A stimulus to exports in Country Y

   ○ An increase in the costs of imports from Country X

   ○ Reducing demand for imports from Country X

   ○ A reduction in the rate of cost push inflation

(2 marks)

3.6   All of the following except one are 'protectionist measures' in international trade.

   Which is the exception?

   ○ Import quotas

   ○ Subsidies for exporters

   ○ Customs procedures

   ○ Tariffs

(2 marks)

3.7   Are the following statements true or false?

Frictional unemployment will be short term	**TRUE**	**FALSE**
Governments can encourage labour mobility if they want to reduce unemployment	**TRUE**	**FALSE**

(2 marks)

3.8   Which **TWO** of the following does government economic monetary policy relate to?

   ☐ Interest rates

   ☐ Taxation

   ☐ Public borrowing and spending

   ☐ Exchange rates

(2 marks)

3.9   Which of the following organisations would benefit from a period of high price inflation?

   ○ An organisation which has a large number of long-term payables

   ○ An exporter of goods to a country with relatively low inflation

   ○ A large retailer with a high level of inventory on display and low rate of inventory turnover

(1 mark)

3.10 Which **THREE** of the following are the goals of macroeconomic policy?

☐ Encouraging economic growth

☐ Low unemployment

☐ Achievement of a balance between exports and imports

☐ Achieving zero inflation

☐ Maximising a currency's foreign exchange value

(2 marks)

3.11 Which of the following is an example of cyclical unemployment?

○ The entry of school leavers into the labour pool each year

○ Lay-offs among agricultural labourers in winter

○ Automation of ticketing services in tourism

○ Recession in the building industry

(2 marks)

3.12 Which word correctly complete this statement?

A surplus on the balance of payments usually refers to a surplus or deficit on the

| ▼ | account.

Pull down list

- Capital
- Current
- Financial

(1 mark)

3.13 Northland, Southland, Eastland and Westland are four countries of Asia. The following economic statistics have been produced for the year 20X7.

Country	Northland	Southland	Eastland	Westland
Change in GDP (%)	−0.30	+2.51	−0.55	+2.12
Balance of payments current account ($m)	+5550.83	−350.47	−150.90	+220.39
Change in consumer prices (%)	+27.50	+15.37	+2.25	+2.15
Change in working population employed (%)	−4.76	+3.78	+1.76	−8.76

Which country experienced stagflation in the relevant period?

○ Northland

○ Southland

○ Eastland

○ Westland

(2 marks)

3.14 Which word correctly completes this statement?

| ▼ | economic growth is determined by supply-side rather than by demand side factors.

Pull down list

• Actual

• Potential

• National

(1 mark)

(Total = 23 marks)

4 Micro-economic factors (50 mins)

4.1 In a free market economy, the price mechanism:

○ Aids government control

○ Allocates resources

○ Measures national wealth

(1 mark)

4.2 The supply curve of a firm operating in a competitive market is its:

○ Marginal cost curve above the average variable cost curve

○ Marginal cost curve above the average total cost curve

○ Average total cost curve beyond the point where the marginal cost curve cuts it from below

○ Average variable cost curve below the average revenue curve

(2 marks)

4.3 A legal minimum price is set which is below the equilibrium price.

What will be the impact of this?

○ Excess of demand over supply

○ Excess of supply over demand

○ Nothing

(1 mark)

BPP
LEARNING
MEDIA

4.4 Which of the following would cause the supply curve for a good to shift to the right (outwards from the origin)?

 ○ A fall in the price of the good

 ○ An increase in the demand for the good

 ○ A fall in production costs of the good

 ○ The imposition of a minimum price

                 (2 marks)

4.5 When the price of a good is held above the equilibrium price, the result will be

 ○ Excess demand

 ○ A shortage of the good

 ○ A surplus of the good

                 (1 mark)

4.6 Which of the following would **NOT** lead directly to a shift in the demand curve for overseas holidays?

 ○ An advertising campaign by holiday tour operators

 ○ A fall in the disposable incomes of consumers

 ○ A rise in the price of domestic holidays

 ○ A rise in the price of overseas holidays

                 (2 marks)

4.7 Which of the following would lead to a fall in the price of good Q which is a normal good?

 ○ A rise in the price of good P, a substitute for good Q

 ○ A fall in the level of household incomes generally

 ○ A fall in the price of good T, a complement to good Q

 ○ A belief that the price of good Q is likely to double in the next three months

                 (2 marks)

4.8 According to the theory of the firm, which of the following statements describes an oligopoly?

 ○ There are no barriers to entry into or exit from the market

 ○ There is only one producer in the market

 ○ There are four producers exerting considerable influence in the market

 ○ There are many producers but they each use product differentiation to distinguish themselves from each other

                 (2 marks)

4.9 Which of the following is **NOT** a substitute for carpets?

 ○ Ceramic floor tiles

 ○ Wooden floorboard

 ○ Carpet underlay

                 (1 mark)

BPP LEARNING MEDIA

4.10   Which of the following is **NOT** a complement to cars?

O Petrol

O Tyres

O Holidays

(1 mark)

4.11   The demand for fashion goods is **NOT** influenced by:

O Price

O Allocative inefficiency among producers

O The distribution of income among households

O Expectation of future price changes

(2 marks)

4.12   If the price of coffee falls, which the following outcomes should be expected to occur?

O A fall in the quantity of coffee demanded

O A rise in the price of tea

O A fall in the demand for drinking cups

O A fall in the demand for tea

(2 marks)

4.13   What is an inferior good?

O A good of such poor quality that demand for it is very weak

O A good for which the cross elasticity of demand with a substitute product is greater than 1

O A good for which demand will fall as household income rises

(1 mark)

4.14   Consider the price and demand for flower vases.

The price of cut flowers goes up sharply.

Which of the following should happen?

O The demand curve for flower vases will shift to the left; their price will rise

O The demand curve for flower vases will shift to the right; their price will rise

O There will be movement in the demand curve for vases; their price will go down

O The demand curve for vases will shift to the left; their price will go down

(2 marks)

4.15   Consider the price and demand for tickets to travel by sea ferry.

The price of travelling by hovercraft (a substitute form of travel) goes up.

Which of the following should happen?

O The demand curve for sea ferry tickets will shift to the left, and their price will go down. More sea ferry tickets will be sold.

O The demand curve for sea ferry tickets will shift to the right, and their price will go up. More ferry tickets will be sold.

○ The demand curve for sea ferry tickets will shift to the right and their price will go down. More sea ferry tickets will be sold.

○ The demand curve for sea ferry tickets will shift to the right and their price will go up. Fewer sea ferry tickets will be sold.

(2 marks)

4.16 The summer demand for hotel accommodation in London comes mainly from foreign tourists. Demand for hotel rooms in London in summer could be reduced by a fall in the price or value of which of the following?

(1) US dollars

(2) Aeroplane tickets

(3) Sterling

○ Item 1 only

○ Items 1 and 2 only

○ Items 2 and 3 only

○ Item 3 only

(2 marks)

4.17 ABC produces a variety of soft drink. It has two competitors but all three producers use product differentiation to distinguish themselves from each other. What type of market is this?

○ Perfect competition

○ Monopoly

○ Monopolistic competition

○ Oligopoly

(2 marks)

4.18 In a certain advanced industrialised country, the government has applied price controls over rents of both public and private rented accommodation for a number of years, and a serious problem of widespread homelessness has built up.

Just recently, the rent price controls have been eased.

Required

Which **TWO** of the following consequences should now occur?

☐ An increase in homelessness

☐ In the longer term, an increase in new building work

☐ The provision of more rented accommodation

☐ Fewer owner-occupied dwellings

(2 marks)

4.19 The demand curve for a resource may shift because of:

○ A change in the demand for a good whose production is dependent on the resource

○ Concerns about potential harmful pollution from the resource

○ A change in the price of a substitute resource

○ All of the above

(2 marks)

4.20 The income elasticity of demand for a product is high.

This means that:

○ Sales will fall only slightly when incomes of households fall

○ Sales will rise sharply when incomes of households rise

○ The good is an inferior good

(1 mark)

4.21 Using the point method, what is the price elasticity of demand of product X as price falls from its current price of $20 to $15?

	Old	New
Price	20	15
Quantity	10	15

Price elasticity of demand = [   ]

(2 marks)

4.22 Consumer surplus is:

○ The excess between what consumers are prepared to pay for a good or service, and the prevailing market price

○ The indirect tax producers pay on a good or service

○ The marginal utility gained by consuming one more unit of a good or service

○ The indirect tax consumers pay on a good or service

(2 marks)

4.23 Which combination of demand and supply curves would be appropriate for a firm attempting to increase its profits by increasing its market share?

○ Inelastic demand, inelastic supply

○ Elastic demand, elastic supply

○ Inelastic demand, elastic supply

○ Elastic demand, inelastic supply

(2 marks)

4.24 If the absolute value of the price elasticity of demand for dry white wine is greater than one, a decrease in the price of all wine would result in:

○ A more than proportional decrease in the quantity of dry white wine purchased

○ A less than proportional decrease in the quantity of dry white wine purchased

○ A less than proportional increase in the quantity of dry white wine purchased

○ A more than proportional increase in the quantity of dry white wine purchased

(2 marks)

4.25   Mr Smith has a limited income which restricts the number of different goods he can buy.

Required

Which of the following describes the position at which Mr Smith's utility from purchasing different goods is maximised?

○ Marginal utility from each good is equal

○ Marginal utility from each good is 0

○ Ratio of marginal utility to price is equal for each good

(1 mark)

(Total = 42 marks)

5 Section A Multi-task questions MTQs   (29 mins)

5.1   (a) Are the following statements about elasticities true or false?

If income elasticity is positive, the commodity is an inferior good	TRUE	FALSE
If two goods are complements, the cross elasticity will be negative	TRUE	FALSE
If price elasticity is greater than 1, demand is inelastic	TRUE	FALSE
Unrelated products have a cross elasticity of infinity	TRUE	FALSE

(2 marks)

(b) Which **THREE** of the following reasons would result in a shift of the demand curve to the right for a normal good?

☐ A fall in the price of substitutes

☐ A change in taste towards a competitor good

☐ An increase in household incomes

☐ An expected future rise in the price of the good

☐ A rise in the price of complements

☐ An increase in population

(2 marks)

(Total = 4 marks)

5.2   (a) A company has recently dismissed employees in the following circumstances:

Sarah was dismissed following disciplinary proceedings, although she was not guilty of negligence, and was not given her contractual period of notice by the company.

Trevor was dismissed from the company immediately after committing an act that was found to be grossly negligent.

Umberto, a relatively new employee who was showing a lot of promise, was dismissed after telling management that he had joined a trade union.

Vanessa, having previously being rated as one of the best performing employees in the company, was dismissed after management discovered she was pregnant.

Required

Match the following types of dismissal to the employees above.

Sarah	**WRONGFUL**	**UNFAIR**	**NEITHER**
Trevor	**WRONGFUL**	**UNFAIR**	**NEITHER**
Umberto	**WRONGFUL**	**UNFAIR**	**NEITHER**
Vanessa	**WRONGFUL**	**UNFAIR**	**NEITHER**

(2 marks)

(b) Are the following statements about redundancy true or false?

In the event of redundancy, an employee with one year's continuous employment is entitled to compensation	**TRUE**	**FALSE**
Redundancy can occur where an employer ceases to carry on business in a particular location	**TRUE**	**FALSE**

(2 marks)

(Total = 4 marks)

5.3   (a) The following are steps that governments can take to influence certain areas.

- Tax incentives for investment
- Equal opportunities legislation
- Forbid takeovers
- Product safety standards

Required

Match the steps above to the areas of government concern below.

Tax incentives for investment	**OUTPUT CAPACITY**	**COMPETI-TION**	**EMPLOY-MENT**	**CONSUMER PROTEC-TION**
Equal opportunities legislation	**OUTPUT CAPACITY**	**COMPETI-TION**	**EMPLOY-MENT**	**CONSUMER PROTEC-TION**
Forbid takeovers	**OUTPUT CAPACITY**	**COMPETI-TION**	**EMPLOY-MENT**	**CONSUMER PROTEC-TION**
Product safety standards	**OUTPUT CAPACITY**	**COMPETI-TION**	**EMPLOY-MENT**	**CONSUMER PROTEC-TION**

(2 marks)

(b) Match the following government policy tools to the policies they relate to.

Borrowing	FISCAL POLICY	MONETARY POLICY
Taxation	FISCAL POLICY	MONETARY POLICY
Interest rates	FISCAL POLICY	MONETARY POLICY
Money supply	FISCAL POLICY	MONETARY POLICY

(2 marks)

(Total = 4 marks)

5.4 (a) GHJ Co is a manufacturing company that makes one product. The production process is labour intensive and as a result the product is highly specialised. GHJ Co also provides its customers with maintenance and after sales service.

Department W uses materials and labour to produce the final product.

Department X stores the final product and delivers it to customers.

Department Y is in charge of advertising and promotion of the final product.

Department Z is responsible for providing spare parts to customers.

Match the primary activities from Porter's value chain to the departments of GHJ Co.

Required

Match the primary activities above to the departments of GHJ Co.

Department W	OPERA-TIONS	AFTER SALES SERVICE	OUTBOUND LOGISTICS	MARKETING AND SALES
Department X	OPERA-TIONS	AFTER SALES SERVICE	OUTBOUND LOGISTICS	MARKETING AND SALES
Department Y	OPERA-TIONS	AFTER SALES SERVICE	OUTBOUND LOGISTICS	MARKETING AND SALES
Department Z	OPERA-TIONS	AFTER SALES SERVICE	OUTBOUND LOGISTICS	MARKETING AND SALES

(2 marks)

(b) Which **TWO** of the following factors indicate that suppliers have high bargaining power in an industry?

☐ There are a large number of suppliers

☐ There is a lack of substitute products available

☐ Switching costs for customers are low

☐ The product supplied is highly differentiated

☐ Product quality is not important to customers

(2 marks)

(Total = 4 marks)

5.5　(a)　Product BB15 has recently reduced its price by 5% which increased the sales volume by 12.5%. This price change also caused a fall in the sales volume of product CC25 by 2.5%.

There was no change in the price of product CC25.

Required

(1)　What is the price elasticity of demand for product BB15? ⬚

(2)　What is the cross elasticity of demand? ⬚

(3)　Products BB15 and CC25 are ⬚　　　　　　　　**(3 marks)**

(b)　Which word from the list below correctly fills in the blank?

For a normal, inferior good, demand curve slopes ⬚ ▾ to the right.

Pull down list

- Downwards
- Horizontally
- Upwards　　　　　　　　**(1 marks)**

　　　　　　　　(Total = 4 marks)

5.6　(a)　Which **THREE** of the following statements reflect the activities of an NGO?

☐ They have targets for customer satisfaction

☐ They are almost always charities

☐ They are aimed at promoting social, political or environmental change

☐ They often raise funds through donations

☐ They are legally constituted organisations with commercial aims

☐ They are measured in terms of effectiveness and efficiency　　**(3 marks)**

(b)　What acronym is generally used for performance measurement of an NGO?

○ VFM

○ ROCE

○ PBIT

○ SWOT　　　　　　　　**(1 mark)**

　　　　　　　　(Total = 4 marks)

　　　　　　　　(Total = 24 marks)

Part B: Business organisation structure, functions and governance

6 Business organisation structure (19 mins)

6.1 Which of the following statements about an organisation chart is **NOT** true?

○ An organisation chart provides a summary of the structure of a business.

○ An organisation chart can improve internal communications within a business.

○ An organisation chart can improve employees' understanding of their role in a business.

○ An organisation chart can indicate functional authority but not line authority within a business.

(2 marks)

6.2 Which of the following is a correct definition of 'span of control'?

○ The number of employees subordinate in the hierarchy to a given manager

○ The number of levels in the hierarchy 'below' a given manager's

○ The number of employees directly responsible to a manager

(1 mark)

6.3 Which of the following terms is **NOT** used by Mintzberg in his description of organisational structure?

○ Strategic apex

○ Support base

○ Technostructure

○ Operating core

(2 marks)

6.4 Y plc is a growing organisation which has recently diversified into a number of significant new product markets. It has also recently acquired another company in one of its overseas markets.

Required

What would be the most appropriate form of organisation for Y plc?

○ Geographical departmentation

○ Divisionalisation

○ Functional departmentation

(1 mark)

6.5 Which of the following principles of classical management is challenged by matrix management?

○ Structuring the organisation on functional lines

○ Structuring the organisation on geographical lines

○ Unity of command

○ Decentralisation of decision-making

(2 marks)

6.6 Which of the following statements about the informal organisation is **NOT** true?

 O The influence of the informal organisation was highlighted by the Hawthorne Studies, in the way group norms and dynamics affected productivity.

 O Informal organisation can pose a threat to employee health and safety.

 O Informal organisation can stimulate innovation.

 O Managers in positions of authority generally cannot be part of the informal organisation.

(2 marks)

6.7 Which of the following is an advantage of centralisation?

 O It helps to develop the skills of junior managers

 O It avoids overburdening top managers in terms of workload and stress

 O Senior managers can take a wider view of problems and consequences

(1 mark)

6.8 Which of the following statements is/are true?

 (1) An informal organisation exists within every formal organisation

 (2) Objectives of the informal organisation are broadly the same the formal organisation

 (3) A strong, close-knit informal organisation is desirable within the formal organisation

 O Statement (1) only

 O Statements (1) and (3) only

 O Statements (2) and (3) only

 O Statement (3) only

(2 marks)

6.9 What is an organisation which has removed the internal barriers which separate hierarchy levels and functions and also between the organisation and its suppliers, customers and competitors known as?

 O Modular organisation

 O Hollow organisation

 O Jobless structure

 O Boundaryless organisation

(2 marks)

6.10 Which of the following statements are true?

 (1) With a shared service centre services are likely to be less tailored

 (2) The IT function is commonly provided using shared service approach

 (3) A shared service centre is not part of the organisation

 O Statement (1) and (3) only

 O Statements (1) and (2) only

 O Statements (2) and (3) only

(1 mark)

(Total = 16 marks)

7 Organisational culture and committees (43 mins)

7.1 BZ Ness Ltd is an organisation with a strongly traditional outlook. It is structured and managed according to classical principles: specialisation, the scalar chain of command, unity of command and direction.

Personnel tend to focus on their own distinct tasks, which are strictly defined and directed. Communication is vertical, rather than lateral. Discipline is much prized and enshrined in the rule book of the company.

Required

From the scenario, what sort of culture does BZ Ness Ltd have, using Harrison's classifications?

O Role culture

O Task culture

O Existential culture

O Power culture

(2 marks)

7.2 Which of the following statements is true?

O Strong values improve corporate performance

O Strong values can replace rules and controls in an organisation

O Strong values minimise conflict within an organisation

O Strong values are dangerous if they filter out 'uncomfortable' environmental information

(2 marks)

7.3 Which word or phrase most accurately completes the definition?

Culture is the collective programming of the mind which distinguishes the members of one

[▼] from another.

Pull down list

• Category of people

• Ethnic group

• Nation

• Social class

(1 mark)

7.4 Which of the following is **NOT** one of the terms used by Hofstede to describe a key dimension of culture?

O Power-distance

O Acquisitive/giving

O Individualism/collectivism

O Uncertainty avoidance

(2 marks)

7.5 Which is the 'deepest' set of underlying factors which determine culture, and the hardest to manage?

○ Values

○ Rituals

○ Assumptions

(1 mark)

7.6 Who defined organisational culture as 'the set of shared, taken-for-granted implicit assumptions that a group holds and that determines how it perceives, thinks about and reacts to its environment'?

○ Maslow

○ Schein

○ Porter

○ Mintzberg

(2 marks)

7.7 Research has indicated that workers in country A display characteristics such as toughness and the desire for material wealth and possessions.

Workers in country B value personal relationships, belonging and the quality of life.

Required

According to Hofstede's theory, these distinctions relate to which of the following cultural dimensions?

○ Masculinity – femininity

○ Power – distance

○ Individualism – collectivism

○ Uncertainty avoidance

(2 marks)

7.8 The research and development (R & D) function of a business:

(1) Is primarily concerned with market research

(2) Can improve existing products as well as developing completely new products

(3) Has been less important for firms manufacturing computers to meet an industry standard than for those firms developing the next generation of computers

(4) Is always undertaken under contract by specialist external consultancies

Required

Which of the above statements are correct?

○ (1) and (2) only

○ (2) and (3) only

○ (1), (3) and (4) only

○ (2) and (4) only

(2 marks)

BPP
LEARNING
MEDIA

7.9 Which of the following words most accurately completes the sentence?

Services have certain qualities which distinguish them from products. Because of their

[▼] , physical elements such as vouchers, tickets, confirmations and

merchandise are an important part of service provision.

Pull down list

- Inseparability
- Intangibility
- Perishability
- Variability

(2 marks)

7.10 U Ltd produces a portfolio of products and focuses its efforts and resources on persuading customers to buy them.

Required

This is an example of which type of 'orientation'?

- ○ Production
- ○ Sales
- ○ Marketing

(1 mark)

7.11 Which of the following is/are objectives of human resource management?

(1) To meet the organisation's social and legal responsibilities relating to the human resource

(2) To manage an organisation's relationship with its customers

(3) To develop human resources that will respond effectively to change

- ○ (1) and (2)
- ○ (1) and (3)
- ○ (1) only
- ○ (1), (2) and (3)

(2 marks)

7.12 Jeff, Jane and Jaitinder work in different departments in the firm XYZ Co. They are members of the permanent 'staff committee' which meets on a monthly basis to discuss staff issues such as pensions and benefits. Their purpose is to listen to communication from staff within their department and raise issues on behalf of their department at committee meetings.

Required

What is the name given to this type of committee?

- ○ Joint committee
- ○ Task force
- ○ Standing committee

(1 mark)

7.13   Josh, Joanne, Ed, and Sue all work for D Co. Josh works in the finance department. Joanne works in the human resources department. Ed is Sue's line manager in the purchasing department.

Required

Which of the staff members would be responsible for payroll administration?

○   Josh

○   Joanne

○   Ed

○   Sue

(2 marks)

7.14   Managers Jill and Paul are talking about how to resolve a business problem. Jill suggests that a committee should be formed to discuss the issues. Paul argues that committees are:

(1)   Time-consuming and expensive

(2)   They invite a compromise instead of a clear-cut decision

Required

Which of these statements is true?

○   Both (1) and (2)

○   (1) only

○   (2) only

○   Neither statement is true

(2 marks)

7.15   Diane carries out routine processing of invoices in the purchasing department of L Co. Joanne is Diane's supervisor.

Lesley is trying to decide how many staff will be needed if some proposed new technology is implemented.

Tracey is considering the new work that L Co will be able to offer and the new markets it could enter, once the new technology is well established.

Required

Which member of L Co carries out tactical activities?

○   Diane

○   Joanne

○   Lesley

○   Tracey

(2 marks)

7.16   Mr Q is manager of a division which is undergoing a business downturn. He tries to shelter the workforce from the effects of downsizing: taking time for consultation, organising counselling and refusing to institute compulsory redundancies.

Required

Which of the following cultural types identified in the Hofstede model does this manager represent?

○   Low power-distance

○   Low masculinity

BPP
LEARNING
MEDIA

○ Low uncertainty avoidance

○ High individuality

(2 marks)

7.17 Which of the following would **NOT** be an objective of stakeholder management in relation to in relation to procurement?

○ Continuity of supply

○ Mutual dependency

○ Information sharing

(1 mark)

7.18 Janet works for a toy company called K Co. She telephones Mary at P Co on a daily basis to order parts. Janet has no contact with customers but does deal with complaint letters from D Group, an organisation against slave labour. D Group believe that K Co use slave labour in the toy manufacturing factories.

Required

Which of the following are internal stakeholders of K Co?

○ Janet only

○ Janet and Mary at P Co

○ Janet and D Group

○ Janet, Mary and D Group

(2 marks)

7.19 Josina has been appointed Chair of a remuneration committee. She is responsible for which of the following duties?

○ Fixing the date and time of the next meeting

○ Giving a ruling on matters in dispute

○ Taking notes during the meeting

(1 mark)

7.20 Ali is responsible for preparing and issuing documents prior to a meeting, then acting on and communicating decisions following the meeting. What is his role?

○ Committee secretary

○ Committee member

○ Committee Chair

(1 mark)

7.21 Which of the following is a role of the Secretary of a committee?

○ Agreeing the minutes of meetings as a true and accurate record

○ Maintaining order at meetings, and ensuring that all members contribute fully to discussions

○ Ascertaining whether specific matters fall within the terms of reference of the committee

(1 mark)

7.22 The audit committee and remuneration committee of a company are examples of which of the following?

○ Ad hoc committees

○ Management committees

○ Executive committees

○ Standing committees

(2 marks)

(Total = 36 marks)

8 Corporate governance and social responsibility (23 mins)

8.1 Which of the following statements about corporate social responsibility is/are true?

(1) CSR guarantees increased profit levels

(2) CSR adds cost to organisational activities and reduces profit levels

(3) Social responsibility may have commercial benefits

(4) Social responsibility is a concern confined to business organisations

○ (1), (2), (3) and (4)

○ (1) and (3)

○ (2) and (4)

○ (3) only

(2 marks)

8.2 Calum, Heidi and Jonas are managers for Zip Co.

They have been told that their salary will be based on company performance and that a bonus scheme will also be introduced.

The bonus will also be related to company performance.

Required

Which of the following theories describes the approach to governance that Zip Co is using?

○ Stewardship theory

○ Agency theory

○ Stakeholder theory

(1 mark)

8.3 Michael has been asked to prepare a presentation for the company directors on good corporate governance.

Which of the following is **NOT** appropriate for him to include in his presentation?

○ Risk management

○ Internal controls

○ Maximising shareholder wealth

○ Accountability to stakeholders

(2 marks)

8.4 Corporate governance is essentially of what significance?

○ Control system

○ Strategic importance

○ Risk management

(1 mark)

8.5 Which of the following is a feature of poor corporate governance?

○ Domination of the board by a single individual

○ Critical questioning of senior managers by external auditors

○ Supervision of staff in key roles

○ Lack of focus on short-term profitability

(2 marks)

8.6 The tasks of which body include: monitoring the chief executive officer; formulating strategy; and ensuring that there is effective communication of the strategic plan?

○ The audit committee

○ The Public Oversight Board

○ The board of directors

○ The nomination committee

(2 marks)

8.7 Which of the following would be in the principles of Corporate Social Responsibility?

(1) Human rights

(2) Employee welfare

(3) Professional ethics

(4) Support for local suppliers

○ (2) and (3) only

○ (2), (3) and (4) only

○ (1), (2) and (4) only

(2 marks)

8.8 Which of the following is subject to the least direct regulation?

○ Employment protection

○ Corporate social responsibility

○ Corporate governance

(1 mark)

8.9 In most countries, what is the usual purpose of codes of practice on corporate governance?

○ To establish legally binding requirements to which all companies must adhere

○ To set down detailed rules to regulate the ways in which companies must operate

○ To provide guidance on the standards of best practice companies should adopt

○ To provide a comprehensive framework for management and administration

(2 marks)

8.10 Who should set directors' reward and incentive packages, according to corporate governance provisions?

  ○ The board of directors

  ○ The nomination committee

  ○ A remuneration committee made up of independent non-executive directors

(1 mark)

8.11 What is the purpose of an Operating and Financial Review (OFR)?

  ○ To provide the board of directors with a narrative statement by the audit committee of its findings on the efficacy of internal operational and financial controls.

  ○ To set out the directors' analysis of the business, in order to provide investors with a historical and prospective view through the eyes of management.

  ○ To provide a statement that the company is a going concern.

(1 mark)

8.12 Which of the following are advantages of having non-executive directors on the company board?

  (1) They can provide a wider perspective than executive directors.

  (2) They provide reassurance to shareholders.

  (3) They may have external experience and knowledge which executive directors do not possess.

  (4) They have more time to devote to the role.

  ○ (1) and (3)

  ○ (1), (2) and (3)

  ○ (1), (3) and (4)

  ○ (2) and (4)

(2 marks)

(Total = 19 marks)

9 Section B MTQs (29 mins)

9.1 (a) Paul, Mary, Alan and Kate are having a board meeting of a newly formed company and they are discussing the orientation of the company.

Paul believes that the company will actively need to persuade customers to buy their products.

Mary believes they should add additional features to their products, without carrying out market research, and this will increase demand from customers.

Alan believes the products will sell as they are and the company should produce as many items as it can.

Kate believes that they should research what customers need and value and adapt the products to meet the findings of the research.

Required

For each board member, select the orientation they are recommending.

Paul

	▼

Mary

	▼

Alan

	▼

Kate

	▼

Pull down list

- Marketing orientation
- Product orientation
- Production orientation
- Sales orientation

(2 marks)

(b) Which of the options below correctly fills the blank?

Breaking up the market into different groups, which each have common needs, wants

and preferences is known as | | ▼ |

Pull down list

- Market segmentation.
- Marketing mix
- Mass marketing
- Undifferentiated marketing

(2 marks)

(Total = 4 marks)

9.2 (a) The main levels of strategy in an organisation are as follows:

- Corporate
- Business
- Operational

Required

Match the appropriate level of strategy above to the strategic questions below.

Which business should we be in?	**CORPORATE**	**BUSINESS**	**OPERATIONAL**
Should we specialise in a profitable product?	**CORPORATE**	**BUSINESS**	**OPERATIONAL**
How best can we market the products?	**CORPORATE**	**BUSINESS**	**OPERATIONAL**
Should we segment the market?	**CORPORATE**	**BUSINESS**	**OPERATIONAL**

(2 marks)

(b) Which **TWO** of the following are advantages of centralisation?

☐ Decision makers have a greater awareness of local problems

☐ Managers are able to take a wider view

☐ Avoids overburdening top managers

☐ Help to develop junior managers

☐ Procedures and documentation can be standardised

(2 marks)

(Total = 4 marks)

9.3 (a) Company W focuses on autonomy of its employees. Task achievement is seen as more important than working relationships. The company is impersonal and defends its business interests. Company X has a strict task structure with written rules and regulations which are adhered to by all employees. Dissent is not tolerated. Company Y has a focus on good working relationships between employees and seeks consensus on all business decisions. Company Z has a flat organisation structure and a high level of employee participation in decision-making.

Required

For each company, select which of Hofstede's four main dimensions of cultural differences is being displayed.

Company W

[▼]

Company X

[▼]

Company Y

[▼]

Company Z

[▼]

Pull down list

• Individualism

• Masculinity

• Power distance

• Uncertainty avoidance

(2 marks)

(b) According to Schein there are three determinants of culture, the first being observable.

Patterns of greeting styles and business formalities are known as [▼]

Concrete expressions, such as office premises design, are [▼]

Pull down list
- Artefacts
- Attitudes
- Behaviour

(2 marks)

(Total = 4 marks)

9.4 (a) The following four components of an organisation were identified by Mintzberg:
- Operating core
- Support staff
- Strategic apex
- Middle line

Required

Match the components above to the following jobs.

Canteen worker	OPERATING CORE	SUPPORT STAFF	STRATEGIC APEX	MIDDLE LINE
Production worker	OPERATING CORE	SUPPORT STAFF	STRATEGIC APEX	MIDDLE LINE
Production manager	OPERATING CORE	SUPPORT STAFF	STRATEGIC APEX	MIDDLE LINE
Director	OPERATING CORE	SUPPORT STAFF	STRATEGIC APEX	MIDDLE LINE

(2 marks)

(b) Which of the following has the greatest influence on a machine bureaucracy?
- O Strategic apex
- O Middle line
- O Technostructure
- O Operating core

(2 marks)

(Total = 4 marks)

9.5 (a) For each of the following tasks, select which department is responsible:

	Financial accounting	Treasury
Arranging an overdraft	O	O
Managing foreign currency exposure	O	O
Recording financial transactions	O	O

	Financial accounting	Treasury
Cash budgeting	○	○
Reporting to shareholders	○	○
Repaying loans	○	○

(3 marks)

(b) Which of the following correctly fills the gap?

Markets for trading short-term financial instruments are known as [　　　　▼] .

Pull down list

- Capital markets
- Money markets
- Venture capital

(1 mark)

(Total = 4 marks)

9.6 (a) Fill in the gaps in the King report's summary of the role of the board below

To define the [　　　▼] of the company

To define the [　　　▼] by which the company will perform its daily duties

To identify the [　　　▼] relevant to the company

To develop a [　　　▼] combining these factors

To ensure [　　　▼] of this strategy

Pull down list

- Implementation
- Purpose
- Stakeholders
- Strategy
- Values

(3 marks)

(b) Which of the following is **NOT** part of the role of a company secretary?

- ○ Establishment and maintenance of a registered office
- ○ Filing of annual returns
- ○ Chairing management committee meetings
- ○ Maintaining statutory books and records

(1 mark)

(Total = 4 marks)

(Total = 24 marks)

10 The role of accounting (54 mins)

10.1 Joseph has just started his first job in an accountancy department. A qualified senior member of staff explains to him what the main aim of accounting is. Which of the following options is the correct aim of accounting?

   ○ To maintain ledger accounts for every asset and liability

   ○ To provide financial information to users of such information

   ○ To produce a trial balance

   ○ To record every financial transaction individually

(2 marks)

10.2 Which of the following statements about accounting information is **NOT** correct?

   ○ Some companies voluntarily provide specially-prepared financial information to employees.

   ○ Accounting information should be relevant, reliable, complete, objective and timely.

   ○ Accountants have a strong obligation to ensure that company accounts conform to accounting standards

   ○ Charities and professional bodies do not have to produce financial statements in the same way as businesses.

(2 marks)

10.3 In a typical finance function, preparation of budgets and budgetary control would usually be the responsibility of which of the following roles?

   ○ The Financial Controller

   ○ The Management Accountant

   ○ The Treasurer

(1 mark)

10.4 Three of the following are outputs of a payroll system, and one is an input to the system. Which is the input?

   ○ Credit transfer forms

   ○ Time sheets

   ○ Payroll analysis

   ○ Pay slips

(2 marks)

10.5 Which of the following is an aim of the control system relating to accounts payable and purchases?

   ○ To ensure that all credit notes received are recorded in the general and payables ledger

   ○ To ensure that goods and services are only supplied to customers with good credit ratings

○ To ensure that all credit notes that have been issued are recorded in the general and receivables ledgers

○ To ensure that potentially doubtful debts are identified

(2 marks)

10.6 Which of the following does company law require a statement of financial position to give?

○ A true and fair view of the profit or loss of the company for the financial year

○ An unqualified (or 'clean') report on the statement of affairs of the company as at the end of the financial year

○ A true and fair view of the statement of affairs of the company as at the end of the financial year

(1 mark)

10.7 All of the following, with one exception, are areas in which an integrated accounting software package has advantages compared to a series of separate (stand-alone) dedicated programs. Which is the exception?

○ Efficiency in updating data

○ Flexibility in preparing reports

○ Data integrity

○ Specialised capabilities

(2 marks)

10.8 Which of the following terms correctly completes this definition?

A [▼] is a program which deals with one particular part of a computerised

business accounting system.

Pull down list

• Database

• Module

• Spreadsheet

• Suite

(2 marks)

10.9 All the following, with one exception, are examples of advantages of a computer-based accounting system over a manual system.

Which statement is the exception?

○ Financial calculations can be performed more quickly and accurately

○ Financial information can be presented to other business departments in a variety of forms

○ There is much stronger provision for data security

○ The system is easier to update as new information becomes available

(2 marks)

BPP
LEARNING
MEDIA

10.10 All of the following, except one, are tasks that can be performed by spreadsheet software. Which is the exception?

   ○ The presentation of numerical data in the form of graphs and charts

   ○ The application of logical tests to data

   ○ The application of 'What if?' scenarios

   ○ Automatic correction of all data entered by the operator into the spreadsheet

(2 marks)

10.11 The preparation and filing of accounts by limited companies each year is required by which of the following?

   ○ Codes of corporate governance

   ○ National legislation

   ○ International Accounting Standards

   ○ Local Accounting Standards

(2 marks)

10.12 All the following statements, except one, are examples of the advantages that a computer-based accounting system used by a management accountant has over a manual system.

Required

Which statement is the exception?

   ○ A computer-based accounting system is easier to update as new information becomes available

   ○ A computer-based accounting system will always reject inaccurate financial information input to the system's database

   ○ Financial calculations can be performed more quickly and accurately

   ○ The management accountant can more readily present financial information to other business departments in a variety of forms

(2 marks)

10.13 Gordon works in the accounts department of a retail business. He and his colleagues are looking at the sales figures for various types of clothing.

The director asks them to use exception reporting to summarise their findings.

Which of the following correctly defines the concept of 'exception reporting' within a business context?

   ○ The reporting of unusual events, outside the normal course of events

   ○ The analysis of those items where performance differs significantly from standard or budget

   ○ The preparation of reports on routine matters on an 'ad hoc' basis

   ○ The scrutiny of all data as a matter of course, save in exceptional circumstances

(2 marks)

10.14 A small company's computer system comprises five desktop personal computers located in separate offices linked together in an intranet within the same building.

The computers are not connected to the Internet and employees are not allowed to take storage media into or out of the building.

Information which the business' owner wishes to keep confidential to herself is stored in one of the computers.

Required

Which of the following statements can be concluded from this information?

○ This company's computer system does not need a back-up storage system

○ This company's computer system does not need a password access system

○ This company's computer system does not receive email from customers or suppliers

(1 mark)

10.15 Which word or phrase correctly completes this sentence?

| ▼ | Systems pool data from internal and external sources and make

information available to senior managers, for strategic, unstructured decision-making.

Pull down list

- Decision Support

- Executive Support

- Expert

- Management Support

(2 marks)

10.16 All the following statements, except one, describe the relationship between data and information. Which is the exception?

○ Information is data which has been processed in such a way as to be meaningful to the person who receives it.

○ The relationship between data and information is one of inputs and outputs.

○ Data is always in numerical form whereas information is always in text form.

(1 mark)

10.17 What element of a database system is represented by the question mark in the **below** diagram?

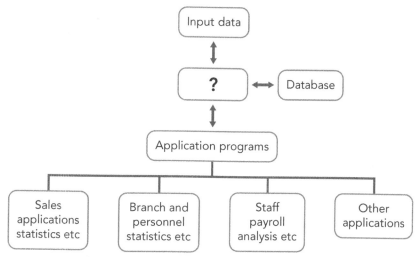

▼

Pull down list

- Data storage
- Database administrator
- Database management system
- Electronic point of sale system

(2 marks)

10.18 Which of the following statements about data security is **NOT** true?

- ○ Loss or corruption of data is almost always non-deliberate.
- ○ New staff in particular pose a threat.
- ○ It is impossible to prevent all threats cost-effectively.
- ○ Smoke detectors are a form of data protection.

(2 marks)

10.19 Which word correctly completes this sentence?

Office Automation Systems are designed mainly to increase the [▼] of data

and information workers.

Pull down list

- Decision-making capability
- Flexibility
- Productivity

(1 mark)

10.20 Which of the following user groups of financial and accounting information are likely to need, and have access to, this information most?

- ○ Managers of the company
- ○ Shareholders of the company
- ○ Financial analysis advisers

(1 mark)

10.21 To whom should the internal audit department of an organisation report?

- ○ The Finance Director
- ○ The audit committee of the board of directors
- ○ The shareholders

(1 mark)

10.22 Which of the following, in the context of computerised accounting systems, is **NOT** true?

- ○ A database is a structured, centralised pool of data which can be accessed by a number of applications.
- ○ A spreadsheet is particularly useful for creating financial models.

○ Computerised systems reduce the risk of errors in financial calculations.

○ Information and Communication Technology (ICT) systems are more efficient than manual systems for any task an accountant may have to perform.

(2 marks)

10.23 Which function in an organisation is responsible for ensuring that only properly authorised purchases which are necessary for the business are made?

○ Goods inwards

○ Finance/accounts

○ Purchasing/procurement

○ Production/operations

(2 marks)

10.24 There is a need for co-ordinated information flow between sections and departments in accounting management. To which of the following should the receivables ledger section give information about overdue debts?

○ Cost accounting staff

○ The credit control department

○ The payables ledger section

(1 mark)

10.25 Which of the following is **NOT** part of the regulatory system?

○ GAAP

○ International financial reporting standards

○ IFAC

○ The European Union

(2 marks)

10.26 International Financial Reporting Standards are issued by which of the following organisations?

○ IASB

○ ASB

○ The European Union

(1 mark)

10.27 Legally binding rules relating to the disclosure and presentation of financial statements are set down in which of the following?

○ National legislation

○ International financial reporting standards

○ Generally agreed accounting principles

○ Rule books of professional accountancy bodies

(2 marks)

(Total = 45 marks)

11 Control, security and audit

(28 mins)

11.1 Which of the following is **NOT** an aim of internal controls?

O To enable the organisation to respond appropriately to business, operational and financial risks

O To eliminate the possibility of impacts from poor judgement and human error

O To help ensure the quality of internal and external reporting

O To help ensure compliance with applicable laws and regulations

(2 marks)

11.2 Which term correctly completes this statement?

Some controls are provided automatically by the system and cannot be by-passed, ignored or overridden: for example, having to input a password to enter a computer system. These are classified as [▼] controls.

Pull down list

• Administrative

• Detect

• Mandated

• Non-discretionary

(2 marks)

11.3 The mnemonic SPAMSOAP is often used to remember the range of financial control procedures. What does the 'O' stand for in this mnemonic?

O Operations

O Organisation

O Oversight

(1 mark)

11.4 Which of the following is **NOT** an internal check?

O Separation of duties for authorising, custody and recording

O Pre-lists, post-lists and control totals

O Bank reconciliations

O Systems for authorising transactions within specified spending limits

(2 marks)

11.5 Which of the following statements about internal audit is true?

O Internal audit is an independent appraisal activity

O Internal audit is separate from the organisation's internal control system

O Internal audit is carried out solely for the benefit of the organisation's stakeholders

O The internal audit function reports to the finance director

(2 marks)

11.6 The use of uninterruptible (protected) power supplies is a method of protecting data and IT systems from what sort of security threat?

    ○ Accidental damage

    ○ Weather

    ○ Hacking

                                                (1 mark)

11.7 Which of the following would be classed as a contingency control in an information system?

    ○ Password-only access to the system

    ○ System recovery procedures

    ○ Audit trails

                                                (1 mark)

11.8 All of the following, except one, are inherent limitations of internal control systems.
Which is the exception?

    ○ The costs of control

    ○ Potential for human error and deliberate override

    ○ The types of transactions controls are designed to cope with

    ○ The independence of controls from the method of data processing

                                                (2 marks)

11.9 Which of the following statements about external auditors is **NOT** correct?

    ○ External auditors are appointed by the shareholders of a company

    ○ The primary responsibility of external auditors is to investigate financial irregularities and report them to shareholders

    ○ External auditors may rely on the work of internal auditors, but first they have to assess its worth

    ○ External auditors are concerned with the financial records and statements of the organisation

                                                (2 marks)

11.10 In the context of audit, what are 'substantive tests' designed to accomplish?

    ○ To establish whether internal controls are being applied as prescribed

    ○ To identify errors and omissions in financial records

    ○ To establish the causes of errors or omissions in financial records

    ○ To establish an audit trail

                                                (2 marks)

11.11 Backing up computer files and storing copies of software in separate locations to the main system are examples of which type of controls?

    ○ Prevent

    ○ Detect

    ○ Correct

                                                (1 mark)

11.12 Which word or phrase correctly completes this definition?

In the context of data security controls, [▼] are records showing who has

accessed a computer system and what operations he or she has performed.

Pull down list
- Archives
- Audit trails
- Passwords

(1 mark)

11.13 Which type of audit is concerned with the monitoring of management's performance, concentrating on the outputs of the system and the efficiency of the organisation?

O   Systems audit

O   Operational audit

O   Probity audit

O   Social audit

(2 marks)

11.14 Which of the following circumstances would cast doubt on the external auditor's ability to rely on the work of internal auditors?

O   There is evidence that management and directors consistently act on internal audit recommendations

O   The internal audit function has a direct line of communication to the audit committee

O   No audit manuals or working papers are available for inspection

O   Internal auditors are recruited on technical qualifications and demonstrated proficiency

(2 marks)

(Total = 23 marks)

12 Identifying and preventing fraud   (32 mins)

12.1 What is the term given to a method of fraud in the accounts receivable area, by which cash or cheque receipts are stolen, and the theft concealed by setting subsequent receipts against the outstanding debt?

O   Collusion

O   Misrepresentation

O   Teeming and lading

(1 mark)

12.2 Which of the following activities create vulnerability to fraud?

(1)   Calculating payslips

(2)   Preparing delivery notes

(3) Paying supplier invoices

(4) Meeting budgets and performance targets

○ (3) only

○ (1) and (3) only

○ (1) and (2) only

○ (1), (2), (3) and (4)

(2 marks)

12.3 X plc has a bad debt policy whereby aged receivables who are obviously not going to pay, are written off. The financial accountant does not enforce this policy.

Required

This might be fraudulent insofar as it creates which of the following effects?

○ It removes funds from the business

○ It results in the understatement of profits and net assets

○ It results in the overstatement of profits and net assets

○ It results in the intentional overstatement of profits and net assets

(2 marks)

12.4 Which word correctly completes this statement?

Dishonesty is a [▼] to act in ways which contravene accepted ethical,

social, organisational or legal norms for fair and honest dealing.

Pull down list

• Motivation

• Pre-disposition

• Stimulus

(1 mark)

12.5 All of the following, with one exception, are internal factors which might increase the risk profile of a business. Which is the exception?

○ Increased competition

○ Corporate restructuring

○ Upgraded management information system

○ New personnel

(2 marks)

12.6 Which of the following would most clearly present a personnel risk of fraud?

○ Segregation of duties

○ High staff morale

○ Staff not taking their full holiday entitlements

○ Consultative management style

(2 marks)

12.7 All of the following, except one, are potential impacts on a business of removal of significant funds or assets. Which is the exception?

- ○ Fall in returns to shareholders
- ○ Reduction in profits
- ○ Increase in working capital
- ○ Reputational damage

(2 marks)

12.8 Which of the following internal controls might be least effective in preventing fraud, if staff are in collusion with customers?

- ○ Physical security
- ○ Requiring signatures to confirm receipt of goods or services
- ○ Sequential numbering of transaction documents
- ○ Authorisation policies

(2 marks)

12.9 Which word or phrase correctly completes this statement?

In a limited company, or plc, it is the ultimate responsibility of [▼] to take reasonable steps to prevent and detect fraud.

Pull down list

- • The audit committee
- • The board of directors
- • The external auditor

(1 mark)

12.10 Which of the following is **NOT** a key risk area for computer fraud?

- ○ Hackers
- ○ Lack of managerial understanding
- ○ Inability to secure access to data
- ○ Integration of data systems

(2 marks)

12.11 Which **TWO** of the following stakeholders will be most directly affected if a business overstates its financial position?

- ☐ Staff
- ☐ Customers
- ☐ Investors
- ☐ Suppliers

(2 marks)

12.12 Which of the following would **NOT** form part of a fraud response plan?

    O Suspending staff suspected of fraudulent activity

    O Investigating the activities and contacts of a suspected fraudster

    O Fraud awareness training and recruitment controls.

(1 mark)

12.13 Only allowing purchasing staff to choose suppliers from an approved list is an example of what sort of fraud prevention measure?

    O Segregation of duties

    O Appropriate documentation

    O Limitation control

    O Check control

(2 marks)

12.14 Which of the following statements about fraud prevention is **NOT** true?

    O Cash sales are an area of high risk of fraud.

    O Performance-based rewards for managers reduce the risk of fraud.

    O Emphasis on the autonomy of operational management may weaken controls.

    O Fraud awareness and ethics education can reduce the risk of fraud

(2 marks)

12.15 Which word(s) completes the sentence?

    [▼] constitutes any financial transactions whose purpose is to conceal the

origins of the proceeds of criminal activity.

Pull down list

- Fraud
- Misrepresentation of results
- Money laundering
- Teeming and lading

(2 marks)

12.16 The initial disposal of the proceeds of an illegal activity into apparently legitimate business activity is known as what?

    O Placement

    O Layering

    O Integration

(1 mark)

(Total = 27 marks)

13 Financial technology (Fintech)

13.1 Landis Co has a team of experts whose role is to analyse vast volumes of data concering many areas of the business that comefrom a wide variety of sources. Landis Co is seeking competitive advantage from:

- ○ An internet gateway
- ○ Big data
- ○ Its accounting information system

(1 mark)

13.2 Which characteristic of big data relates to the ability to stream data in real-time?

- ○ Veracity
- ○ Volume
- ○ Variety
- ○ Velocity

(2 marks)

13.3 Which of the following accounting tasks could data analytics help to make more effective?

- ○ Processing routine transactions
- ○ Asset management
- ○ Risk management
- ○ Payroll processing

(2 marks)

13.4 Which word correctly completes this statement?

[▼] is a source of big data that originates from public sector data (for example transport, government financial and public service data).

Pull down list
- Machine-generated data
- Open data
- Processed data

(1 mark)

13.5 Which of the following is a disadvantage of using cloud accounting software?

- ○ Cloud accounting software only allows one user to access the system at any one time
- ○ Financial data held in the cloud must be manually transferred between individual computers
- ○ Upgrading cloud accounting software is expensive and time-consuming
- ○ Users of cloud accounting software are completely reliant on the provider of the software to ensure their data is secure and to take backups of it

(2 marks)

13.6 Which of the following technologies allows unconnected organisations and individuals people to trust a shared record of events?

O Cloud computing

O Data analytics

O Distributed ledger (Blockchain)

O Artifical intelligence

(2 marks)

13.7 Which of the following is an area of an accountant or auditor's work that is made more effective by automation?

O Downloading bank transactions into the accounting system

O Report writing

O Forming an audit opinion

O Posting transactions to nominal codes

(2 marks)

13.8 Which of the following is an area of an accountant or auditor's work that is made more effective by artificial intelligence?

O Report writing

O Forming an audit opinion

O Downloading bank transactions into the accounting system

O Posting transactions to nominal codes

(2 marks)

13.9 Which word or phrase correctly completes this statement?

Distributed ledgers reduce the need for auditors to [▼] because they have a

source of information that they can trust.

Pull down list

• Check for material misstatement

• Form an audit opinion

• Verify the ownership of assets

(1 mark)

(Total = 15 marks)

14 Section C MTQs   **(29 mins)**

14.1 (a) The following are reasons why people might be interested in financial information about a large public company.

• Assessing how effectively management is running the company

• To advise clients

• To assess tax payable by the company

• To assess the ability of the company to pay its debts

Required

For each of the following users of financial information, match the appropriate reason for wanting the information from the list above:

Assessing how effectively management is running the company	SUPPLIERS	TAX AUTHORI- TIES	SHARE- HOLDERS	FINANCIAL ANALYSTS
To advise clients	SUPPLIERS	TAX AUTHORI- TIES	SHARE- HOLDERS	FINANCIAL ANALYSTS
To assess tax payable by the company	SUPPLIERS	TAX AUTHORI- TIES	SHARE- HOLDERS	FINANCIAL ANALYSTS
To assess the ability of the company to pay its debts	SUPPLIERS	TAX AUTHORI- TIES	SHARE- HOLDERS	FINANCIAL ANALYSTS

(2 marks)

(b) Only businesses need to prepare financial statements.

O True

O False

(1 mark)

(c) Which of the following correctly fills the blank?

The statement of financial position must give [　　　　　　▼] view of the company

at the end of the financial year.

Pull down list

- A GAAP compliant
- A true and fair
- An informative

(1 mark)

(Total = 4 marks)

14.2 (a) QRT Co has just implemented a new computerised accounting package and also reinforced some of its accounting controls.

The new system has the following features:

(1) All accounting entries must balance or they cannot be entered.

(2) A module exists so that non-current asset purchases can be authorised by the relevant member of management.

(3) Users are set up with passwords in order to login to the system.

(4) An audit trail is produced so all transactions can be traced to the time of posting and the individual who entered them.

Required

For each of the following controls, identify if they are discretionary or non-discretionary.

	Disc.	Non-disc.
Balancing of accounting entries	○	○
Authorisation of non-current asset purchase	○	○
Password access to the system	○	○
Review of the audit trail	○	○

(2 marks)

(b) Which of the following correctly fills the blank?

[　　　　　▼] audit is testing and evaluating internal controls of an organisation.

Pull down list

- A systems
- A transactions
- An operational

(1 mark)

(c) A control system consisting of sufficient controls will be entirely effective.

○ True

○ False

(1 mark)

(Total = 4 marks)

14.3 (a) The external auditor should design audit procedures to have a reasonable expectation of detecting fraud. Everything else is the responsibility of the directors.

Required

Which **TWO** of the following are advantages of computerised accounting systems over manual systems?

☐ The risk of errors is eradicated

☐ Processing is faster

☐ Corrections can be made quicker

☐ Information is less accessible

(2 marks)

(b) Which word fills in the blank above?

A [　　　　　▼] is a program that deals with a particular part of the accounting system.

Pull down list

- Database
- Module
- Spreadsheet

(1 mark)

(c) A database does not need updating once it has been set up.

○ True

○ False

(1 mark)

(Total = 4 marks)

14.4 (a) Which **TWO** of the following are examples of physical access controls?

☐ Door locks

☐ Automatic system back ups

☐ Intruder alarms

☐ Authorisation of purchases

☐ Physical inspection of inventory

(2 marks)

(b) Check digits, control totals and limit checks are examples of which type of control?

○ Output control

○ Processing control

○ Input control

(1 mark)

(c) Which word fills in the blank above?

| ▼ | controls help an organisation recover in the event of a disaster.

Pull down list

• Contingency

• Integrity

• Security

(1 mark)

(Total = 4 marks)

14.5 (a) Stella is an external auditor who has observed some cash transactions that don't have any supporting documentation. Upon further investigation she discovered that these payments are made into bank accounts of the Finance Director's family. She discusses this with the audit manager and they jointly decide not to take any further action.

James is also an external auditor and has discovered a fraud at one of his clients and has decided he will make a report to his nominated officer. At the same time he decides to inform the financial controller of the client about making the report.

Required

Which of the following offences has been committed by Stella? | ▼ |

Which of the following offences has been committed by James? | ▼ |

Pull down list

• Failure to report

• No offence has been committed

• Tipping off

(2 marks)

(b) Elyse is transferring amounts of money from business to business to disguise the fact that the money was originally the proceeds from criminal activity.

Laura is in the process of banking several small amounts of illegally obtained money with a variety of banks in order to avoid anti-money laundering requirements.

Required

Which of the following phases of money laundering is being undertaken by Elyse?

[▼]

Which of the following phases of money laundering is being undertaken by Laura?

[▼]

Pull down list

- Integration
- Layering
- Placement

(2 marks)

(Total = 4 marks)

14.6 (a) Which of these is an example of an 'internal check'?

- O Adherence to internal policies
- O Completeness of the accounting records
- O Safeguarding of assets
- O Use of control totals

(1 mark)

(b) Categorise the following as relating to the work of internal or external audit:

	Internal	External
Work relates to the financial statements, and the financial records that underlie them	O	O
Designed to add value and improve operations	O	O
Enables an opinion to be expressed on the financial statements	O	O
Report is to those charged with governance	O	O
Work relates to the operations of the organisation	O	O
Independent of the company and its management	O	O

(3 marks)

(Total = 4 marks)

(Total = 24 marks)

15 Leading and managing (42 mins)

15.1 Which of the following types of power correctly completes this statement?

Leaders may be distinguished from managers by the fact that they do not depend on

| ▼ | in the organisation.

Pull down list

- Expert power
- Physical power
- Position power

(1 mark)

15.2 Which of the following writers is **NOT** a member of the school of management thought to which the others belong?

- O FW Taylor
- O Elton Mayo
- O Abraham Maslow
- O Frederick Herzberg

(2 marks)

15.3 Monica is a manager in the finance department of P Co and she has several staff working for her. She has become quite friendly with most of her staff and they like her and appreciate that she does everything she can to attend to their needs.

Required

Which type of managerial style does Monica have?

- O Impoverished
- O Task management
- O Country club
- O Dampened pendulum

(2 marks)

15.4 According to Fielder, which of the following are true of psychologically distant managers?

(1) They judge their staff on the basis of performance

(2) They are primarily task-oriented

(3) They prefer formal consultation methods rather than seeking staff opinions

(4) They are closer to their staff

- O (1) and (2)
- O (2) and (3)
- O (1), (2) and (3)
- O (1), (2), (3) and (4)

(2 marks)

15.5   What is delegated by a superior to a subordinate?

○ Authority

○ Power

○ Responsibility

(1 mark)

15.6   Which of the following is **NOT** a technique of scientific management or Taylorism?

○ Micro-design of jobs

○ Work study techniques to establish efficient methods

○ Multi-skilled teamworking

○ Financial incentives

(2 marks)

15.7   What is the key contribution of the human relations approach to management?

○ Awareness of the importance of group dynamics and worker attitudes as an influence on productivity

○ Concern for productivity and efficiency

○ Awareness of the many different variables that influence and constrain a manager's behaviour

○ Proof of a comprehensible, clear link between job satisfaction, worker motivation and business success

(2 marks)

15.8   Which of the following leadership styles gives the most discretion or decision-making power to subordinates?

○ Autocratic

○ Consultative

○ Democratic

○ Persuasive

(2 marks)

15.9   Of Mintzberg's nine managerial roles, which is being exercised by a manager who gathers information from contacts within and outside the organisation?

○ Leader

○ Monitor

○ Spokesperson

○ Disseminator

(2 marks)

15.10 Which word or phrase correctly completes this definition?

[▼]   is the role at the interface between the operational core (non-managerial

workers) and management.

Pull down list

- Junior management
- Middle line
- Supervision

(1 mark)

15.11 According to research, which of the following statements is true of a consultative style of management, compared to other styles?

    ○ It is most popular among subordinates

    ○ It is most popular among leaders

    ○ It encourages the highest productivity

(1 mark)

15.12 Which of the following terms is used to describe the 'right' to perform an action in an organisation?

    ○ Responsibility

    ○ Authority

    ○ Influence

    ○ Power

(2 marks)

15.13 Which of the following is an 'interpersonal' role of management, in Mintzberg's classification of nine managerial roles?

    ○ Spokesperson

    ○ Figurehead

    ○ Negotiator

    ○ Resource allocator

(2 marks)

15.14 John Adair's action-centred leadership model is part of which school of thought?

    ○ Trait theories

    ○ Style theories

    ○ Contingency theories

(1 mark)

15.15 Are the following statements true or false?

	True	False
Adair's leadership model focuses on what leaders do and not what they are	○	○
The Ashridge leadership model proposes a democratic approach to leadership	○	○

(2 marks)

15.16 Which leadership approach sees the leadership as made up of three interrelated variables: task needs, individual needs of group members and needs of the group as a whole?

○ Action-centred leadership

○ Contingency theory

○ The managerial grid

○ Dispersed leadership

(2 marks)

15.17 Which managerial function is referred to in this definition?

[▼] is the managerial function concerned with establishing a structure of

tasks; grouping and assigning them to appropriate units; and establishing lines of

information and reporting to support performance.

Pull down list

• Organising

• Planning

• Controlling

(1 mark)

15.18 Which of the following is **NOT** one of Fayol's five functions of management?

○ Planning

○ Organising

○ Motivating

○ Commanding

(2 marks)

15.19 According to Drucker, which of the following is a management task?

○ Informational

○ Developing people

○ Decisional

(1 mark)

15.20 Which of the following writers put forward specific differences between the role of the manager and the role of the leader?

○ Bennis

○ Heifetz

○ Fielder

○ Blake and Mouton

(2 marks)

15.21 Which of the following theorists suggested that leaders can emerge, rather than be formally designated?

○ Kotter

○ Heifetz

O Adair

O Mintzberg

(2 marks)

(Total = 35 marks)

16 Recruitment and selection   (36 mins)

16.1 Which of the following would be classed as a 'selection' activity rather than a 'recruitment' activity?

O Job description

O Designing application forms

O Screening application forms

(1 mark)

16.2 A recruitment manager has prepared a statement of the key duties, tasks and reporting responsibilities involved in a particular job, as the basis for job interviewing.

Required

What name would be given to such a statement?

O Job analysis

O Job description

O Job advertisement

O Personnel specification

(2 marks)

16.3 In the context of personnel specifications, the Seven Point Plan (Rodger) does **NOT** explicitly include which of the following headings?

O Physical make-up

O Interests

O Motivation

O Circumstances

(2 marks)

16.4 What is the current trend in human resource management?

O Centralise recruitment and selection within HR

O Devolve recruitment and selection to line managers

O Devolve recruitment and selection to the Board

(1 mark)

16.5 Selection tests such as IQ tests and personality tests may not be effective in getting the right person for the job for several reasons.

Which of the following criticisms of the tests is **NOT** justified, however?

O Test results can be influenced by practice and coaching rather than genuine ability

O Subjects are able to deliberately falsify results

○ Tests do not completely eliminate bias and subjectivity

○ Tests are generally less accurate predictors of success than interviews

(2 marks)

16.6 In a selection interview, the interviewer asks: 'Surely you'd agree that objectivity is a key requirement for an auditor?'

Required

What sort of question is this?

○ Open

○ Closed

○ Problem-solving

○ Leading

(2 marks)

16.7 Which of the following is a disadvantage of a large panel or selection board interview compared to individual or one-to-one interviews?

○ A number of people see the candidate at one sitting

○ Specialists can ask a questions about technical areas of the work

○ Questions tend to be more varied and more random

○ There is less opportunity for personal rapport with the candidate

(2 marks)

16.8 In the context of selection interviews, which of the following describes the 'halo effect'?

○ A tendency for people to make an initial judgement based on first impressions, and then letting this colour their later perceptions.

○ An effect whereby the interviewer changes the behaviour of the applicant by suggestion

○ A tendency to mentally assign people to a group and then attribute to them the traits assumed to be characteristic of the group as a whole

○ An effect whereby the interviewer attributes to the applicant beliefs, attitudes or feelings which he has himself

(2 marks)

16.9 Which word correctly completes this sentence?

Selection tests which focus on aptitude, intelligence and personality factors are called

[▼] tests.

Pull down list

• Proficiency

• Psychometric

• Sensitive

• Standardised

(2 marks)

16.10 In the context of selection, what is an assessment centre?

   O   A place where candidates are taken to undergo group assessments

   O   A series of tests and interviews undergone by an individual candidate over several days

   O   A series of tests, interviews and activities undergone by a group of candidates over several days

   O   A technique for assessing large numbers of candidates, usually for junior positions, in a cost-effective manner

                                                                                        (2 marks)

16.11 Which of the following statements about reference checking is true?

   O   References provide objective information about a job candidate

   O   Personal references are particularly valuable in assessing the qualities of a candidate

   O   At least two employer references are desirable

                                                                                        (1 mark)

16.12 All of the following, except one, are areas of human resource management that benefit from job descriptions. Which is the exception?

   O   Job evaluation

   O   Training needs analysis

   O   Recruitment

   O   Employee flexibility

                                                                                        (2 marks)

16.13 A financial consultancy firm has a job vacancy for a junior office assistant at one of its offices. Which of the following would be the most suitable external medium for the job advertisement?

   O   Accountancy journal

   O   National newspapers

   O   Local newspapers

                                                                                        (1 mark)

16.14 A policy of internal promotion, as opposed to external recruitment, can have positive and negative effects. Which of the following would be negatively effected by such a policy?

   O   Innovation

   O   Succession planning

   O   Induction times

                                                                                        (1 mark)

16.15 Which of the following is **NOT** a primary aim of a job selection interview?

   O   Comparing the applicant against job requirements

   O   Getting as much information as possible about the applicant

   O   Giving the applicant information about the job and organisation

   O   Making the applicant feel (s)he has been treated fairly

                                                                                        (2 marks)

16.16 In which of the following circumstances would an organisation be better off carrying out its own recruitment, rather than using recruitment consultants?

   O The organisation has a strong, traditional culture, but is now looking to introduce greater innovation and flexibility

   O The organisation does not have a specialist recruitment function, but is looking to recruit on a large scale for the first time

   O The organisation uses outside consultants in many areas of its business, and is used to managing their services effectively

   O The organisation has complex cultural, business and technical selection criteria for its staff, but is considering using a consultancy for the first time, because it requires new people urgently in order to exploit an opportunity

(2 marks)

16.17 Which word correctly completes this sentence?

| ▼ | are capacities that lead to behaviours that meet job demands within the

parameters of the organisational environment.

Pull down list

- Attributes
- Competences
- Skills

(1 mark)

16.18 The first stage in the recruitment process is:

   O To write a job description

   O To write a person specification

   O To identify a vacancy

   O To liaise with recruitment consultants

(2 marks)

(Total = 30 marks)

17 Diversity and equal opportunities   (19 mins)

17.1 Sound business arguments can be made for having an equal opportunities policy. Which of the following reasons apply?

(1) To show common decency and fairness in line with business ethics

(2) To widen the recruitment pool

(3) To attract and retain the best people for the job

(4) To improve the organisation's image as a good employer

   O (1), (2) and (3) only

   O (2) and (3) only

   O (1) and (3) only

   O (1), (2), (3) and (4)

(2 marks)

17.2 Which of the following correctly describes the purpose of current Equal Pay legislation?

○ To ensure that there is no element of sexual or racial discrimination in determining pay rates

○ To provide that job evaluation must be used in determining pay rates

○ To provide that women have the right to equal pay to work of equal value to that of men

○ To ensure that women have the right to equal pay to men in the same job

(2 marks)

17.3 Which of the following statements are true or false?

	True	False
Taking active steps to encourage people from disadvantaged groups to apply for jobs and training is classed as positive discrimination.	○	○
Diversity in the workplace means implementing an equal opportunities policy.	○	○

(2 marks)

17.4 Members of a religious minority in a workplace are frequently subjected to jokes about their dress and dietary customs, and a bit of name-calling, by non-religious workmates.

They find this offensive and hurtful – even though their colleagues say it is 'just a bit of fun'.

Required

What type of discrimination (if any) would this represent?

○ Victimisation

○ Indirect discrimination

○ Harassment

(1 mark)

17.5 Which of the following is a potential business benefit of a corporate diversity policy?

○ Compliance with equal opportunities legislation

○ Respect for individuals

○ Better understanding of target market segments

○ Efficiency in managing human resources

(2 marks)

17.6 Which of the following statements about disability discrimination law is **NOT** true?

○ The requirements only effect employers of more than 20 employees

○ Employers must adjust working arrangements or the physical features of premises to remove any disadvantage to disabled people

○ For an individual to be defined as a disabled person, the physical or mental impairment must have an adverse effect of more than 12 months' duration

○ Public bodies have additional duties to protect and promote equality for disabled people

(2 marks)

17.7 Which of the following would constitute direct discrimination?

○ Setting age limits or ranges in an employment advertisement

○ Offering less favourable terms to workers on flexible hours contracts

○ Using word-of-mouth recruitment in a predominantly male workforce

(1 mark)

17.8 A job interviewer asks a woman about her plans to have a family. She eventually does not get the job, because she lacks qualifications which are listed as essential in the person specification. However, she later finds out that men who attended interviews were not asked questions about their plans to have a family.

Required

Which of the following statements correctly describes the situation?

○ The woman would have a successful claim of direct sexual discrimination

○ The woman would have a successful claim of indirect sexual discrimination

○ The organisation has laid itself open to a claim of indirect sexual discrimination, but such a claim would not be successful

○ The organisation has not laid itself open to any claim of discrimination

(2 marks)

17.9 Which words correctly complete this sentence?

The concept of [▼] is based on the belief that the dimensions of individual

difference on which organisations currently focus are crude and performance-irrelevant,

and that an organisation should reflect the range of differences within its customer and

labour markets.

Pull down list

- Cultural divergence
- Equal opportunity
- Managing diversity

(1 mark)

17.10 Which of the following is an example of 'positive discrimination' rather than 'positive action' on equal opportunities?

○ Selecting a certain number of people from ethnic minorities for jobs, regardless of job-relevant selection criteria

○ Using ethnic languages in job advertisements

O   Setting targets for the number of people from ethnic minorities that the organisation would like to see in managerial positions

(1 mark)

(Total = 16 marks)

18 Individuals, groups and teams

(32 mins)

18.1   Which of the following is most clearly a sign of an ineffective group?

O   There is disagreement and criticism within the group

O   There is competition with other groups

O   Members passively accept work decisions

O   Individuals achieve their own targets

(2 marks)

18.2   A team leader is having difficulties with conflict in the team, due to 'clashes' or incompatibilities in the personalities of two of its members. The leader draws up a list of options for managing the problem.

Required

Which option, from the following list, would be the least practicable?

O   Educate the members about personality differences

O   Encourage the members to modify their personalities

O   Remove one of the members from the team

(1 mark)

18.3   At the Soli-Darretty Bros factory, a project team has been put together by management. The team are engaged in debating how they are going to approach the task, and who is going to do what.

Some of their first ideas have not worked out but they are starting to put forward some really innovative ideas: they get quite excited in brainstorming sessions, and are uninhibited in putting forward their views and suggestions.

Factions are emerging, not only around different ideas, but around two dominating individuals who always seem to disagree.

Required

At what stage of Tuckman's group development model is this team?

O   Forming

O   Storming

O   Norming

(1 mark)

18.4   Which word correctly completes this definition?

| ▼ | are mental states (made up of thoughts, feelings and intentions) which influence an individual's response to all objects and situations with which they are related.

Pull down list

- Attitudes
- Emotional intelligences
- Perceptions
- Personality traits

(2 marks)

18.5 For which of the following applications is teamworking **NOT** best suited?

○ Ideas generation for innovation

○ Co-ordination of different functions

○ Crisis decision-making

○ Co-ordination of geographically dispersed workers

(2 marks)

18.6 If a team is bogged down in argument, and discussion is turning hostile, which of the following types of contribution would the team leader seek to discourage?

○ Bringing-in

○ Blocking

○ Summarising

○ Testing understanding

(2 marks)

18.7 Which of the following is **NOT** a key tool of team building?

○ Members identify with the team

○ Members are as alike as possible

○ Members commit to shared objectives

(1 mark)

18.8 Grant is a member of a project team. His colleagues in the team rely on him to read and check complex project documentation.

Grant has a keen eye for detail and often identifies minor details in documents that others miss but may be of significance. Despite the diligent approach, Grant always meets his deadlines.

However, some of Grant's colleagues feel frustrated when he refuses to involve others.

He can hold up progress as he will not agree to the team signing off project documents until all of his concerns are fully discussed.

Required

According to Belbin's team roles theory, Grant is an example of which of the following?

○ Implementer

○ Completer – finisher

○ Monitor – evaluator

○ Shaper

(2 marks)

18.9 What is the most important attribute of a 'group', which distinguishes it from a random crowd of people?

○ Purpose

○ Conformity

○ Identity

(1 mark)

18.10 In Belbin's model of team roles, which of the following is most important for a well-functioning team?

○ A mix and balance of team roles

○ Nine members, so that all roles are filled

○ A focus on functional/task roles, not process roles

○ As few members as possible

(2 marks)

18.11 A team is winding up a challenging project that it has been working on for some time. Next week, the same team will go on to a new project with quite different challenges.

Required

Which stage of the group development model is this team likely to be going through?

○ Norming

○ Dorming

○ Adjourning

(1 mark)

18.12 Which of the following would be an effective technique for encouraging healthy team solidarity?

○ Discouraging competition with other groups

○ Encouraging competition within the group

○ Encouraging members to express disagreements

○ Discouraging members from expressing disagreements

(2 marks)

18.13 An organisation has set up a team in which any member of the team can perform the full range of its tasks.

The manager is able to share out tasks between members according to who is available to do a given job when it is required.

Required

What sort of team organisation does this describe?

○ Multi-disciplinary team

○ Multi-skilled team

○ Self-managed team

○ Virtual team

(2 marks)

18.14 Team-member Tom is one of those people who is dynamic and thrives on pressure.

He tends to be the one who challenges and pushes other team members, sometimes annoying or upsetting them – but also getting the team past difficult periods.

Required

Which of Belbin's team roles does Tom exercise?

O   Plant

O   Co-ordinator (chair)

O   Implementer

O   Shaper

(2 marks)

18.15 A team is having a brainstorming session and one member suggests 'Let's move on to something else as we're getting nowhere'. What type of contribution is this?

O   Proposing

O   Supporting

O   Blocking

O   Shutting out

(2 marks)

18.16 Team-leader Arnica has given a briefing stating the current situation and asking for suggestions to move the project on. What stage is the team current at?

O   Forming

O   Storming

O   Norming

O   Performing

(2 marks)

(Total = 27 marks)

19 Motivating individuals and groups   (36 mins)

19.1   Phil T Luker & Son offers its employees a reward package which includes salary and company car. Its factory is safe and clean and rather smart. The work is technically challenging and employees are encouraged to produce innovative solutions to problems.

Required

Which of the rewards offered by the firm is a form of intrinsic reward?

O   The salary

O   The car

O   The work

(1 mark)

19.2   Which of the following is **NOT** a category in Maslow's hierarchy of needs theory?

O   Physiological needs

O   Freedom of inquiry and expression needs

BPP
LEARNING
MEDIA

○ Need for affiliation

○ Safety needs

(2 marks)

19.3 Keepham (Hungary) Co offers its employees:

(1) Sensible company policies

(2) Good salaries and bonuses

(3) Considerate supervision

(4) Training programmes

According to Herzberg's two-factor theory, which of these things will satisfy employees in such a way as to motivate them to superior effort in the long-term?

○ (2) only

○ (4) only

○ (2) and (4) only

○ (1), (2), (3) and (4)

(2 marks)

19.4 What term is given, in motivation theory, to the things people value and choose to pursue?

○ Goals

○ Innate needs

○ Satisfaction

(1 mark)

19.5 Willy Dewitt-Ornott works in Sales. There is always a sales competition at the year end and the winner is likely to be made team leader. Willy's quite certain that he will be able to win and that he will have more responsibility, which he would like. However, he would also have to work much longer hours, and he is quite reluctant to do this for family reasons.

Required

If an expectancy equation were used to assess Willy's motivation to work hard at the end of the year, based on the information given, which of the following results would you expect to see?

○ Valence would be high, expectancy high, motivation high

○ Valence would be high, expectancy low, motivation low

○ Valence would be around 0, expectancy high, motivation low

○ Valence would be around 0, expectancy high, motivation high

(2 marks)

19.6 All of the following, except one, are alternative terms for the same thing. Which is the exception?

○ Motivator factor

○ Hygiene factor

○ Environmental factor

○ Maintenance factor

(2 marks)

19.7 Which of the following is the dimension missing from the above list?

The five core dimensions which contribute to job satisfaction are skill variety, task identity,

task significance, [_____ ▼] and feedback.

Pull down list

- Advancement
- Autonomy
- Recognition
- Rewards

(2 marks)

19.8 Participation can motivate employees by making them take 'ownership' of the task and increasing their commitment.

In which of the following circumstances, however, would this **NOT** happen?

○ Participation is genuine

○ The purpose of participation is made clear

○ Everyone is allowed to participate equally

○ Efforts at participation are maintained for a reasonable period

(2 marks)

19.9 The management of Guenguiss Cans Co runs a 'tight ship', with clocking-on timekeeping systems, close supervision and rules for everything.

'Well,' says the general manager, 'if you allow people to have any freedom at work, they will take advantage and their work rate will deteriorate'.

Required

Which of Douglas McGregor's 'theories' does this management team subscribe to?

○ Theory X

○ Theory Y

○ Theory Z

(1 mark)

19.10 Application of process theories to motivation in practice involves all but one of the following measures. Which is the exception?

○ Clarifying intended results

○ Giving feedback on actual results

○ Immediacy of reward following results

○ Consistency of reward for results

(2 marks)

19.11 Which of the following is a potential problem with individual performance-related pay (PRP) as a motivator?

○ Its effect on organisational communication

○ Its relevance to business objectives

BPP
LEARNING
MEDIA

○ The fact that it does not relate to individuals' wage or salary grades

○ Its effect on team motivation

(2 marks)

19.12 The following, with one exception, are claimed as advantages for job enrichment as a form of job re-design.

Which is the exception?

○ It increases job satisfaction

○ It enhances quality of output

○ It replaces monetary rewards

○ It reduces supervisory costs

(2 marks)

19.13 According to Maslow's hierarchy of needs, which of the following is the final 'need' to be satisfied?

○ Self-realisation

○ Self-actualisation

○ Esteem needs

○ Physiological needs

(2 marks)

19.14 Job evaluation puts a relative value on jobs primarily on the basis of which of the following factors?

○ Equity

○ Job content

○ Market rates of pay

(1 mark)

19.15 In Vroom's expectancy theory, what is meant by 'valence'?

○ The strength of an individual's preference for a given outcome

○ The strength of an individual's motivation to act in a certain way

○ The strength of an individual's belief that acting in a certain way will obtain the desired outcome

(1 mark)

19.16 Eva Moor-Drudgery used to pack chocolate bars into boxes of three dozen.

Her job has been redesigned, so that she now packs them, applies a 'sell-by' date stamp, cellophanes the box and applies a promotional sticker.

Required

Of which form of job redesign is this an example?

○ Job rotation

○ Job enlargement

○ Job enrichment

(1 mark)

19.17 Which job design technique was advocated by the scientific management school?

○ Empowerment

○ Micro-division of labour

○ Division of labour

○ Job enlargement

(2 marks)

19.18 Javed manages a team in which individuals with strong personalities often have heated disagreements, which can lead to open conflict and disruption of work processes.

Javed called the team together and explained to them that the outputs of the team should take priority and that every individual team member should try to put their personal feelings aside for the benefit of the company.

He persuaded them that they would be better off by modifying their behaviour, as the team's effort was more important in meeting the objectives of the organisation, than the personal agendas of each person in it.

Required

Which of the following is Javed's approach to addressing conflict?

○ Integration

○ Compromise

○ Denial

○ Dominance

(2 marks)

(Total = 30 marks)

20 Training and development   (34 mins)

20.1 Trainee Sara is unhappy in her current training programme, because it is too 'hands on': she is required to attempt techniques before she has had a chance to study the underlying principles first. She spends the evenings trying to read ahead in the course textbook.

Required

Which of Honey and Mumford's learning styles is Sara's preferred style?

○ Reflector

○ Pragmatist

○ Theorist

(1 mark)

20.2 Which of the following is **NOT** a characteristic of a 'learning organisation'?

○ The generation and transfer of knowledge

○ Support for learning and development by all members

○ A scientific approach to problem-solving, in order to minimise risk and error

○ Willingness to continuously transform itself in response to a changing environment

(2 marks)

BPP
LEARNING
MEDIA

20.3 Which of the following statements about training would be the foundation of an effective training policy?

   ○ Training is the responsibility of the HR department

   ○ Training is all cost and no quantifiable benefit

   ○ The important thing is to do lots of training

   ○ Training can be an effective solution to some performance problems

(2 marks)

20.4 Which word correctly completes this definition?

[▼] is 'the planned and systematic modification of behaviour through learning events, programmes and instruction which enable individuals to achieve the level of knowledge, skills and competence to carry out their work effectively'.

Pull down list

   • Conditioning

   • Education

   • Training

(1 mark)

20.5 The learning cycle developed by David Kolb is a process for .... learning.

Required

Which of the following words correctly completes this sentence?

   ○ Programmed

   ○ Experiential

   ○ Action

   ○ Reflection

(2 marks)

20.6 All the following, with one exception, are clear benefits of training and development for an organisation.

Which is the exception?

   ○ Increased organisational flexibility

   ○ Less need for detailed supervision

   ○ Enhanced employability of staff members

   ○ Improved succession planning

(2 marks)

20.7 Which of the following are 'on the job' training methods?

   (1) Day-release

   (2) Job rotation

(3) Coaching

(4) Temporary promotion

○ Method (3) only

○ Methods (1) and (3) only

○ Methods (2), (3) and (4) only

○ Methods (1), (2), (3) and (4)

(2 marks)

20.8 You have been asked to comment on the most effective approach for training accounts staff in the use of a new payroll system.

Which of the following arguments would you put forward for choosing an on-the-job approach?

○ Ability of learners to concentrate on the learning process

○ Risk of errors

○ Relevance to the informal customs and practices of the department

○ Application of learned skills to the job

(2 marks)

20.9 The effectiveness of a training scheme may be measured at different levels.

Which of the following levels would be most appropriate for a team leader seeking to evaluate a training programme designed to improve the productivity of her section?

○ Level 1: trainee reactions

○ Level 2: trainee learning

○ Level 3: job behaviour

○ Level 5: ultimate value

(2 marks)

20.10 Which word or phrase correctly completes this sentence?

[_____ ▼] development is a process whereby employees are offered a wide range of developmental opportunities, rather than focusing on skills required in the current job.

Pull down list

• Career

• Management

• Personal

(1 mark)

20.11 Peter has been identified, using Honey & Mumford's learning styles questionnaire, as a Pragmatist learner. He is now preparing a personal development plan to improve his sales skills.

Required

Which of the following training methods would Peter prefer and include in his plan?

○ On-the-job coaching by his supervisor

○ A group workshop in 'interpersonal skills practice'

○ Personal development journaling

○ A computer-based training module on sales

(2 marks)

20.12 The HR manager of a firm has been asked to explain to the finance director the quantifiable benefits of training programmes. Which of the following might she hesitate to put forward?

○ Increased speed of working

○ Increased accuracy of work

○ Increased employee satisfaction

(1 mark)

20.13 Which of the following statements is correct?

(1) The growth or realisation of a person's ability and potential through the provision of learning and educational experiences.

(2) The planned and systematic modification of behaviour through learning events, programmes and instruction which enable individuals to achieve the level of knowledge, skills and competences to carry out their work effectively.

○ 1 is the definition of development and 2 is the definition of training

○ 1 is the definition of education and 2 is the definition of development

○ 1 is the definition of training and 2 is the definition of development

○ 1 is the definition of education and 2 is the definition of training

(2 marks)

20.14 Which of the following documents would be part of a formal training needs analysis exercise?

○ An email reminding you that a new piece of legislation is about to come into effect

○ A health and safety officer's report showing that a department failed its assessment in a recent fire evacuation drill

○ A set of competence standards for your job or department

○ Feedback from a colleague about the standard of your work

(2 marks)

20.15 What term is used for this learning technology?

[▼] is learning through a network of computers or the internet (but not stand-alone CD-Rom or tuition software), so that learning support is available from online tutors, moderators and discussion groups.

Pull down list

• Blended learning

• Computer based assessment

• Computer based training

• E-learning

(2 marks)

20.16 The stages of Kolb's experiential learning cycle are as follows.

(1) Draw conclusions from the experience

(2) Have an experience

(3) Plan the next steps

(4) Reflect on the experience

Required

Which is the correct order?

○ (2), (4), (1), (3)

○ (2), (3), (4), (1)

○ (2), (4), (3), (1)

(1 mark)

20.17 What is a competence framework used for?

○ To identify present level of competence

○ To identify training needs

○ To evaluate training success or failure

(1 mark)

(Total = 28 marks)

21 Performance appraisal   (26 mins)

21.1 Which of the following is **NOT** a purpose of performance appraisal?

○ Job evaluation

○ Identification of training needs

○ Succession planning

(1 mark)

21.2 A manager is assessing the performance of her team members.

In accordance with the appraisal system of the organisation, she has been given a list of characteristics and performance elements, with notes on how to interpret and apply the terms: 'integrity', 'punctuality' and so on.

She is required to comment on how each appraisee measures up in terms of each factor.

Required

Which appraisal technique is this organisation using?

○ Overall assessment

○ Grading

○ Behavioural incident

○ Guided assessment

(2 marks)

21.3 All of the following, except one, are sound principles for devising performance measures. Which is the exception?

○ They should be related to actual key tasks of the job

○ They should be easily achievable

○ They should be within the control of the individual

○ They should be observable or measurable

(2 marks)

21.4 In an appraisal interview, the manager tells the subordinate how he has been assessed – good and bad – and then gives him a chance to put questions, suggest improvement targets, explain shortcomings and identify problems.

Required

Using Maier's classification, what is the name given to this approach to appraisal interviewing?

○ Tell and sell

○ Tell and listen

○ Problem solving

○ Sell and listen

(2 marks)

21.5 Which of the following is likely to be the most objective approach to appraisal?

○ Self appraisal

○ Peer appraisal

○ Upward appraisal

○ 360-degree feedback

(2 marks)

21.6 Which two words correctly completes this definition?

[▼] is 'a process to establish a shared understanding about what is to be

achieved, and an approach to managing and developing people in order to achieve it'.

Pull down list

• Peer appraisal

• Performance appraisal

• Performance management

(1 mark)

21.7 Which of the following are meaningful criteria for measuring the effectiveness of an appraisal scheme?

(1) Serious intent

(2) Fairness

(3) Efficiency

(4) Co-operation

(5) Results

○ (2), (3) and (5) only

○ (3) and (5) only

○ (1), (2), (3) and (4) only

○ (1), (2), (3), (4) and (5)

(2 marks)

21.8 Which word or phrase correctly completes this sentence?

| ▼ | is the name given to gathering of appraisals from the individual,

superiors, subordinates, peers and co-workers and customers.

Pull down list

• Management by objectives

• Multi-source feedback

• Performance management

(1 mark)

21.9 Appraisal is a complex human relations and political exercise.

Required

Which of the following is **NOT** necessarily a helpful factor in the design of an appraisal scheme?

○ The purpose of the system is positive and clearly expressed

○ There is reasonable standardisation throughout the organisation

○ Time is allowed for appraisee preparation and appraiser training

○ There is an implied link between assessment and reward

(2 marks)

21.10 Which of the following is **NOT** a barrier to effective appraisal?

○ Appraisal is seen as a way of wrapping up unfinished business for the year

○ Appraisal is seen as conforming to Human Resource procedures

○ Appraisal is seen as an opportunity to raise workplace problems and issues

○ Appraisal is seen as an annual event

(2 marks)

21.11 Which of the following criteria would **NOT** be suitable for evaluating an appraisal system?

○ Serious intent

○ Fairness

○ Bonuses awarded

(1 mark)

BPP
LEARNING
MEDIA

21.12 Which of the following is an advantage to all employees of having a formal appraisal system?

○ Suitable promotion candidates are identified

○ It provides a basis for medium- to long-term HR planning

○ Individual objectives are related to the objectives of the whole organisation

○ It provides a basis for reviewing recruitment and selection decisions

(2 marks)

21.13 A sales team is assessed according to the number of sales calls made, number of leads generated, and number and value of sales made.

Required

Which appraisal technique is described in this example?

○ Behavioural incident

○ Rating scale

○ Guided assessment

○ Results-oriented

(2 marks)

(Total = 22 marks)

22 Section D MTQs   **(29 mins)**

22.1 (a) Peter, Gloria, Shirley and Matthew are part of a newly formed team.

Peter is a reliable employee who likes to take ideas from other people and turn them into actions. He is not very flexible and tends to be resistant to change or new possibilities.

Gloria is a dynamic individual who responds best when under pressure. She is driven to overcome any obstacles, but has a tendency to hurt other people's feelings.

Shirley is single-minded and dedicated to her work. She has a lot of specific knowledge, but only contributes to discussions on these areas and lacks the ability to see the bigger picture.

Matthew is strategically minded. He likes to see all the available options before judging them. He has a proven track record of good judgements, but can be overly critical and does not inspire others that he works with.

Required

For each team member listed below, select the appropriate Belbin team role from the list below:

Peter

▼

Gloria

▼

Shirley

▼

Matthew

▼

Pull down list

- Implementer
- Monitor-Evaluator
- Shaper
- Specialist

(2 marks)

(b) Which word correctly fills in the blank?

[▼]   occurs when an individual is penalised for giving information in a discrimination claim against an employer.

Pull down list

- Harassment
- Indirect discrimination
- Victimisation

(1 mark)

(c) Encouraging individuals from disadvantaged groups to apply for jobs and training is known as positive action.

- ○ True
- ○ False

(1 mark)

(Total = 4 marks)

22.2 (a) Indicate whether the following are extrinsic rewards, intrinsic rewards or incentives.

	Extrinsic reward	Intrinsic reward	Incentive
A feeling of achievement	○	○	○
A promise of additional time off for meeting a target	○	○	○
Working conditions	○	○	○
Salary	○	○	○

(2 marks)

(b) Which **TWO** of the following steps would be classified as job enrichment?

- ☐ Giving an employee freedom to decide how the job should be done
- ☐ Increasing the number of tasks an employee participates in
- ☐ Transferring an employee from one job to another
- ☐ Encouraging employee participation in planning decisions of superiors
- ☐ Dividing a job up into a small number of sequential tasks

(2 marks)

(Total = 4 marks)

22.3 (a) Shaun likes to understand basic principles and take a hands-off approach based on logical argument. He wants to participate in a structured training programme which is run by teachers.

Louise needs to work at her own pace and tends to be fairly slow and cautious in her learning. She likes to observe things, take time to think about them and then produces a carefully thought-out conclusion.

Susan only likes to study if she can see a link to a real practical problem. She likes to learn new techniques through on-the-job training, but tends to discard good ideas which require some development to work properly.

Tony is flexible and optimistic, but does not have any patience with theories. He wants to receive hands-on training and enjoys practical problems.

Required

Honey and Mumford classified the four following learning styles:

- Theorists
- Reflectors
- Activists
- Pragmatists

Match the learning styles above to the following individuals below.

Theorists	SHAUN	LOUISE	SUSAN	TONY
Reflectors	SHAUN	LOUISE	SUSAN	TONY
Activists	SHAUN	LOUISE	SUSAN	TONY
Pragmatists	SHAUN	LOUISE	SUSAN	TONY

(2 marks)

(b) Which **TWO** of the following are off-the-job training methods?

☐ Job rotation

☐ Computer-based training

☐ Temporary promotion

☐ Demonstration

☐ College courses

(2 marks)

(Total = 4 marks)

22.4 (a) George, Helen, Josh and Leigh are all on development programmes.

George is learning skills that are not directly required in his current role, but should allow him to contribute more flexibly and innovatively to the organisation in the future whichever role he is in.

Helen is gaining experience of each of the different functions in her company as well as a variety of position and work settings as preparation for increased responsibility in the future.

Josh is receiving training to ensure his professional standards in his accountancy work are maintained and enhanced through education, development and training.

Leigh is partway through a series of planned secondments within her department and has recently been working in two project group for implementing new systems.

The following are all different approaches to development:

- Management development
- Personal development
- Professional development
- Career development

Required

Match the development approaches above to the following individuals below.

Management development	GEORGE	HELEN	JOSH	LEIGH
Personal Development	GEORGE	HELEN	JOSH	LEIGH
Professional development	GEORGE	HELEN	JOSH	LEIGH
Career development	GEORGE	HELEN	JOSH	LEIGH

(2 marks)

(b) Which **TWO** of the following are necessary for a training programme to be effective?

☐ Training should be expensive

☐ There should be clear objectives

☐ Training should be off-the-job

☐ There should be timely feedback

☐ Training should be on-the-job

(2 marks)

(Total = 4 marks)

22.5 (a) Company W assess the performance of its sales staff by the number of clients visited and the number of products they each sell.

Company X rates its managerial staff. Each manager is awarded a score from 1 (excellent) to 4 (poor), based on feedback from subordinates and superiors.

Company Y appraises the performance of its staff through assessors commenting on a number of desired characteristics and performance elements.

Company Z compares attributes displayed by its staff to a series of attributes that indicate either unsatisfactory or unsatisfactory performance in their job role.

The following are different types of appraisal techniques

- Guided assessment
- Grading
- Behavioural-incident method
- Results-oriented scheme

Required

Match the appraisal techniques above to the following companies below.

Guided Assessment	COMPANY W	COMPANY X	COMPANY Y	COMPANY Z
Grading	COMPANY W	COMPANY X	COMPANY Y	COMPANY Z

Behavioural-incident method	COMPANY W	COMPANY X	COMPANY Y	COMPANY Z
Results-oriented scheme	COMPANY W	COMPANY X	COMPANY Y	COMPANY Z

(2 marks)

(b) The manager does not criticise, but instead discusses issues with the employee.

The employee is encouraged to think things through and is committed to improvement.

Required

Which of Maier's three approaches to appraisal interviews is this an example of?

○ Tell and sell

○ Tell and listen

○ Problem-solving

(1 mark)

(c) Performance appraisal can be used to identify potential candidates for promotion.

○ True

○ False

(1 mark)

(Total = 4 marks)

22.6 (a) What type of power describes the behaviour of a manager who is refusing a request for one of his team members to help with the workload of another department?

○ Expert power

○ Negative power

○ Coercive power

○ Physical power

(1 mark)

(b) Fiedler, Heifetz and Bennis are theorists who wrote about management and leadership.

Match each of the statements below with each theorist's findings.

	Fiedler	Heifetz	Bennis
Individuals at all levels can exert a leadership influence	○	○	○
There are 'psychologically close' and 'psychologically distant' managers	○	○	○
The manager 'does things right' while the leader 'does the right thing'	○	○	○

(3 marks)

(Total = 4 marks)

(Total = 24 marks)

> **Part E: Personal effectiveness and communication in business**

23 Personal effectiveness and communication (37 mins)

23.1 If a supervisor in the Sales department requests the help of the HR Director in a complex disciplinary matter, what direction is the communication flow?

○ Vertical

○ Horizontal

○ Diagonal

(1 mark)

23.2 What name is given to the process whereby an individual defines objectives and formulates action plans for learning with a view to improving his or her own effectiveness?

○ Coaching

○ Mentoring

○ Counselling

○ Personal development planning

(2 marks)

23.3 The following, with one exception, are potential problems for time management.

Which is the exception?

○ An open door policy of management

○ A sociable work group

○ An assertive style of communication

(1 mark)

23.4 Jared is the leader of a virtual team which stays in contact via email. Team members send all messages to Jared, who forwards them to the rest of the network. Which communication pattern is reflected in this situation?

○ The circle

○ The 'Y'

○ The wheel

○ The all-channel

(2 marks)

23.5 You are a sales representative who routinely visits customers in their homes and places of business to present the latest products to them, as well as take orders (where inventory is available).

Required

Which of the following technology tools will most directly enhance your effectiveness?

○ Computer telephony integration

○ Electronic Data Interchange (EDI)

○ Mobile communications

(1 mark)

23.6 Which of the following areas is **NOT** an advantage of using email as a communication tool?

○ Security

○ Speed

○ Multiple recipients

○ Versatility

(2 marks)

23.7 Which of the following words correctly completes this statement.

Counselling is essentially a/an [▼] role.

Pull down list

• Advisory

• Non-directive

• Task-related

(1 mark)

23.8 Which of the following is **NOT** an attribute of communication through an informal organisational network or 'grapevine'?

○ Fast

○ Selective

○ Accurate

○ Up-to-date

(2 marks)

23.9 All of the following, except one, are measures for encouraging upward communication in an organisation.

Which is the exception?

○ Suggestion schemes

○ Management by Walking Around

○ Exception reporting

(1 mark)

23.10 In the radio signal model, which of the following shows the correct order in which a message is transmitted?

○ Feedback, Sender, Decoded message, Coded message, Receiver

○ Sender, Decoded message, Coded message, Feedback, Receiver

○ Coded message, Sender, Decoded message, Receiver, Feedback

○ Sender, Coded message, Decoded message, Receiver, Feedback

(2 marks)

23.11 Which of these communication mechanisms improves upward communication?

○ Notice boards

○ Organisation manual

○ Team meetings

○ Team briefings

(2 marks)

23.12 What is the technical term given to a fault in the communication process where the meaning of the message is lost 'in translation' from intention to language, or from language to understanding?

○ Noise

○ Redundancy

○ Distortion

○ Feedback

(2 marks)

23.13 According to Leavitt, which of the following communication patterns is the fastest in terms of problem solving?

○ Y

○ Circle

○ Chain

○ Wheel

(2 marks)

23.14 Which of the following defines coaching?

○ Developing the individual by helping to build on skills and overcome weaknesses

○ Provision of one-way instruction on formal tasks required to carry out the immediate job

○ Offering career guidance in order to maximise the individual's potential

○ Provision of objective advice to overcome the individual's personal problems

(2 marks)

23.15 Which of the following statements about non-verbal communication is **NOT** true?

○ Non-verbal cues can be used to reinforce or undermine spoken messages

○ People pay less attention to non-verbal cues than to what is being said

○ Non-verbal cues include tone of voice and silences

○ Non-verbal cues are a key source of feedback

(2 marks)

23.16 In the context of work planning and personal development planning, a SMART framework is often used as a checklist of the characteristics of effective goals.

Required

What does the 'M' in SMART stand for?

○ Manageable

○ Measurable

○ Motivational

(1 mark)

23.17 ABC has promised customer DEF that a product will be delivered on a certain date. The product is in fact delivered nearly a month late. As a direct result DEF misses an important deadline and has to pay penalties.

Required

In what way has ABC failed DEF?

○ Failed to communicate

○ Failed to meet deadlines

○ Failed to comply with job specifications

○ Failed to deliver the exact product needed

(2 marks)

23.18 When considering a personal development programme, what should be the first stage?

○ Planning a learning and development programme

○ Establishing learning targets

○ Broadening the employee's knowledge and experience

○ Setting up a competence framework

(2 marks)

23.19 Which of the following may give rise to a source of positive or constructive conflict?

○ Hostility between employees

○ The task is lost sight of due to individual arguments

○ A dispute focuses attention on individual contributions

(1 mark)

(Total = 31 marks)

24 Section E MTQs   (29 mins)

24.1 (a) Which **TWO** of the following would show that a task is important to an organisation?

☐ The task will satisfy a key customer

☐ The task comes in an email marked urgent

☐ The task will add value to the organisation

☐ The task has already been delegated by two superiors

(2 marks)

(b) Are the following statements true or false?

	True	False
A meeting without a clear objective will always give value to everyone attending for the time taken.	○	○
Time management can be improved by setting aside times when an individual is not contactable by others.	○	○

(2 marks)

(Total = 4 marks)

24.2 (a) Trevor, Joss, Michael and Leona are all managers in HGF Co experiencing conflict in their teams.

Trevor responds to conflict by encouraging the individuals to bargain and negotiate.

Joss puts emphasis on the task in hand and stresses that the group effort must be superior to individual effort.

Michael likes to use his power as manager to force a settlement on his team. This causes some resentment amongst his team members.

Leona ignores the conflict in the hope that the issue is trivial and the team will then continue to operate as normal.

The following are management responses to conflict:

- Denial
- Compromise
- Dominance
- Integration / Collaboration

Required

Match the management responses above to the managers below.

Denial	TREVOR	JOSS	MICHAEL	LEONA
Compromise	TREVOR	JOSS	MICHAEL	LEONA
Dominance	TREVOR	JOSS	MICHAEL	LEONA
Integration / Collaboration	TREVOR	JOSS	MICHAEL	LEONA

(2 marks)

(b) Are the following statements about conflict resolution true or false?

	True	False
Compromises result in all parties being satisfied	O	O
A win-win situation is rare, but is the best solution to conflict resolution	O	O
A lose-lose situation is not possible	O	O
Win-lose situations can result in damaged relationships within the team	O	O

(2 marks)

(Total = 4 marks)

24.3 (a) Indicate whether each of the following are data or information.

	Data	Information
Completed questionnaires for market research	O	O
Company website page	O	O
Calculations showing whether an investment is profitable	O	O
An individual employee's test score	O	O

	Data	Information
Variance reports for a department manager	○	○
The average employee assessment grade for a company	○	○

(3 marks)

(b) A five-year cash forecast would be classified as which level of information?

○ Operational

○ Management

○ Strategic

(1 mark)

(Total = 4 marks)

24.4 (a) On 1 August, the financial controller of XYZ Co is told it is her responsibility to let everyone in the finance department know about a compulsory meeting to be held on 15 September. The financial controller sends an email to all members of the finance department, informing them about the time, date, place and purpose of the meeting. The email is sent on 13 September.

Required

Which of the following desirable qualities of formal communication is lacking in this scenario?

○ Clarity

○ Recipient

○ Medium

○ Timing

(2 marks)

(b) Which **THREE** of the following statements about informal communication are true?

☐ The grapevine operates outside the place of work

☐ Information is not divulged randomly

☐ It can bypass secretive management

☐ The grapevine fills a gap created by an ineffective formal communication system

☐ It is less current than formal communication

☐ It relates to internal politics

(2 marks)

(Total = 4 marks)

24.5 (a) Which **TWO** of the following are examples of misunderstanding in the communication process?

☐ Slang is used in task instructions

☐ A meeting goes on for too long for participants to pay attention to everything in the meeting

☐ An email sent to all employees using IT jargon

☐ The sender of an email has not included details of the location of the meeting

☐ A manager is constantly dealing with queries from subordinates and misses a meeting

(2 marks)

(b) Which of the following correctly fills the blank?

| ▼ | occurs when an individual thinks that they have been wrongly

treated by a colleague or supervisor.

Pull down list

- A grievance
- Direct discrimination
- Indirect discrimination

(1 mark)

(c) The meaning of a message is lost at the coding and decoding stage.

Required

Which of the following is the correct term for this loss of meaning?

O Feedback

O Distortion

O Noise

(1 mark)

(Total = 4 marks)

24.6 (a) Peggy, Operations Director at X Ltd, has delegated the task of identifying reasons for recent bottlenecks in manufacturing processes to Susan. This will involve Susan in interviewing relevant operators, foremen and supervisors, and also liaising with other departments, to establish why the bottlenecks are occurring. Peggy would like a report on her desk in two weeks' time as she is due to report to the board. Susan is worried about the project, as she is very busy with her routine workload.

Required

Place the steps below in the correct order, so that Susan can plan her time effectively.

- Identification of information sources within the business
- Collation of information
- Establishing priorities with Peggy
- Sequencing of interviews with relevant staff
- Delegation of routine tasks
- Report writing

(3 marks)

(b) Jim has been asked to coach John in certain technically demanding aspects of his accounting role in order to improve John's performance.

Which of the following is **NOT** part of this role?

O Showing John where to find company information on accounting standards

O Demonstrating the company's new accounting software

O Inviting John to the annual audit planning meeting

O Helping John to prepare for his upcoming appraisal

(1 mark)

(Total = 4 marks)

(Total = 24 marks)

25 Ethical considerations   (41 mins)

25.1   Which term correctly completes this sentence?

Managers are said to have a [▼] responsibility (or duty of faithful service) in respect of the entities whose purposes they serve.

Pull down list

- Ethical
- Fiduciary
- Financial

(1 mark)

25.2   What is the name given to an approach to ethical decision-making which considers the 'right' decision to be the one which results in the greatest good to the greatest number of people in a given situation?

- ○ Utilitarianism
- ○ Deontology
- ○ Virtue ethics

(1 mark)

25.3   X plc is trying to get a trading permit, for which it qualifies.

Unfortunately, there is a backlog at the issuing office, and X plc has been notified that there will be a delay in the processing of its permit.

The divisional manager offers a donation to the issuing office's staff welfare fund, if the official concerned will expedite the paperwork.

Required

Which of the following statements is true of this action?

- ○ It is not unethical, because the money is offered for positive purposes.
- ○ It is not unethical, because X plc is legally entitled to the benefit it is claiming.
- ○ It constitutes bribery.
- ○ It constitutes grease money.

(2 marks)

25.4   Which of the following is an approach to ethics which combines a concern for the law with an emphasis on managerial responsibility?

- ○ Compliance based
- ○ Integrity based
- ○ Environmental based
- ○ Economic based

(2 marks)

25.5 What two words correctly complete the sentence?

Farrah works in the sales tax section of the accounts department of BCD Co. When the finance director is on holiday, Farrah notices that BCD Co has not been paying the correct quarterly amounts to the authorities. Farrah had suspected this for some time and decides to contact the authorities to tell them about the fraud. This disclosure is known as

[▼]

Pull down list

- Confidentiality breach
- Corporate conscience
- Whistle blowing

(1 mark)

25.6 Which of the following would raise ethical issues for a manufacturer of fast-moving consumer goods?

(1) The materials used in manufacture of the goods

(2) The quality of the goods

(3) How the goods are advertised

(4) How much its raw materials suppliers pay their staff

(5) How the goods are packaged

○ (2) and (3) only

○ (1), (2) and (3) only

○ (2), (3) and (5) only

○ (1), (2), (3), (4) and (5)

(2 marks)

25.7 Which of the following words correctly complete this statement?

Reliability, responsibility [▼] , courtesy and respect are the personal qualities expected of an accountant.

Pull down list

- Accountability
- Ambition
- Social responsibility
- Timeliness

(2 marks)

25.8 You have been asked to work on a major investment decision that your company will be making, and discover that your brother-in-law is the managing director of a firm that may benefit from the outcome of the decision.

You have no intention of allowing this to influence the advice you give your firm, and you know that your brother-in-law will not try to influence you in any way.

Required

What professional quality would make you consider handing this task to a colleague, or otherwise raising questions with your superiors?

O Scepticism

O Accountability

O Independence of mind

O Independence in appearance

(2 marks)

25.9 Which of the following would **NOT** represent an ethical objective in employment practices?

O Guarantee of minimum wages

O Proactive health, safety and welfare promotion

O Promotion of workforce diversity

O Employability training

(2 marks)

25.10 Of the three main sources of rules that regulate the behaviour of businesses, the minimum level of acceptable behaviour is set by which?

O Non-legal rules and regulations

O Ethics

O The law

O Society

(2 marks)

25.11 The directors' deliberations must be balanced by taking into account everyone who has a legitimate interest in the company and respecting their rights and views.

Required

This statement describes which concept?

O Fairness

O Openness

O Probity

(1 mark)

25.12 Which of the following statements is a definition of probity?

O Open and clear disclosure of all relevant information

O Telling the truth and not misleading stakeholders

O Accepting the blame or credit for decisions

O Answerable in some way for the consequences of its actions

(2 marks)

25.13 Holders of public office should not place themselves under any obligation to outside individuals or organisations that might influence them in the performance of their official duties.

Required

This statement refers to which concept?

O Independence

O Reputation

O Integrity

(1 mark)

25.14 Which of the following is **NOT** part of a corporate code of ethics?

O Professional ethics

O Organisational culture

O Organisational self-interest

(1 mark)

25.15 Abner is the lead partner on the audit of DEF Inc.

The client often gives Abner corporate hospitality at major sporting events and small gifts, such as a bottle of spirits, on his birthday.

Required

Which threat does this represent?

O Self-interest

O Self-review

O Advocacy

O Intimidation

(2 marks)

25.16 XYZ carries out the audit of Delta Products Inc. Delta Products Inc is in financial trouble and XYZ has had to qualify the audit report for the past two years.

The managing director of Delta blames the qualified audit reports for her firm's continuing problems. She is threatening to sue XYZ for poor work if they qualify the audit report for this year.

Required

What threat does this represent?

O Familiarity

O Intimidation

O Self-interest

O Self-review

(2 marks)

25.17 Which of the following is **NOT** a conflict of interest?

O An ACCA member is in direct competition with a client on a contract

O An ACCA member is married to a director of the client

○ An ACCA member is an officer of the client company but does not deal with the client's affairs

○ An ACCA member is part of a joint venture with a competitor of the client

(2 marks)

25.18 You have been asked to prepare management accounts while a colleague is on holiday.

Your supervisor tells you that the accounts should be printed out and left on each manager's desk.

Required

You query whether the accounts should be put in an envelope marked 'confidential' but you are told not to bother in order to save costs.

What problem does this cause you?

○ Confidentiality

○ Unprofessional behaviour

○ Objectivity

○ Integrity

(2 marks)

25.19 Which of the following statements reflects a relativist view of ethics?

○ There is an unchanging set of ethical principles that apply in all situations

○ The subject to all ethical situations is the self

○ The ethics appropriate for a given situation will depend on the conditions at the time

(1 mark)

25.20 Which of the following statements is a criticism of absolutism?

○ It is based on a fundamental contradiction

○ It takes no account of changing norms in society

○ It leads to a culture of anything goes

○ It promotes the pursuing of short-term selfish desires

(2 marks)

25.21 A deontological approach to an ethical decision focuses on which of the following?

○ The desired virtues of the decision taker

○ The duties of the decision taker

○ The consequences arising from the decision

(1 mark)

(Total = 34 marks)

26 Section F MTQs

(29 mins)

26.1 (a) Which **TWO** of the following are criticisms of relativism?

☐ It takes no account of evolving norms

☐ It leads to a philosophy of anything goes

☐ It makes short-term desires equivalent to longer-term interests

☐ It is based on a fundamental contradiction

☐ A consensus may not be possible

(2 marks)

(b) Indicate whether the following statements about social responsibility true or false.

	True	False
Social responsibility action is likely to have an adverse effect on shareholders' interests in the short term	O	O
An environmental audit involves assessing the opportunities and threats to an organisation	O	O
Only governments are concerned with social responsibility	O	O
Guaranteeing employees a minimum 'living wage' is an example of social responsibility	O	O

(2 marks)

(Total = 4 marks)

26.2 (a) Indicate whether the following statements about ethics true or false.

	True	False
The teleological view of ethics is based on duty	O	O
Bribery can sometimes be legal	O	O
Virtue ethics suggests that managers should incorporate values such as fairness and loyalty into their decision-making	O	O
An accountant's ethical behaviour serves to protect the public interest	O	O

(2 marks)

(b) Which **TWO** of the following are criticisms of absolutism?

☐ It takes no account of evolving norms

☐ It leads to a philosophy of anything goes

☐ It makes short-term desires equivalent to longer-term interests

☐ It is based on a fundamental contradiction

☐ Whatever source is used, human interpretation will lead to different views

(2 marks)

(Total = 4 marks)

26.3 (a) The following are qualities you can see in an accountant

Required

Which **FOUR** of the following are personal qualities expected of an accountant?

☐ Reliability

☐ Courtesy

☐ Scepticism

☐ Accountability

☐ Independence

☐ Respect

☐ Timeliness

☐ Social responsibility   **(2 marks)**

(b) Which **TWO** of the following are fundamental principles from ACCA's Code of Ethics?

☐ Integrity

☐ Leadership

☐ Objectivity

☐ Truthfulness

☐ Accountability

(2 marks)

(Total = 4 marks)

26.4 (a) YRT Co is a firm of external auditors which has Company W, Company X, Company Y and Company Z among its audit clients.

Company W is currently being sued by one of its suppliers. YRT Co has offered legal services and will defend them in this legal case. The audit partner of Company X has been a member of the external audit team for the past 15 years and has good relationships with the senior management of Company X. Company Y's financial controller is the daughter of YRT Co's audit manager. Company Z does not have an experienced financial department and so YRT Co helps to prepare the financial statements of Company Z in advance of the external audit.

The following are types of conflicts of interest:

• Familiarity threat

• Advocacy threat

• Self-review threat

• Self-interest threat

Required

Match the types of conflict of interest above to the companies below.

Familiarity threat	COMPANY W	COMPANY X	COMPANY Y	COMPANY Z
Advocacy threat	COMPANY W	COMPANY X	COMPANY Y	COMPANY Z
Self-review threat	COMPANY W	COMPANY X	COMPANY Y	COMPANY Z
Self-interest threat	COMPANY W	COMPANY X	COMPANY Y	COMPANY Z

(2 marks)

(b) Which of the following would give rise to a threat of intimidation?

○ Litigation against the external auditor by an audit client

○ Provision of taxation services as well as audit services

○ An audit partner is on the board of a client

(1 mark)

(c) Which of the following correctly fills the blank?

Ethics are a set of [▼] that guide behaviour.

Pull down list

- Legal guidelines
- Moral principles
- Professional regulations

(1 mark)

(Total = 4 marks)

26.5 (a) JKL Co is a small firm of external auditors with a small number of clients. Almost 20% of its revenue comes from one client. The client still has not settled the invoice from the previous year's audit in the hope that this will strengthen their position in negotiating a lower price for this year's audit.

Required

Which **TWO** of the following conflicts of interest exist in this situation?

- ☐ Self-review threat
- ☐ Advocacy threat
- ☐ Self-interest threat
- ☐ Familiarity threat
- ☐ Intimidation threat

(2 marks)

(b) Indicate whether the following statements true or false?

	True	False
When dealing with ethical dilemmas ACCA students must follow ACCA's code of conduct.	O	O
Professional ethics should not be followed at the expense of contractual obligations.	O	O
There is a public expectation that accountants will act ethically.	O	O
A prospective audit firm quoting a significantly lower fee for assurance work than the current auditors charge does not raise a threat of a conflict of interest.	O	O

(2 marks)

(Total = 4 marks)

26.6 (a) Corporate codes of ethics are published by organisations in order to communicate values to stakeholders.

Required

Indicate why each of the following stakeholders might be interested in what an organisation does.

	Employees	Local communities	Customers
Decisions of this stakeholder may be influenced by ethical considerations	O	O	O
Standards of behaviour expected of this stakeholder should be communicated to them	O	O	O
This stakeholder may need reassurance that the organisation will act as a 'good citizen'	O	O	O

(3 marks)

(b) The Chair's report of Fairmind states that "We are a competitive business, yet we are fair and open. Obtaining information about competitors by deception is strongly condemned. Making disparaging comments about competitors should be avoided."

Required

Which of the following safeguards would be most effective in ensuring that these standards are maintained?

O   A system of fines for employees who are in breach of the code

O   Effective education and training for all staff

O   External review of Fairmind's ethics policy

O   Rewarding employees who report on colleagues' ethical breaches

(1 mark)

(Total = 4 marks)

(Total = 24 marks)

27 Mixed Bank 1 (46 mins)

27.1 Systems are sometimes described as either open or closed.

Required

When a system is closed it is:

- O Incapable of further technical enhancement
- O Protected from unauthorised access
- O Isolated from its external environment

(1 mark)

27.2 A company has placed a job advertisement for a full time employee and a part time employee. The part time employee's terms are less favourable than the full-time employee's terms. What type of discrimination is this?

- O Direct discrimination
- O Indirect discrimination
- O Victimisation

(1 mark)

27.3 What is the main focus and role of the accounting function?

- O To pay employee salaries
- O To provide information to external auditors
- O To record financial information
- O To estimate how much to spend on production

(2 marks)

27.4 Which of the following is a benefit of decentralisation?

- O Decisions are made at one place in the organisation
- O Reductions in bureaucracy
- O Better crisis management
- O Improves the motivation of junior managers

(2 marks)

27.5 A narrow span of control would be suitable where

- O The team is not dispersed across a wide area
- O The work is of a routine nature
- O There is little similarity between team members' work
- O The team is very experienced

(2 marks)

27.6 When analysing the current situation in a business, a consultant will review the general environment surrounding it.

Required

Which of the following would not be included in this analysis?

O New legislation coming into effect in six months' time

O Activities of overseas competitors

O Interest rates

O Independence of the non-executive directors

(2 marks)

27.7 How might the purchasing manager work closely with the accounting function?

O Processing expense claims

O Seeking prompt payment from customers

O Managing the prompt payment of suppliers

O Recording staff salaries

(2 marks)

27.8 Many organisations are described as bureaucratic.

When the term was first coined, bureaucracy was regarded as being highly efficient and there are still cases where a bureaucratic approach is appropriate.

However, bureaucracy has some undesirable features.

Required

Which of the following are undesirable features of bureaucracy?

(1) It relies on the expertise of its members – not through standardised skills but by the importance of the mix of skills

(2) Committees and reports slow down the decision-making process

(3) Innovation is difficult

(4) Over-prescriptive rules produce a simplistic approach to problems

O (1), and (3) only

O (1), (3) and (4) only

O (2), (3) and (4) only

O (1) and (2) only

(2 marks)

27.9 Mr Warner, your department manager, is weighing up the benefits and disadvantages of off-the-shelf packages that have been customised so that they fit the organisation's specific requirements.

Required

Which of the following options are disadvantages of customisation?

(1) It may delay delivery of the software

(2) The user is dependent on the supplier for maintenance of the package

(3) The company will not be able to buy 'add-ons' to the basic package

(4) It may introduce bugs that do not exist in the standard version

○ (1) and (2) only

○ (1), (2) and (3) only

○ (1) and (4) only

○ (2) and (3) only

(2 marks)

27.10 In the short run, firms will continue to supply customers provided that they cover:

○ Fixed costs

○ Marginal costs

○ Variable costs

(1 mark)

27.11 Which of the following is **NOT** an advantage of a matrix structure?

○ Dual authority

○ Greater flexibility

○ Employee motivation

○ Improved communications

(2 marks)

27.12 Which of the following parties has the main responsibility for good corporate governance?

○ The board of directors

○ The audit committee

○ The non-executive directors

(1 mark)

27.13 Which of the following statements is **NOT** true in respect of the relationships between directors, shareholders and auditors?

○ Auditors are the agents of shareholders

○ Shareholders are accountable to auditors

○ Auditors report to shareholders on the financial statements prepared by directors

○ Directors are accountable to shareholders

(2 marks)

27.14 Which of the following statements correctly describes the principal purpose of the external audit of a company within the UK?

○ To assist management in the preparation of the company's periodic financial statements

○ To examine and express an opinion on the company's periodic financial statements

○ To prevent and detect fraud within the company

(1 mark)

27.15 A record showing who has accessed a computer system is called:

○ An audit trail

○ A computer trail

○ A password trail

(1 mark)

27.16 Alf Sparks is a manager of a small team designing and building a new management information system.

The various levels of management that will be using the system will all have different information requirements but the qualities of good information are the same at each level. He is describing these qualities to his team.

Required

Which of the following would be included in his explanation?

(1) Comprehensive

(2) Relevant

(3) Accurate

(4) Authoritative

○ (1), (2) and (3) only

○ (2), (3) and (4) only

○ (1) and (4) only

○ (3) and (4) only

(2 marks)

27.17 External auditors may place reliance on internal auditors' work.

Required

Is this statement correct?

○ External auditors need to assess the work of internal audit first

○ Internal auditors are not independent and so cannot be relied upon

○ Yes, always

(1 mark)

27.18 Which of the following costs, in regards to an information system, are capital costs?

(1) Hardware purchase costs

(2) Routine system maintenance costs

(3) Software purchase costs

(4) Installation costs

○ (1), (2) and (3) only

○ (2) and (4) only

○ (2), (3) and (4) only

○ (1), (3) and (4) only

(2 marks)

27.19 Who appoints external auditors?

- O Chair
- O Finance director
- O Shareholders

(1 mark)

27.20 Control over cash receipts will concentrate on three main areas.

Required

Receipts must be [▼] promptly

The record of receipts must be [▼]

The loss of receipts through theft or accident must be [▼]

Pull down list

- Banked
- Complete
- Prevented

(2 marks)

27.21 There are three broad pre-requisites or 'pre-conditions' that must exist in order to make fraud a possibility.

Required

What are they?

- O Deception, criminality and opportunity
- O Dishonesty, criminality and opportunity
- O Dishonesty, motivation and opportunity
- O Deception, motivation and opportunity

(2 marks)

27.22 The identification within a client company of financial problems, a dominant chief executive, poor internal control, unusual transactions, or a high-technology environment, are **all** indicative of:

- O Increased scope for potential fraud
- O A higher than normal risk audit
- O Inadequacies in the systems of reporting
- O The presence of going concern problems

(2 marks)

27.23 Data and information come from sources both inside and outside an organisation.

Required

Which of the following represent data or information captured from within the organisation?

(1) Information about personnel from the payroll system

(2) Market information on buying habits of potential customers from the marketing manager

(3) Information on decisions taken from the minutes of a meeting

(4) Value of sales from the accounting records

○ (1), (2) and (3) only

○ (2) and (4) only

○ (2) and (3) only

○ (1), (3) and (4) only

(2 marks)

(Total = 38 marks)

28 Mixed Bank 2 (48 mins)

28.1 Which of the following did Henri Fayol include in his five functions of management?

(1) Motivating

(2) Co-ordinating

(3) Commanding

(4) Controlling

○ (1), (2) and 3) only

○ (2), (3) and (4) only

○ (1) and (4) only

○ (3) and (4) only

(2 marks)

28.2 Which of the statements below describes contingency theory?

○ Organisational design will be determined by a number of factors all of which depend on the others

○ Companies must plan for changes to their organisation

○ Companies should focus on the short-term as the future is uncertain

(1 mark)

28.3 Peter Drucker grouped management activities or operations into five categories.

Required

Which of the following is **NOT** one of those categories?

○ Setting objectives

○ The job of measurement

○ Planning and control

(1 mark)

28.4 Different types of power may be exercised within an organisation any different individuals.

Required

Which type of power is associated with formal authority?

○ Resource power

○ Expert power

○ Position power

(1 mark)

28.5 Rensis Likert identifies four management styles. What are they?

○ Benevolent autocratic, participative, democratic, exploitative autocratic

○ Benevolent authoritative, participative, exploitative authoritative, democratic

○ Exploitative autocratic, benevolent autocratic, participative, laissez faire

○ Benevolent autocratic, consultative participative, exploitative, laissez faire

(2 marks)

28.6 A company has established a project team to design a new information system.

The team has had a few meetings to discuss how they are going to tackle the work, and who would do what, but some early ideas have been unsuccessful.

Group members are still putting forward a number of very innovative ideas, but they often disagree strongly with each other. The group members appear to be dividing into two 'camps' each of which has an unofficial 'leader'. These two individuals agree about very little and appear to dislike each other.

According to Tuckman, which stage in development has the project team reached?

○ Norming

○ Performing

○ Storming

(1 mark)

28.7 In the context of human resource planning, which **TWO** of the following documents are the outputs of a process of job analysis?

(1) Human resource plan

(2) Job description

(3) Person specification

(4) Performance appraisal

○ (1) and (2)

○ (1) and (3)

○ (2) and (4)

○ (2) and (3)

(2 marks)

28.8 Belbin described the most effective character mix in a team.

This involves eight necessary roles, which should ideally be balanced and spread in a team.

Required

A person who is highly strung, extrovert and passionate about the task fits into which of Belbin's roles?

○ Plant

○ Completer Finisher

○ Resource investigator

○ Shaper

(2 marks)

28.9 Which of the following team member roles is **NOT** from Belbin's list of group rules?

○ Shaper

○ Plant

○ Attacker

○ Finisher

(2 marks)

28.10 Which of the following are positive aspects of teamworking?

(1) Control

(2) Work organisation

(3) Knowledge generation

(4) Decision making

○ (1), (2) and (3)

○ (1) and (2)

○ (1), (2) and (4)

○ All four

(2 marks)

28.11 Tuckman identified four stages in group development, which occur in a particular order. What is the order in which the stages occur?

○ Forming, storming, norming, performing

○ Forming, storming, performing, norming

○ Storming, norming, forming, performing

○ Storming, forming, performing, norming

(2 marks)

28.12 'The justification for empowering workers, or removing levels in hierarchies that restrict freedom, is that not only will the job be done more effectively but the people who do the job will get more out of it in terms of growth, challenge, responsibility and self-fulfilment'.

Required

The thinking is in line with which management writer?

○ Herzberg

○ Fayol

○ Taylor

○ Weber

(2 marks)

28.13 Bruce has been on a training course to help him develop his negotiation skills and learn some new techniques.

Required

He has been practising three of these back in the office – can you identify them?

(1) Look for a wide variety of possible solutions

(2) Try to develop options that would result in mutual gain

(3) Create a trusting supportive atmosphere in group

(4) Define the problem carefully

O (1), (2) and (3)

O (2), (3) and (4)

O (1), (2) and (4)

O (1), (3) and (4)

(2 marks)

28.14 There are many different methods of communication, each with its own features and limitations.

Can you identify the three features/advantages of conversation as a communication technique from the list below?

(1) Requires little or no planning

(2) Gives a real impression of feelings

(3) Complex ideas can be communicated

(4) Usually unstructured so can discuss a wide range of topics

O (1), (2) and (3)

O (2), (3) and (4)

O (1), (2) and (4)

O (1), (3) and (4)

(2 marks)

28.15 Which of the following would Herzberg class among 'hygiene factors'?

(1) Salary

(2) Job security

(3) Gaining recognition

(4) Challenging work

O (2) and (4) only

O (1) only

O (1), (2), (3) and (4)

O (1) and (2) only

(2 marks)

28.16 Vocabulary and style should contribute to the clarity of message in a presentation.

It is recommended that short simple sentences are used and the presenter should avoid certain expressions.

Required

Which of following list should be avoided?

(1) Acronyms

(2) Jargon

(3) Colloquialisms

(4) Double meanings

○ (2) and (3) only

○ (2), (3) and (4) only

○ (1), (2) and (4) only

○ (3) and (4) only

(2 marks)

28.17 Electronic mail has so many features and advantages that it is easy to forget that there may be limitations associated with it.

Can you identify the disadvantages of email from the list below?

(1) People may not check their email regularly

(2) Complex images do not transmit well

(3) Requires some computer literacy to use effectively

(4) Lack of privacy – can be forwarded without your knowledge

○ (1), (2) and (3) only

○ (2), (3) and (4) only

○ (1), (2) and (4) only

○ (1), (3) and (4) only

(2 marks)

28.18 For a formal meeting, in which order would you expect the following items to appear on the agenda?

Subjects for discussion ▼

Minutes of previous meeting ▼

Date of next meeting ▼

Any other business ▼

Apologies for absence ▼

Matters arising ▼

Pull down list

- 1
- 2
- 3
- 4
- 5
- 6

(1 mark)

28.19 A 360° (or multi-source) appraisal collects feedback on an individual's performance from sources such as the person's immediate superior and also his or her immediate subordinates. Identify these other sources from the list below.

(1) Peers

(2) Customers

(3) Self-appraisal

(4) Family and friends

○ (1), (2) and (3) only

○ (2), (3) and (4) only

○ (1), (2) and (4) only

○ (1), (3) and (4) only

(2 marks)

28.20 What type of appraisal occurs when employees judge managers?

○ Peer

○ Traditional

○ Upward

(1 mark)

28.21 Which of the following is **NOT** a general aim of an appraisal system?

○ Identify potential

○ Deal with grievances

○ Reward attainment

○ Measure performance

(2 marks)

28.22 Which of the following is the person least likely to be requested to fill out feedback forms for use in a 360 degree appraisal of a sales account manager?

○ Accounts payable clerk

○ Credit sales clerk

○ Direct customer

(1 mark)

28.23 Which of the following is **NOT** a characteristic of a learning organisation?

○ Learning climate

○ Enabling accounting

○ Reward flexibility

(1 mark)

28.24 Upward appraisal is used by some businesses. This involves staff giving their opinions on the performance of their managers. There are problems with this method, which include three of the following.

Required

Can you identify them?

(1) Employee point scoring

(2) Fear of reprisal

(3) The chance of bias is increased

(4) Lack of authority

  ○ (1), (2) and (3) only

  ○ (2), (3) and (4) only

  ○ (1), (2) and (4) only

  ○ (1), (3) and (4) only

(2 marks)

(Total = 40 marks)

29 Mixed Bank 3 (48 mins)

29.1 Which of the following is an acronym used to describe the key elements of an organisation's external environment?

  ○ PERT

  ○ PEST

  ○ SWOT

(1 mark)

29.2 Henry Mintzberg categorised five basic components of an organisation.

Required

Which **TWO** of the following statements describes the work of the technostructure of an organisation?

  ☐ Designing systems

  ☐ Organising and controlling work

  ☐ Standardising work

  ☐ Securing inputs

(2 marks)

29.3 Which of the following is a correct definition of the term 'span of control'?

  ○ The number of employees reporting to one manager

  ○ The number of managers to whom one employee reports

  ○ The number of levels in the hierarchy

  ○ The number of employees at each level of the organisation

(2 marks)

29.4 To whom is the internal auditor accountable?

  ○ The directors of the company

  ○ The employees of the company

  ○ The shareholders of the company

(1 mark)

29.5 SPAMSOAP is a mnemonic word for the eight types of internal control employed by an organisation.

Required

Which **TWO** of the following are types of internal control included in SPAMSOAP?

☐ Output

☐ Arithmetic

☐ Preventative

☐ Physical

(2 marks)

29.6 Which **TWO** of the following are typical responsibilities of the financial accountant in a large organisation?

☐ Inventory valuation

☐ Sales invoicing

☐ Project appraisal

☐ Payroll

(2 marks)

29.7 Who was responsible for developing the 'Situational Leadership' model?

○ Blake and Mouton

○ Katz and Kahn

○ Hersey and Blanchard

○ Tannenbaum and Schmidt

(2 marks)

29.8 Which of the following statements accurately describes a multi-disciplinary team?

○ All team members collaboratively decide how to organise their work

○ All team members have different skills and specialisms which they pool

○ All team members can perform any and all of the group's tasks

○ All team members are jointly responsible for the leadership of the team

(2 marks)

29.9 Which **TWO** of the following are examples of content theories of motivation?

☐ Maslow's hierarchy of needs

☐ Vroom's expectancy theory

☐ Herzberg's two factor theory

☐ Adam's equity theory

(2 marks)

29.10 Which **TWO** of the following are examples of 'on the job' training?

☐ Formal training courses

☐ Mentoring by a colleague

☐ Self study courses

☐ Secondments to other departments

(2 marks)

29.11 If a manager in the purchasing department requests the help of the Human Resources Director in preparing for a difficult appraisal, what direction is the communication flow?

O Vertical

O Horizontal

O Diagonal

(1 mark)

29.12 Honey and Mumford classified four different learning styles.

Required

Which of the following statements accurately describes the reflector?

O Prefers to understand principles

O Prefers to think things through first

O Prefers to try things 'hands on'

O Prefers to see practical examples

(2 marks)

29.13 Which of the following words completes this sentence appropriately?

'An organisation is a social arrangement which pursues collective [▼] , which controls its own performance and which has a boundary separating it from its environment.'

Pull down list

• Ambitions

• Duties

• Goals

(1 mark)

29.14 Which **TWO** of the following are included in Mintzberg's organisational components?

☐ Strategic apex

☐ Technicians

☐ Specialists

☐ Support staff

(2 marks)

29.15 Which of the following is/are examples of weak financial control procedures?

○ Suppliers not being paid on time

○ Debtors not paying within credit limits

○ Excessive bad or doubtful debts

○ All of the above

(2 marks)

29.16 In a typical finance function, budgets and budgetary control would usually be the responsibility of which of the following roles?

○ The Financial Controller

○ The Management Accountant

○ The Chief Executive

(1 mark)

29.17 Which function in an organisation is responsible for ensuring that only properly authorised purchases which are necessary for the business are made?

○ Dispatch

○ Internal audit

○ Purchasing/procurement

(1 mark)

29.18 What is the term given to a method of fraud in the accounts receivable area, by which cash or cheque receipts are stolen, and the theft concealed by setting subsequent receipts against the outstanding debt?

○ Collaboration

○ Topping and tailing

○ Teeming and lading

○ Understating sales

(2 marks)

29.19 Which of the following are purposes of a receivables control account?

(1) A sales ledger control account provides a check on the arithmetical accuracy of the personal ledger

(2) A sales ledger control account helps to improve separation of duties

(3) A sales ledger control account ensures that there are no errors in the personal ledger

(4) Control accounts deter fraud

○ (1), (2) and (3) only

○ (2), (3) and (4) only

○ (1), (2) and (4) only

○ (1), (3) and (4) only

(2 marks)

29.20 Which of the following terms correctly completes this definition?

A [▼] is a program which deals with one particular part of a computerised business accounting system.

Pull down list

- Module
- Spreadsheet
- Suite

(1 mark)

29.21 Power arising from an individual's formal position in the organisation is called:

- ○ Coercive power
- ○ Legitimate power
- ○ Expert power
- ○ Negative power

(2 marks)

29.22 What is the most important attribute of a 'group', which distinguishes it from a random crowd of people?

- ○ Leadership
- ○ Goals
- ○ Function
- ○ Identity

(2 marks)

29.23 Which of Belbin's nine roles does the following description apply to? Single-minded, self-starting, dedicated.

- ○ Chair
- ○ Specialist
- ○ Co-ordinator
- ○ Teamworker

(2 marks)

29.24 Which of the following is a category in Maslow's hierarchy of needs theory?

- ○ Self determination
- ○ Need for affiliation
- ○ Safety needs

(1 mark)

(Total = 40 marks)

30 Mixed Bank 4

30.1 William Ouchi identified three types of control.

   Required

   Which of the following is **NOT** one of those?

   ○ Bureaucratic control

   ○ Market control

   ○ Output control

   ○ Clan control

   (2 marks)

30.2 From the list below, identify the one that doesn't have the attributes of a group.

   ○ The finance department of an organisation

   ○ An orchestra

   ○ A football team

   ○ Five pop fans

   (2 marks)

30.3 Which of the following is most clearly a sign of an ineffective group?

   ○ Internal disagreement and criticism

   ○ Passive acceptance of work decisions

   ○ Competition with other groups

   (1 mark)

30.4 A leader may be distinguished from a manager by lack of dependency on:

   ○ Position power

   ○ Expert power

   ○ Personal power

   ○ Physical power

   (2 marks)

30.5 Delegation is needed in organisations to enable a distribution of work in the organisation.

   Required

   Which **TWO** of the following are reasons why managers may be reluctant to delegate?

   ☐ Doesn't trust staff to carry out delegated tasks

   ☐ Wants to control all activities under his or her responsibility

   ☐ The organisation is dynamic and turbulent with constant changes

   ☐ Is new and doesn't know how competent staff are

   (2 marks)

30.6 Bill has been on a training course to learn negotiation skills. Which **THREE** of the following are negotiation skills?

☐ Look for a wide variety of possible solutions

☐ Define the problem carefully

☐ Evaluate progress towards objectives

☐ Monitor the behaviour of others

☐ Try to develop objectives resulting in mutual gains

(2 marks)

30.7 Leadership involves activities that are generally people-centred.

Required

Which of the following is **NOT** a leadership activity?

O Creating the culture

O Inspiring and motivating others

O Reconciling individual needs with the requirements of the organisation

O Allocating scarce resources

(2 marks)

30.8 Which of the following describes an employee duty, rather than an employer duty under Health and Safety legislation?

O To keep all plant and machinery up to a necessary standard

O To ensure all work practices are safe

O To take reasonable care of themselves

(1 mark)

30.9 Every organisation has a boundary that separates it from its environment.

Required

From an organisation's point of view, which **TWO** of the following would be part of the organisation's environment?

☐ Shareholders

☐ Customers

☐ Sales team

☐ Purchasing department

(2 marks)

30.10 Which **TWO** of the following disciplinary actions may be used only if it is (they are) provided for in the employee's contract of employment?

☐ Suspension without pay

☐ Dismissal

☐ Demotion

☐ Suspension with pay

(2 marks)

30.11 Which type of culture according to Handy's cultural models would best fit with a matrix structure?

○ Person

○ Role

○ Power

○ Task

(2 marks)

30.12 Which **TWO** of the following said 'Culture is the way we do things around here'.

☐ Handy

☐ Schein

☐ Harrison

☐ Deal and Kennedy

(2 marks)

30.13 Which **TWO** of the following are connected stakeholders to an organisation?

☐ Employees

☐ Suppliers

☐ Managers

☐ Customers

(2 marks)

30.14 Henry Mintzberg categorised five basic components of an organisation.

Required

Which of the following statements describes the work of the strategic apex of an organisation?

○ Ensuring the organisation pursues its objectives and serves the needs of its owners and stakeholders

○ Securing inputs and processing and distributing them as outputs

○ Organising, planning and controlling work and acting as an interface

(1 mark)

30.15 Which **TWO** of the following are typical responsibilities of the management accountant in a large organisation?

☐ Processing sales invoices

☐ Reconciling cash balances with bank statements

☐ Planning and preparing budgets

☐ Appraisal of capital investment projects

(2 marks)

30.16 Lack of control over which of the following activities can lead to the fraudulent practice of teeming and lading?

○ Non-current asset register

○ Budgetary system

○ Inventory management

○ Sales ledger and receipts

(2 marks)

30.17 Which of the following statements identifies three broad requisites for fraud?

○ Collusion, opportunity, motivation

○ Dishonesty, opportunity, motivation

○ Opportunity, collusion, dishonesty

(1 mark)

30.18 Which type of audit is concerned with the evaluation and testing of the internal controls within an organisation?

○ Systems

○ Management

○ Transactions

(1 mark)

30.19 To which of the following cultural types did Charles Handy give the name of the Greek god Dionysus?

○ Power/club culture

○ Person culture

○ Role culture

○ Task culture

(2 marks)

30.20 Which of the following describes the 'impoverished' style of management identified by Blake and Mouton's managerial grid?

○ High concern for people and a low concern for the task

○ Low concern for people and a high concern for the task

○ Low concern for people and low concern for the task

(1 mark)

30.21 According to Belbin, the success of a group can depend on the balance of individual skills and personality types.

Required

Which of the following statements are characteristics of the 'shaper'?

○ Calm, self confident and controlled – coordinating and operating through others

○ Concerned with the relationships within the group, supportive and tends to diffuse conflict

○ Highly-strung, outgoing and dynamic and committed to the task

○ Orderly, conscientious, anxious and ensures that timetables are met

(2 marks)

30.22 Which of the following statements describes the correct sequence between sender and receiver within the communication cycle?

○ Encoded message, medium, decoded message

○ Medium, encoded message, decoded message

○ Decoded message, encoded message, medium

(1 mark)

30.23 According to the Ashridge studies on leadership style, what is most important to subordinates about the style of their leader?

○ Consultation

○ Direction

○ Consistency

(1 mark)

30.24 Which **TWO** of the following must be in a job description?

☐ Reporting lines

☐ Salary

☐ Hours of work

☐ Job content

(2 marks)

(Total = 40 marks)

31 Mixed Bank 5 (48 mins)

31.1 Which **TWO** of the following are advantages of computerised accounting packages over manual systems?

☐ They make it easier to see where a mistake has been made

☐ They can be used by non-specialists

☐ They provide more consistent processing than manual systems

☐ They are less expensive to implement

(2 marks)

31.2 Which of the following is normally subject to the most direct government regulation?

○ Employment protection

○ Corporate social responsibility

○ Corporate governance

(1 mark)

31.3 Fish and chips are considered complementary products. If the price of fish rises, what will the impact be in demand for chips?

○ Rises

○ Stays the same

○ Falls

(1 mark)

31.4 For which **TWO** of the following does the external auditor have responsibility?

☐ Evaluating the efficiency of systems and procedures

☐ Reporting to shareholders

☐ Detecting fraud

☐ Giving an opinion on financial statements

(2 marks)

31.5 A medium sized manufacturing firm produces a number of reports, for example, production and materials reports, marketing reports, personnel reports and financial reports.

Which **TWO** of the following would you expect to see in a production and materials report?

☐ Transport costs

☐ Wastage rates

☐ Labour utilisation figures

☐ Sales analyses

(2 marks)

31.6 Which of the following is a feature of a structured decision?

○ There is a formal process for decision-making

○ The decision variables are very complex

○ The information needed for decision-making is unpredictable

○ The manager's experience and intuition play a large part in making the decision

(2 marks)

31.7 Who was responsible for developing the 'two-factor theory' of motivation?

○ Herzberg

○ Maslow

○ Vroom

(1 mark)

31.8 Which of the following statements describes coercive power?

○ Power associated with a particular role or status

○ Power associated with physical force or punishment

○ Power associated with control over physical resources

○ Power associated with individual personality and attitudes

(2 marks)

31.9 Which **TWO** of the following are parts of the job of a supervisor?

☐ Managing team performance

☐ Co-ordinating departmental objectives

☐ Developing strategic plans

☐ Organising the work of others

(2 marks)

BPP
LEARNING
MEDIA

31.10 Which of the following employee selection methods has the highest 'predictive validity': that is, which is best at predicting a candidate's performance in the job?

○ Interviews

○ Personality testing

○ Assessment centres

○ Work sampling

(2 marks)

31.11 Which words correctly complete this sentence?

The concept of [▼] is based on the belief that the types of individual difference which are protected by anti-discrimination legislation are crude and irrelevant to successful performance, and that an organisation can benefit from embracing all kinds of difference.

Pull down list

• Diversification

• Equal opportunity

• Managing diversity

(1 mark)

31.12 Kolb provides a useful descriptive model of adult learning.

Required

Which of the following is the correct sequence of the four stages of the learning cycle?

○ Active experimentation, observation and reflection, abstract conceptualisation, concrete experience

○ Concrete experience, abstract conceptualisation, active experimentation, observation and reflection

○ Abstract conceptualisation, observation and reflection, active experimentation, concrete experience

○ Concrete experience, observation and reflection, abstract conceptualisation, active experimentation

(2 marks)

31.13 Which of the following features of organisational structure is **NOT** associated with flexibility and adaptability?

○ Horizontal structure

○ Shamrock organisation

○ Scalar chain

(1 mark)

31.14 Which of the following is the role of the secretary of a committee?

   ○ Guiding discussion in committee meetings

   ○ Selecting members of the committee

   ○ Taking and circulating minutes of the meeting

   ○ Determining the agenda of the meeting

(2 marks)

31.15 Which of Handy's 'gods' is associated with 'power culture'?

   ○ Zeus

   ○ Apollo

   ○ Athena

   ○ Dionysus

(2 marks)

31.16 Which of the following factors help shape an organisation's culture?

   (1) The person who founded the organisation

   (2) The failures and successes experienced by the organisation

   (3) Recruitment and selection

   (4) The industry the organisation is in

   (5) Labour turnover

   ○ (2) and (4) only

   ○ (1), (2) and (4) only

   ○ (2), (3) and (4) only

   ○ (1), (2), (3), (4) and (5)

(2 marks)

31.17 In the context of the different levels of objectives that an organisation may pursue, environmental protection regulations would represent which of the following categories?

   ○ Primary economic objective

   ○ Non-economic, social objective

   ○ Responsibility

   ○ Boundary

(2 marks)

31.18 Three of the following are recognised advantages of a framework-based approach to ethical codes. Which is the exception?

   ○ Encourages proactive discussion of issues

   ○ Encourages consistent application of rules

   ○ Suits complex situations and evolving environments

   ○ Encourages professional development

(2 marks)

31.19 The following, with one exception, are 'building blocks' for team building. Which is the exception?

  O   Diverse mix of personalities

  O   Members do not challenge or criticise

  O   Regular reviews of performance

(1 mark)

31.20 Which of the following would be identified as a problem with the role of non-executive director?

  O   External stakeholder security

  O   Time available to devote to the role

  O   Objective viewpoint

(1 mark)

31.21 In the context of corporate social responsibility, which **TWO** of the following might 'sustainability' involve?

  ☐   Using local suppliers

  ☐   Maintaining long-term relationships with suppliers

  ☐   Minimising energy consumption

  ☐   Ethical employment practices

(2 marks)

31.22 Which word correctly completes this sentence?

[▼] is the study of the aggregated effects of the decisions of individual economic units (such as households or businesses).

Pull down list

  •   Demographics

  •   Globalisation

  •   Macro-economics

(1 mark)

31.23 Government can directly affect an organisation by influencing

  (1)   Demand

  (2)   Capacity expansion

  (3)   Competition

  O   (1) and (2)

  O   (1) and (3)

  O   (2) and (3)

  O   (1), (2) and (3)

(2 marks)

31.24 In relation to fraud prevention, what objective should external auditors have in designing and implementing their audit procedures?

    ○ A reasonable prospect of detecting irregular statements or records

    ○ The identification of every inconsistency or error within the records

    ○ To provide a systematic check of every recorded transaction

    ○ To verify pre-determined samples of all types of records

(2 marks)

(Total = 40 marks)

32 Mixed Bank 6   (46 mins)

32.1 Which of the following groups are the owners of a limited company?

    ○ Non-executive directors

    ○ Stakeholders

    ○ Shareholders

(1 mark)

32.2 Which of the following describes the meaning of Mintzberg's term: 'technostructure'?

    ○ Analysts such as accountants and workplanners, whose objective is to effect standardisation in the organisation

    ○ The range of technology needed for effective organisational performance

    ○ The organisation of shopfloor workers and their supervisors in a manufacturing environment

    ○ The central strategy-setting component of organisation structure

(2 marks)

32.3 Z plc sources a range of complex components from suppliers which are critical to the quality of Z plc's final product. Any disruption to the supply of these components will mean that Z plc cannot maintain its service levels to its own customers.

Required

In the purchasing of these components, which **TWO** of the following will **NOT** be a component of Z plc's supply strategy?

    ☐ Long-term partnership relations with key suppliers of the components

    ☐ A small number of suppliers of the components

    ☐ Outsourcing production of the product to low-cost countries

    ☐ Consolidating purchases of the components and sourcing from a single supplier to reduce sourcing costs

(2 marks)

32.4 In the Anthony hierarchy, which of the following is the term given to the process of establishing means to corporate ends, mobilising resources and innovating?

    ○ Strategic management

    ○ Tactical management

    ○ Operational management

(1 mark)

32.5 Which two words correctly complete this definition?

| ▼ | is the system by which organisations are directed and controlled by their senior officers.

Pull down list

- Corporate governance
- Executive directorship
- Internal controls
- Strategic management

(2 marks)

32.6 Which of the following statements is true of a 'progressive tax'.

○ It takes a higher proportion of a poor person's salary than of a rich person's.

○ It takes the same proportion of income in tax from all levels of income.

○ It takes a higher proportion of income in tax as income rises.

(1 mark)

32.7 In employment protection law, which of the following would constitute unfair dismissal?

○ Dismissal because the employer has ceased to carry on the business

○ Dismissal because the employer has relocated the place of work

○ Dismissal because demand for the type of work done by the employee(s) is expected to decline

○ Dismissal because the employee is pregnant

(2 marks)

32.8 Various groups of people might be interested in financial information about an organisation, for various reasons.

Required

Match up each of the following groups with the primary nature of their interest in financial information.

Ability to maintain and repay loans	SHARE-HOLDERS	FINANCIERS	EMPLOYEES	PUBLIC
Potential social contributions and impacts	SHARE-HOLDERS	FINANCIERS	EMPLOYEES	PUBLIC
Management stewardship	SHARE-HOLDERS	FINANCIERS	EMPLOYEES	PUBLIC
Attainment of performance objectives	SHARE-HOLDERS	FINANCIERS	EMPLOYEES	PUBLIC

(2 marks)

32.9 The website of a university contains a dedicated site for academic researchers, giving them access to the university's archived material, if they register and obtain a password to enter the site.

Required

Of which type of network is this an example?

- ○ Internet
- ○ Intranet
- ○ Extranet

(1 mark)

32.10 Which of the following is a feature of an ineffective job advertisement?

- ○ It narrows the pool of people who might go on to apply for the job
- ○ It provides all information necessary to make an application
- ○ It maximises the attractiveness of the job and organisation to potential applicants
- ○ It is relevant and appropriate to the nature of the job and the desired applicants

(2 marks)

32.11 There are three pre-requisites for fraud: motivation, opportunity and dishonesty. Match each of these with the most immediate control strategy from the following list.

Recruitment reference checking	MOTIVATION	OPPORTU-NITY	DISHON-ESTY
Disciplinary codes	MOTIVATION	OPPORTU-NITY	DISHON-ESTY
Internal checks and controls	MOTIVATION	OPPORTU-NITY	DISHON-ESTY

(2 marks)

32.12 In which of the following areas does a database system have significant advantages?

- ○ Data security
- ○ Data privacy
- ○ Development cost
- ○ Data management

(2 marks)

32.13 Which word correctly completes the sentence?

[_____ ▼] Studies is the name given to experimental social research initiated by Elton Mayo, which identified the influence exercised by social needs and informal groups in the workplace, and gave rise to the human relations school of management.

Pull down list

- Ashridge
- Hawthorne

- Hofstede
- Mintzberg

(2 marks)

32.14 In strategic planning, what is the purpose of environmental scanning?

○ To monitor PEST factors

○ To appraise SWOT factors

○ To monitor competitive forces

(1 mark)

32.15 What is the main focus of International Accounting Standards (IASs)?

○ Financial control

○ Accountancy training

○ Financial reporting

○ Corporate governance

(2 marks)

32.16 A large supermarket chain has purchased land for a new out-of-town shopping development in an area of recognised natural beauty.

The organisation is now preparing plans for infrastructure development (road access, parking, power) and construction.

		Level of interest	
		Low	High
Power	High	C	D
	Low	A	B

Required

Into which quadrant of the above power/interest matrix would the organisation place local nature appreciation groups, and what strategy does this indicate?

○ Consult and involve

○ Keep informed

○ Keep satisfied

○ Minimal effort

(2 marks)

32.17 What is a fraud response plan?

　　O　A strategy for preventing and controlling fraud

　　O　A framework of disciplinary rules and sanctions to be applied when fraud is discovered

　　O　A strategy for investigating and dealing with the consequences of suspected or identified fraud

(1 mark)

32.18 In which of the following areas is economic growth most clearly beneficial, as an objective of macro-economic policy?

　　O　Employment

　　O　Public services

　　O　Environment

(1 mark)

32.19 According to Warren Bennis, which **TWO** of the following attributes distinguishes a leader, as opposed to a manager?

　　☐　Administers and maintains

　　☐　Focuses on people

　　☐　Innovates

　　☐　Focuses on systems

(2 marks)

32.20 Comfy Dentiality, a large dental practice, is concerned with the security of its patient records. The manager amends the disciplinary rules of the practice, so that unauthorised disclosure of data by personnel can be made grounds for dismissal.

Required

What type of approach to data security does this reflect?

　　O　Correction

　　O　Detection

　　O　Threat avoidance

　　O　Deterrence

(2 marks)

32.21 The diagram below is of an appraisal system.

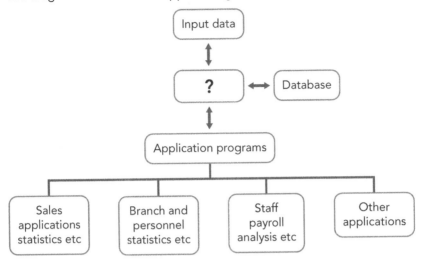

Required

Match the following labels to Boxes A, B and C.

Assessment interview	A	B	C
Follow up action	A	B	C
Criteria for assessment	A	B	C

(2 marks)

32.22 What set of environmental factors is most directly influenced by birth and mortality rates?

○ Political

○ Economic

○ Social

○ Technological

(2 marks)

32.23 Which word correctly completes this sentence?

In the context of rewarding team performance, team-based rewards and bonuses are more

effective if individual team members' contributions and work patterns are [▼]

Pull down list

• Independent

• Interdependent

• Isolated

(1 mark)

(Total = 38 marks)

33 Mixed Bank 7

33.1 In a payroll system, which of the following actions would **NOT** require authorisation, as a standard control measure?

○ Engagement or discharge of employees

○ Changes in pay rates

○ Statutory deductions from pay

○ Overtime payments

(2 marks)

33.2 At a chocolate manufacturing company, one of the production mixers has recently been made redundant. Fellow shop-floor staff are outraged: he was 'the only one who knew anything about chocolate' and they had relied on his judgement for years. Protests are ignored. A week later, cement is found in a batch of crunchy bars. Two weeks later, staff refuse to work overtime. The mixer is finally reinstated.

Required

Which **TWO** types of power are illustrated in this scenario by the mixer and the shop floor staff?

☐ Position power

☐ Expert power

☐ Personal power

☐ Negative power

(2 marks)

33.3 In a particular work team, Jemima is acknowledged to be the 'ideas' person who 'thinks outside the box' with creative solutions to difficult problems. However, she tends to look at the big picture, not at the details. Frank spots the gaps in Jemima's suggestions, and encourages the team to consider other options.

Required

Match each character in this scenario with the role that they occupy in Belbin's team role model.

Jemima		**MONITOR-EVALUATOR**	**TEAM WORKER**	**PLANT**
Frank		**MONITOR-EVALUATOR**	**TEAM WORKER**	**PLANT**

(2 marks)

33.4 Which of the following statements about outsourcing is true?

○ In order to maintain control, the organisation should outsource activities in areas of its own core competence.

○ Outsourcing to external contractors harnesses specialist expertise, but at the cost of lost economies of scale.

○ Outsourcing carries commercial and reputational risks.

(1 mark)

33.5 Victor Vroom's 'expectancy theory' is an example of which type of motivational theory?

    O Content theory

    O Process theory

    O Hierarchy theory

(1 mark)

33.6 In the context of improving organisational communication, which of the following would be helpful measures in addressing the problem of information overload on managers?

    O Using email

    O Introducing reporting by exception

    O Holding regular staff meetings

    O Speed reading training for managers

(2 marks)

33.7 Which of the following is represented by Blake and Mouton's managerial grid?

    O The balance in a manager's leadership style between concern for the task and concern for people and relationships

    O The success of a manager's performance, for the purposes of appraisal

    O A manager's position on the continuum between concern for task and concern for people and relationships

    O A matrix organisation structure, combining functional and line authority

(2 marks)

33.8 In the context of selection interviewing, which **TWO** of the following types of question might you use to pin down a candidate who seems reluctant or unable to give a definite answer?

    ☐ Open

    ☐ Closed

    ☐ Leading

    ☐ Probing

(2 marks)

33.9 In the context of motivation, workers may have the attitude that work is not an end in itself, but a means to other ends, through earning financial rewards.

Required

What term is given to this attitude?

    O Theory Y

    O Job enrichment

    O Instrumental orientation

(1 mark)

33.10 In the context of performance appraisal, what does the term 'tell and listen' refer to?

○ An approach to appraisal interviewing

○ An approach to upward appraisal

○ A barrier to effective appraisal

(1 mark)

33.11 Which of the following statements about training and development is false?

○ A gap between current performance and required performance is a learning gap which requires training.

○ Training and development activities can have measurable benefits for organisations.

○ Education may form part of training, which in turn may form part of employee development.

○ A 'learning organisation' is one which facilitates the learning of all its members.

(2 marks)

33.12 According to the hierarchy of needs (a motivational theory put forward by Maslow) which **TWO** of the following rewards might you pursue in order to have your esteem needs satisfied?

☐ Opportunity to undertake further professional development

☐ Award of a departmental prize for your performance

☐ Receiving praise on an achievement from your work team

☐ Being invited to join colleagues for lunch

(2 marks)

33.13 If a team has been functioning for some time, it may grow complacent with its performance, and start to devote more attention to relationship and power issues within the group.

Required

In the group development model, which of the following terms would be used for this stage of the team's development?

○ Forming

○ Norming

○ Dorming

○ Storming

(2 marks)

33.14 In a typical recruitment and selection process, in what order would the following steps be carried out.

Assign each a number in the sequence, from 1 (first) to 5 (last).

(i) Preparing job descriptions

(ii) Selection interviewing

(iii) Reference checking

(iv) Selection testing

(v) Preparing person specifications

○ 1(i), 2(ii), 3(iii), 4(iv), 5(v)

○ 1(ii), 2(iv), 3(i), 4(iii), 5(iv)

○ 1(iii), 2(i), 3(v), 4(ii), 5(iv)

○ 1(i), 2(v), 3(ii), 4(iv), 5(iii)   **(2 marks)**

33.15 Which word correctly completes this sentence?

One of the distinctions between coaching and mentoring is that a [▼] is not

usually the immediate superior of the person being helped.

Pull down list

• Coach

• Mentor

(1 mark)

33.16 A popular approach to self development is for employees to reflect on work incidents, and assess whether and how they might adjust their behaviour to gain more successful outcomes in future.

Required

On which school of learning theory is this approach based?

○ Behaviourist psychology

○ Cognitive psychology

○ Contingency theory

○ Learning styles

(2 marks)

33.17 Which **TWO** of the following factors establish the independence of an internal auditor?

☐ The auditor's mandatory authority

☐ The auditor's involvement in the activities being appraised

☐ The auditor's own professionalism

☐ The auditor's freedom from accountability

(2 marks)

33.18 A manager is coming up to retirement in a year's time.

In which of the following circumstances would the organisation be most likely to consider external recruitment, rather than internal promotion, to fill the position?

○ The organisation has a policy of staff development and succession planning

○ The organisation is looking to introduce a culture of innovation for the first time

○ The organisation has a very strong managerial culture, which it wishes to preserve

(1 mark)

33.19 In which of the following areas is there an advantage to using formal off-the-job training courses as opposed to on-the-job or experiential learning methods?

○ Level of risk for acquiring new skills

○ Relevance of learning to the job

○ Application of learning to the job

○ Continuity of work effort

(2 marks)

33.20 Which word or words correctly complete this statement?

[▼] occurs when a person is penalised for giving information or taking action is pursuit of a claim of discrimination.

Pull down list

• Direct discrimination

• Indirect discrimination

• Victimisation

(1 mark)

33.21 Which of the following would be considered a potentially sensitive or negative element of an effective equal opportunities policy?

○ Flexible working and career break programmes

○ Monitoring numbers and performance of ethnic minority staff

○ Diverse job interview panels

○ Counselling and disciplinary policies on discrimination

(2 marks)

33.22 Which of the following checks would the external audit function be responsible for?

○ Separation of duties for independent proving of work

○ Arithmetic checks on the accuracy of data recording and calculation

○ Creating and preserving records that confirm accounting entries

○ Considering whether directors act on internal audit information

(2 marks)

33.23 The effectiveness of training programmes can be evaluated using a five-level model by Hamblin.

Assign the correct number from 1 to 5 to each of the following levels.

(i) Ultimate value

(ii) Changes in job behaviour

(iii) Trainee reactions

(iv)   Trainee learning

(v)   Impact on organisational results

- ○ 1(i), 2(ii), 3(iii), 4(iv), 5(v)
- ○ 1(iii), 2(iv), 3(ii), 4(v), 5(i)
- ○ 1(ii), 2(iii), 3(iv), 4(i), 5(v)
- ○ 1(iii), 2(i), 3(v), 4(ii), 5(iv)

(2 marks)

33.24 In the context of data security, which **TWO** of the following are examples of physical access controls to protect computer equipment or data storage media?

- ☐ Card entry systems
- ☐ Back-up controls
- ☐ Personal identification numbers
- ☐ Logical access systems

(2 marks)

33.25 An organisation's employees are one of its connected stakeholders.

- ○ True
- ○ False

(1 mark)

(Total = 42 marks)

Answers

1 Business organisations and their stakeholders

1.1 'An organisation is a social arrangement which pursues collective │ goals │ , which controls

its own performance and has a boundary separating it from its environment.'

Rationale: Collective goals or aims are a feature of organisations.

Pitfalls: Watch out for closely related terminology like 'goals' and 'tactics'. You might have thought 'tactics' would fit here, but they are the lower level plans of functions: they may not be shared by the organisation as a whole.

Ways in: If you didn't know the definition, you could have got to the answer by ruling out the other options. Stakeholders doesn't fit 'pursues'; profits are not the objective of all organisations; and tactics are at a lower level than goals.

1.2 The correct answer is: Synergy

Rationale: Synergy is the 2 + 2 = 5 factor, and is one of the key reasons for the formation of teams and organisations.

Pitfalls: You need to read all the options carefully, especially if they look similar and all 'sound' plausible.

Ways in: You should be able to define the other options, to confirm that they do not fit the definition given.

1.3 The correct answer is: For organisations that have limited company status, ownership and control are legally separate.

Rationale: In a limited company, the owners (shareholders) are separate from the managers of the concern (board of directors).

Pitfalls: Some options look plausible because of the wording. 'Limited' doesn't mean 'only being allowed to trade up to' – but looks as if it might. The second half of the statement about partnerships is true – but this doesn't mean that the first half is also true.

Ways in: You should have been able to rule out A (no company's turnover is limited), C (sole traders do have personal liability for debts: they do not have 'limited liability') and D (ordinary partnerships are different from limited companies).

1.4 The correct answer is: A public sector organisation

Rationale: Such an organisation is part of the public sector. The voluntary sector comprises charities and other organisations whose members are volunteers. Private sector comprises non-governmental organisations, such as limited companies.

Pitfalls: Watch out for 'public' and 'private' sector terms – and be able to distinguish clearly between them.

1.5 The correct answer is: (1), (2), (3) and (4)

Rationale: All these groups have a legitimate stake in the enterprise: the government, as a regulator; employees, as participants in the business; and environmental pressure group and local residents, because of potential impacts.

Pitfalls: Don't forget external stakeholders!

1.6 The correct answer is: Stakeholders who do not have a contractual relationship with the organisation

Rationale: Secondary stakeholders are stakeholders who do **not** have a contractual relationship with the organisation.

Primary stakeholders are stakeholders who do have a contractual relationship with the organisation.

ANSWERS

1.7　The correct answer is: A local authority

Measures such as value for money or efficiency are often used in not-for-profit organisations such as local authorities.

1.8　The correct answer is: Co-operative

Rationale: A co-operative is a business which is owned by its workers or customers, who share the profits. Others features include open membership, democratic control, distribution of surplus in proportion to purchases and promotion of education.

2 Business environment and legal framework

2.1　The correct answer is: PEST

Rationale: PEST stands for Political, Economic, Socio-cultural and Technological.

Pitfalls: SWOT (Strengths, Weaknesses, Opportunities, Threats) is a related exercise, as PEST data is fed into the O/T part of the business appraisal.

Ways in: You could eliminate as many distractors as you could identify: SMART (Specific, Measurable, Attainable, Relevant, Time-bounded) refers to objective-setting.

2.2　The correct answer is: Offering financial incentives to public officials to use their influence on the organisation's behalf

Rationale: This would be interpreted as corruption. The other options are usually legitimate methods of influence. Although giving lawmakers non-executive directorships may be questionable in some parts of the world, in others like the UK it is perfectly legitimate.

2.3　Demographics　is an analysis of statistics on birth and death rates, age structures of people and ethnic groups within a community.

Rationale: The statement defines demographics. Ergonomics is a study of the interaction of humans and their environments (used in design of office equipment and furniture, for example).

Psychographics is the study of psychological factors (used in selection testing, for example). Economics is the study of economies.

Ways in: You could eliminate as many distractors as you could define in other ways.

2.4　The correct answer is: Technological

Rationale: Virtual organisation is the collaboration of geographically dispersed individuals and teams, specifically using the latest information and communication technology (ICT) enablers: the Internet, web-conferencing and so on.

2.5　The correct answer is: Erasure

Rationale: Erasure is also known as the right 'to be forgotten'. Data subjects may request information held about them be destroyed.

Ways in: Think about what the other terms mean. Rectification means to change for errors or misstatements, portability means that the data can be moved.

2.6　The correct answer is: Selection for redundancy on the basis of age

Rationale: This constitutes unfair selection for redundancy (on the basis of recent age discrimination legislation): redundancy is potentially fair grounds for dismissal as long as the basis of selection is fair.

Misconduct and incompetence are potentially fair grounds: there should be a reasonable attempt at performance or disciplinary management (warnings, training etc).

You may have hesitated over marriage to an employee of a key competitor, but this is an example of 'substantial reasons' that would be considered by a tribunal.

Ways in: You could narrow the options by considering that there must be **some** way for companies to dismiss incompetent or deliberately obstructive employees.

2.7   The correct answer is: (1), (2) and (3) only

Rationale: Increasing diversity has an impact on HR policies in regard to equal opportunity and prevention of discrimination. Falling birth rates creates an aging workforce and skill shortages. All organisations need to take account of environmental regulation and consumerism. An increase in single-member households will impact on **some** organisations: notably, those which market goods and services to this segment (eg single-serve pack sizes), but the questions said 'most' organisations.

Pitfalls: You need to think through a range of compliance, marketing and skilling issues when appraising socio-cultural factors.

2.8   The correct answer is: Government regulation of the industry

Rationale: The other forces are bargaining power of suppliers and rivalry amongst current competitors in the industry.

Pitfalls: The five forces model is basic: you really need to learn the details ...

2.9   The correct answer is: Marketing

Rationale: Socio-economic groupings are often the basis on which markets are segmented, so that products/services and marketing messages can be targeted appropriately (to people with the right levels of income, aspiration, education and so on). You might have paused over Human Resources, because social class includes education factors, but the data cannot be used to predict skill availability.

2.10   The correct answer is: Procurement

Rationale: Procurement, technology development, HR management and infrastructure are support activities. Inbound and outbound logistics, operations, marketing/sales and service are primary activities.

2.11   The correct answer is: Automation and artificial intelligence allow the accountant to focus their time on verifying low-level transactions.

Rationale: Automation and artificial intelligence support the automatic and intelligent processing of transactional information to free the accountant to work on value-adding services rather than focussing on low-level transactions. The other options are all correct statements concerning the impact of technology on the role of accountants.

2.12   The correct answer is: Sheila

Steve, Sam, and Sunny all have support roles and the words 'administration' and 'information technology' should have immediately indicated a support role for Steve and Sam. Sunny's procurement role is not so clear cut but the responsibilities for dealing with the suppliers are sufficient to conclude that Sunny also has a support role.

2.13   The correct answer is: As early as possible after employment

Rationale: After the first few weeks of employment is incorrect because waiting a few weeks leaves the employee open to risks in those weeks. The other options are incorrect because there is no certainty that the job will be offered or accepted.

2.14   The correct answer is: Low switching costs in the market

Rationale: Low switching costs means that it will be easy for customers to change from existing suppliers to a new supplier: this would facilitate entry to the market. The other options should clearly pose difficulties to a new entrant: not yet big enough to benefit from economies of scale (against competitors who are); high start-up costs; high degree of recognition of and loyalty to existing brands.

2.15   The correct answer is: Delegating

Rationale: Outsourcing (contracting some of the firm's activities to external providers) and delayering (removing levels of the organisation hierarchy) are strategies for downsizing (reducing the number of staff permanently or directly employed by the firm).

Delegating is the process whereby a superior gives a subordinate part of his or her own authority to make decisions.

BPP
LEARNING
MEDIA

2.16 The correct answer is: Concern with health and diet

Rationale: Health and safety legislation may **reflect** a cultural trend (increasing expectation of quality of working life, say), but it is a compliance issue. Increasing age of the population is a demographic trend.

2.17 The correct answer is: Lifestyle

Rationale: Lifestyle is generally considered a reflection of economic status and conditions, not a determinant of them. (For market segmentation purposes, for example, lifestyle factors are often measured in terms of attitudes, interests and opinions, rather than purely economic factors.)

2.18 The correct answer is: False

Rationale: Technological developments, such as automation and AI, mean that the role of the accountant and auditor to record and verify day-to-day transactions has become *less* important as the role switches to more high-level tasks such as report writing.

3 The macro-economic environment

3.1 The correct answer is: Exchange rates

Rationale: Exchange rates are a target of monetary policy: government policy on the money supply, the monetary system interest rates, exchange rates and the availability of credit. Fiscal policy is government policy on the three other options.

Pitfalls: This whole syllabus area is full of fine distinctions in terminology, which lend themselves to testing in a Multiple Choice and Objective Testing format.

Ways in: If you knew that there was a distinction between fiscal and monetary policy, you might have identified exchange rates as the only monetary issue.

3.2 The correct answer is: The government is running a budget surplus.

Rationale: A budget surplus occurs when a government's income exceeds its expenditure: there is a negative PSNCR or PSDR. When a government's expenditure exceeds its income, so that it must borrow to make up the difference, there is a positive PSNCR and we say that the government is running a budget deficit.

Ways in: If you recognised that a negative PSNC means no borrowing, you might have been able to start eliminating some options ...

3.3 Indirect taxes are collected by the Revenue authority from a business, which attempts to

pass on the tax to consumers in the price of goods.

Rationale: The definition clearly distinguishes an indirect tax (eg sales tax) from a direct tax, which is paid direct by a person to the Revenue authority (eg income tax, corporation tax, capital gains tax and inheritance tax). Progressive refers to the proportion of income taken by a tax.

3.4 The correct answer is: Increasing taxation

Rationale: Increasing taxation lowers demand in the economy because people have less of their own money after tax for consumption or saving/investment. Increasing public expenditure should increase the level of consumer demand. Decreasing taxation has the opposite effect. Lowering interest rates should stimulate investment (by companies) and consumer expenditure, even if only after a time lag.

3.5 The correct answer is: A reduction in the rate of cost push inflation

Rationale: An increase in the exchange rate makes a country's exports more expensive to overseas buyers, and imports cheaper: it therefore has the opposite of the first three effects. The lower cost of imports, however, is likely to reduce the rate of domestic inflation.

Pitfalls: The permutations of increases/decreases in interest rate can be confusing: ensure that the logic makes sense to you!

Ways in: You could group the second and third options together (increased cost = reduce demand): since both cannot be the answer, and there is only one answer, neither of these options can be correct. This gets you quite a long way towards the solution ... So if you don't know an answer, don't panic: logic can often help!

3.6　The correct answer is: Subsidies for exporters

Rationale: Subsidies for exporters will encourage domestic exports, but will not help to protect domestic producers against overseas producers. The other options are tariff (taxes and duties on goods entering the country) and non-tariff barriers to trade.

3.7　The correct answers are:

Frictional unemployment will be short term	**TRUE**	
Governments can encourage labour mobility if they want to reduce unemployment	**TRUE**	

Rationale: Frictional unemployment occurs when there is difficulty in matching workers quickly with jobs. This means that frictional unemployment is temporary and short term. A government can encourage labour mobility by offering individuals financial assistance with relocation expenses and by improving the flow of information on vacancies.

3.8　The correct answers are:

- Interest rates
- Exchange rates

Rationale: Government policy on taxation, public spending and public borrowing relates to fiscal policy. Government policy on interest rates and exchange rates are part of the monetary policy.

3.9　The correct answer is: An organisation which has a large number of long-term payables

Rationale: Debts lose 'real' value with inflation: a company that owes a lot of money would effectively pay less (in real terms) over time. The other organisations would suffer because: inflation would make exports relatively expensive and imports relatively cheap; business might be lost due to price rises; and the cost of implementing price changes would be high.

3.10　The correct answers are:

- Encouraging economic growth
- Low unemployment
- Achievement of a balance between exports and imports

Rationale: The four main objectives of macroeconomic policy relate to economic growth, stable (not zero) inflation, unemployment and the balance of payments (balance between exports and imports).

3.11　The correct answer is: Recession in the building industry

Rationale: Recession is part of the business cycle: demand for output and jobs falls, and unemployment rises until recovery is well under way. The first option is an example of frictional unemployment; the second option is seasonal unemployment; the third option is technological unemployment.

Pitfalls: It is easy to confuse cyclical with seasonal unemployment, or frictional unemployment that occurs on a seasonal basis. You need to associate cyclical employment firmly with **business** cycles.

3.12　A surplus on the balance of payments usually refers to a surplus or deficit on the　 current

account.

Rationale: It is particularly tempting to equate a trade surplus or deficit with a 'profit' or 'loss' for the country, but this is not the case.

BPP
LEARNING
MEDIA

3.13   The correct answer is: Northland

Rationale: Stagflation occurs when economic growth (defined by the change in national income in a period) is low or negative, and inflation is high. So the relevant figures are percentage change in GDP and change in consumer prices. Northland and Eastland both experienced negative growth, however, Northland had a high level of price inflation as well.

3.14 | Potential | economic growth is determined by supply-side rather than by demand side factors.

Rationale: Potential growth is the rate at which the economy would grow if all resources were utilised: it is therefore determined by factors in the capacity of the economy (supply side), such as increases in the amount of resources available, or in the productivity or resources. Actual growth is determined both by growth in output (supply side) **and** aggregate demand (demand side).

4 Micro-economic factors

4.1   The correct answer is: Allocates resources

Rationale: In a free market economy, it is the interaction of supply and demand through the price mechanism that determines what should be produced and who should get it.

4.2   The correct answer is: Marginal cost curve above the average variable cost curve

Rationale: The supply curve for a perfectly competitive firm is its marginal cost curve above the average variable cost curve. The firm will not continue to produce if price is less than average variable cost.

4.3   The correct answer is: Nothing

Rationale: A minimum price (floor price) only leads to excess supply if it is set **higher** than the equilibrium price.

4.4   The correct answer is: A fall in production costs of the good

Rationale: The other options relate to movements **along** the supply curve.

4.5   The correct answer is: A surplus of the good

Rationale: The effect of price being above the equilibrium (market clearing) price is that supply will extend and demand will contract.

4.6   The correct answer is: A rise in the price of overseas holidays

Rationale: A rise in the price of overseas holidays will lead to a movement along the demand curve rather than a shift in the demand curve.

4.7   The correct answer is: A fall in the level of household incomes generally

Rationale: Generally, if incomes fall, demand will fall.

4.8   The correct answer is: There are four producers exerting considerable influence in the market

Rationale: The first option is one of the conditions for a perfect market, the second is a monopoly and the fourth is monopolistic competition.

4.9   The correct answer is: Carpet underlay

Rationale: Carpet underlay is a complement to carpet.

4.10   The correct answer is: Holidays

Rationale: An increase in demand for cars will lead to an increase in demand for petrol and tyres. It will not increase the demand for holidays although people may use their cars to go on holiday.

4.11   The correct answer is: Allocative inefficiency among producers

Rationale: This is a supply-side factor.

4.12 The correct answer is: A fall in the demand for tea

Rationale: Coffee and tea are substitute products. Thus, a fall in the price of coffee will result in higher demand for coffee and lower demand for its substitute product, tea.

The price of tea might therefore fall. Demand for drinking cups is probably insufficiently related to the consumption of coffee to make them a complementary product to coffee. Even so, lower coffee prices would be likely to raise the demand for drinking cups rather than reduce it.

4.13 The correct answer is: A good for which demand will fall as household income rises

Rationale: The term 'inferior good' is a technical term in economics. An example of such a good might be small 'starter' homes.

4.14 The correct answer is: The demand curve for vases will shift to the left; their price will go down

Rationale: It is assumed that cut flowers and flower vases are complementary goods. The rise in price of cut flowers will have an adverse effect on demand for flower vases, and the demand curve for flower vases will shift to the left. Given no change in supply conditions for vases, the new equilibrium price for vases will be lower.

4.15 The correct answer is: The demand curve for sea ferry tickets will shift to the right, and their price will go up. More ferry tickets will be sold.

Rationale: As sea ferry tickets and hovercraft tickets are substitute goods, an increase in the price of hovercraft tickets will cause a shift to the right (increase in demand) for sea ferry tickets. Given no change in supply conditions, the consequence will be an increase in the number of sea ferry tickets sold, at a higher price than before.

4.16 The correct answer is: Item 1 only

Rationale: A fall in the price of **sterling** would make London hotels cheaper for foreign tourists. A fall in the price of aeroplane tickets would make London cheaper to visit for foreign tourists. Events 2 and 3 would lead to a **rise** in demand for hotel rooms. In contrast, a fall in the value of the US dollar would make the UK more expensive to visit for US tourists and tourists from other countries where the US dollar is widely used, and demand for hotel rooms in London would fall.

4.17 The correct answer is: Oligopoly

Rationale: This is an example of oligopoly.

4.18 The correct answers are:

- In the longer term, an increase in new building work
- The provision of more rented accommodation

Rationale: When rent controls are eased, the effect is similar to raising or removing minimum prices in the rented housing market. We should expect higher rents, more supply of housing, and a closing of the gap between demand for rented housing and supply of rented accommodation. The reverse of the first option should happen, and homelessness should decrease. Given widespread homelessness, it is unlikely that the easing of rent controls will have any effect on demand for owner-occupied dwellings.

4.19 The correct answer is: All of the above

Rationale: All of the options may cause the demand curve for a resource to shift.

4.20 The correct answer is: Sales will rise sharply when incomes of households rise

Rationale: The income elasticity of demand measures the responsiveness of demand to changes in consumers' incomes. An 'inferior' good has a negative income elasticity: as incomes fall, more is bought.

4.21 The correct answer is: 2

Rationale: Percentage change in quantity = 50%. Percentage change in price = 25%.

4.22 The correct answer is: The excess between what consumers are prepared to pay for a good or service, and the prevailing market price

BPP
LEARNING
MEDIA

ANSWERS

Rationale: Consumer surplus is the excess between what consumers are prepared to pay for a good or service and the prevailing market price they have to pay to purchase it.

4.23 The correct answer is: Elastic demand, elastic supply

Rationale: To increase market share requires greater quantities of the firm's products to be both demanded and supplied. To sell more, a firm needs to lower price. For this to be profitable, demand must be elastic. To produce more, supply must also be elastic.

4.24 The correct answer is: A more than proportional increase in the quantity of dry white wine purchased

Rationale: Assuming a normal good, a decrease in price results in a greater quantity being demanded. Given that demand is price elastic, the increase in quantity will be proportionally greater than the price fall.

4.25 The correct answer is: Ratio of marginal utility to price is equal for each good

Rationale: Imagine you can buy a second car for $10,000 or buy a bike for $100 and they both give you the same extra utility. You wouldn't choose to buy the car as you're paying much more to achieve the same utility as you could get from buying the bike. If you get 10 times more utility for one thing compared to another you'd be prepared to pay 10 times more for it.

5 Section A Multi-task questions MTQs

5.1 (a) The correct answers are:

If income elasticity is positive, the commodity is an inferior good		**FALSE**
If two goods are complements, the cross elasticity will be negative	**TRUE**	
If price elasticity is greater than 1, demand is inelastic		**FALSE**
Unrelated products have a cross elasticity of infinity		**FALSE**

False. An inferior good would have negative income elasticity.

True. If price elasticity is greater than 1, demand is said to be inelastic.

False. If price elasticity is less than 1, demand is said to be inelastic.

False. Unrelated products has a cross elasticity of zero.

(b) The correct answers are:

- An increase in household incomes
- An expected future rise in the price of the good
- An increase in population

5.2 (a) The correct answers are:

Sarah	**WRONGFUL**		
Trevor			**NEITHER**
Umberto		**UNFAIR**	
Vanessa		**UNFAIR**	

Wrongful dismissal relates to the method of dismissal.

(b) The correct answers are:

In the event of redundancy, an employee with one year's continuous employment is entitled to compensation		**FALSE**
Redundancy can occur where an employer ceases to carry on business in a particular location	**TRUE**	

There is no entitlement to compensation with less than 2 years' continuous employment.

5.3 (a) The correct answers are:

Tax incentives for investment	**OUTPUT CAPACITY**			
Equal opportunities legislation			**EMPLOY-MENT**	
Forbid takeovers		**COMPETI-TION**		
Product safety standards				**CONSUMER PROTEC-TION**

Tax incentives will encourage investment which will increase output capacity.

Forbidding takeover will mean more competitors in an industry and encourages competition. Equal opportunities will positively influence employment.

Product safety standards will ensure a minimum safety level for consumers.

(b) The correct answers are:

Borrowing	**FISCAL POLICY**	
Taxation	**FISCAL POLICY**	
Interest rates		**MONETARY POLICY**
Money supply		**MONETARY POLICY**

5.4 (a) The correct answers are:

Department W	**OPERA-TIONS**			
Department X			**OUTBOUND LOGISTICS**	
Department Y				**MARKETING AND SALES**
Department Z		**AFTER SALES SERVICE**		

ANSWERS

(b) The correct answers are:

- There is a lack of substitute products available
- The product supplied is highly differentiated

If there are a lack of substitutes then the customer has less choice of suppliers and similarly if the product is highly differentiated.

5.5 (a) (1) What is the price elasticity of demand for product BB15? 12.5%/−5% = −2.5

(2) What is the cross elasticity of demand? −2.5%/−5% = +0.5

(3) Products BB15 and CC25 are substitutes

Since the cross elasticity of demand is positive, the products are substitutes.

(b) For a normal, inferior good, demand curve slopes downwards to the right.

An inferior good still has a downward sloping demand curve, but less of the product is demanded when incomes rise.

5.6 (a) The correct answers are:

- They are aimed at promoting social, political or environmental change
- They often raise funds through donations
- They are measured in terms of effectiveness and efficiency

The description 'NGO' generally applies to groups whose primary aim is not a commercial one, aimed at promoting social, political or environmental change. NGOs are not necessarily charities, although they tend to raise funds through donations. They are measured in terms of effectiveness and efficiency, rather than customer satisfaction or profit targets.

(b) The correct answer is: VFM

NCOs are measured on their effectiveness and efficiency in how they manage their resources – 'value for money'

6 Business organisation structure

6.1 The correct answer is: An organisation chart can indicate functional authority but not line authority within a business.

Rationale: Line authority can easily be shown on the organisation chart.

Pitfalls: You may have hesitated if you didn't know the difference between functional authority (where an expert department has authority over the activities of other departments in the areas of its expertise eg the HR department setting recruitment policy for the sales and production departments) and line authority (direct authority flowing down the chain of command). However, you only needed to know the meaning of line authority to see that the statement was untrue.

Ways in: You may have paused to ask whether an organisation chart can improve internal communications, but it does in one key way: by highlighting the length and complexity of lines of communication between people who need to co-ordinate their work.

6.2 The correct answer is: The number of employees directly responsible to a manager

Rationale: This is the definition of span of control: all the others are distractors.

Pitfalls: All the distractors are plausible: note the need to think them through carefully. The first option is close to the correct definition – but if you think about it, the number of subordinate employees includes **all** those below the manager, whereas span of control is direct reports only.

6.3 The correct answer is: Support base

Rationale: Support base is not one of Mintzberg's components of organisation structure: the other correct terms are middle line and support staff.

Pitfalls: The basic terminology of well-known models is must-learn material!

6.4 The correct answer is: Divisionalisation

Rationale: While there may be elements of functional and geographical organisation, Y plc's situation suits divisionalisation: more or less autonomous product and regional businesses, with co-ordination from head office. 'Diversification' and 'acquisition' are good pointers to divisionalisation.

Pitfalls: Don't get sidetracked by the link between 'overseas markets' and 'geographical'.

6.5 The correct answer is: Unity of command

Rationale: Matrix organisation is based on dual command: the classical principle of unity of command is 'one person, one boss'.

6.6 The correct answer is: Managers in positions of authority generally cannot be part of the informal organisation.

Rationale: The first option is a fact. The second option is true, because of informal 'short cuts' which are often developed and shared, by-passing health and safety rules and procedures. The third option is true, because the 'grapevine' encourages knowledge sharing and multi-directional communication. The fourth option is not true: managers can feed information into the grapevine and be part of their own informal networks.

6.7 The correct answer is: Senior managers can take a wider view of problems and consequences

Rationale: A centralised organisation is one in which authority is concentrated in one place. If all decisions are made in the same place then it will be easier for the decision-makers to see the 'bigger picture' and therefore understand the consequences of their decisions.

The first two options are advantages of decentralisation, where decisions are delegated.

6.8　The correct answer is: Statement (1) only

Rationale: Statement (2) is not true, because the informal organisation has its own agenda. Statement (3) is not true, because a strong informal organisation with its own agenda can undermine the formal organisation: create damaging rumours, safety/quality shortcuts, distractions from task goals etc.

6.9　The correct answer is: Boundaryless organisation

Rationale: This describes a boundaryless organisation. A hollow organisation splits people and activities into core and non-core. In modular organisations different elements or components of the product or service the organisation produces are outsourced to different suppliers. In a jobless structure the employee becomes not a job-holder but a seller of skills.

6.10　The correct answer is: Statements (1) and (2) only

Rationale: The shared service centre is created within the organisation and is a part of it, although its relationship is similar to that of an external service provider.

7　Organisational culture and committees

7.1　The correct answer is: Role culture

Rationale: The role culture is a bureaucratic or mechanistic culture, as described in the scenario. Task culture is project-focused; existential culture is person-focused; and power culture is leader-focused.

Pitfalls: If you didn't know Harrison's model well, you might have confused 'focus on the task' (see in the scenario) with a task culture, or the strong central leadership with a 'power' culture.

7.2　The correct answer is: Strong values are dangerous if they filter out 'uncomfortable' environmental information

Rationale: This is a problem with strong cultures (and ultra-cohesive groups).

Pitfalls: The other statements are plausible: you need to come up with counter-arguments to show that they are not always true. B is most plausible because it makes a limited claim that values 'can' replace rules: think of health and safety or financial controls, however, to disprove the claim.

Ways in: You could rule out two of the statements because they are dogmatic (so that just one counter-example would make them untrue).

7.3　Culture is the collective programming of the mind which distinguishes the members of one

> category of people | from another.

Rationale: There are many spheres of culture: nation, ethnic group and social class are only three of them. 'Culture' applies to categories of people including genders, social classes and organisations.

7.4　The correct answer is: Acquisitive/giving

Rationale: The fourth dimension in Hofstede's model is masculinity-femininity.

7.5　The correct answer is: Assumptions

Rationale: Assumptions are foundational ideas that are no longer even consciously recognised or questioned by the culture, but which 'programme' its ways of thinking and behaving. Values and beliefs are the next level up: they are consciously held concepts which give meaning to the next level up again – observable factors such as rituals, artefacts and behaviour.

7.6　The correct answer is: Schein

Rationale: This is just a case of learning who is associated with which theory and definition.

7.7 The correct answer is: Masculinity – femininity

Rationale: Make sure that you learn the distinctions between the cultural dimensions.

7.8 The correct answer is: (2) and (3) only

Rationale: R & D tends to be concerned with product research (not market research), and many organisations have internal R & D functions.

Pitfalls: Be aware of the difference between product and market research.

Ways in: If you were able to rule out statement (1), you were only left with two options to choose from – and you should be able to rule out statement (4) if you know any organisations with an internal R & D department, leaving you with the correct option.

7.9 Services have certain qualities which distinguish them from products. Because of their

intangibility , physical elements such as vouchers, tickets, confirmations and

merchandise are an important part of service provision.

Rationale: Intangibility refers to the fact that there are no material or physical aspects to a service: physical elements help to reduce this effect, and make the provision concrete for the customer. Inseparability and perishability refer to the fact that services are created and consumed at the same time: they cannot be stored – and pose challenges to demand forecasting and scheduling. Variability refers to the fact that services are specific to the situation and cannot easily be standardised.

Ways in: What do physical elements **do** for a customer purchasing eg a train ride or legal advice? If you knew the meaning of the term 'intangible', the answer to this question would get you to the correct answer.

7.10 The correct answer is: Sales

Rationale: A sales orientation assumes that customers must be persuaded to buy the products that the firm produces. A production orientation assumes that customer will buy whatever is produced: the focus of the firm is on meeting demand. A marketing orientation seeks to determine the needs, wants and values of customers and to produce what customers want to buy.

Pitfalls: Don't confuse selling and marketing!

7.11 The correct answer is: (1) and (3)

Rationale: HRM is concerned with the most effective use of human resources. It deals with staffing levels, motivation, employee relations and employee services. It is the marketing function which manages an organisation's relationship with its customers, not HRM. Note that increasingly, HRM is undertaken by line managers as well or instead of HR departments.

7.12 The correct answer is: Standing committee

Rationale: A standing committee is formed for a particular purpose on a permanent basis. Joint committees are formed to co-ordinate the activities of two or more committees: they need not be permanent. Task forces are specifically **not** permanent: they fulfil their allocated task and then wind up.

Pitfalls: The confusion of related terminology is often the target of testing.

7.13 The correct answer is: Josh

Rationale: HR and line departments generally provide details of salary/wage rates, time sheets etc – but the finance department generally administers payroll, so Josh is likely to be responsible.

7.14 The correct answer is: Both (1) and (2)

Rationale: Time, expense and compromise decisions are some of the disadvantages of a committee so Paul is correct. There are, however, many advantages to committees as well.

7.15 The correct answer is: Lesley

Rationale: Diane and Joanne work at operational level as they are concerned with routine activities. Lesley is at an intermediate level and is managing resources. She is therefore part of tactical management. Tracey is concerned with direction setting for the business and is therefore part of strategic management.

7.16 The correct answer is: Low masculinity

Rationale: Low masculinity (or femininity) is about high regard for values such as focus on relationships and quality of working life, and the acceptability of such values for both men and women: Mr Q's nurturing style would score on this dimension. His approach does not really say anything about power-distance (command-and-control v delegation-and-involvement). There are elements of uncertainty-avoidance in his attempt to minimise staff insecurity – but this would be high UA, not low UA.

Pitfalls: Don't confuse the masculine/feminine dimension with straightforward gender stereotypes!

7.17 The correct answer is: Mutual dependency

Rationale: Dependency increases stakeholder power and creates risks and constraints. A buyer would not necessarily want a supplier to be dependent on its business (for ethical reasons), any more than it would want to be dependent on a supplier (for bargaining and supply risk reasons).

Pitfalls: You may have hesitated over information-sharing, because of intellectual property and confidentiality issues – but it is necessary for high-interest, high-power 'key players'.

7.18 The correct answer is: Janet only

Rationale: Internal stakeholders include employees and management and so Janet is the only internal stakeholder. Customers and suppliers (like Mary at P Co) are connected stakeholders. Pressure groups such as D Group are external stakeholders.

7.19 The correct answer is: Giving a ruling on matters in dispute

Rationale: All the other options are duties of the Committee secretary.

7.20 The correct answer is: Committee secretary

Rationale: You should have been able to rule out the chair of a committee. An ordinary committee member will receive communications, not produce them.

7.21 The correct answer is: Ascertaining whether specific matters fall within the terms of reference of the committee

Rationale: The Secretary does not agree the minutes, and may indeed sometimes not be a committee member at all.

7.22 The correct answer is: Standing committees

Rationale: Ad hoc committees are non-permanent committees, often formed for a particular purpose.

The terms 'management committee' and 'executive committee' are generally interchangeable.

They refer to the committee of executives that will meet regularly to formulate, implement and review operational matters.

In a large company, they usually include the two or three executives who serve as executive directors as well as other senior managers who are not executive directors.

Standing committees are a permanent feature of the governance of a company and include the audit committee and the remuneration committee (larger companies also have a nomination committee and perhaps a risk committee).

Standing committees meet regularly (though not necessarily monthly).

8 Corporate governance and social responsibility

8.1 The correct answer is: (3) only

Rationale: Statement (1) is incorrect, because there is no such 'guarantee'; statement (2) because it is not necessarily so, and statement (4) because other organisations (eg charities, government bodies) are often more concerned with social responsibility than businesses.

Ways in: It is always worth checking to see if logic helps. Words like 'guarantee' often signal an untrue statement, because they make such extreme claims.

And if statement (1) is therefore incorrect, you've halved your options. It should then be obvious that (4) is incorrect (if you think about a hospital, say).

8.2 The correct answer is: Agency theory

Rationale: Agency theory suggests that managers will look after the performance of the company if doing so serves their own interests: hence performance incentives and rewards. Stewardship theory views the managers as stewards of the assets of the firm. Stakeholder theory argues that managers have a duty of care to a range of organisational shareholders.

Ways in: You could have ruled out stakeholder theory as irrelevant, and then worked on the implications of stewardship and agency.

8.3 The correct answer is: Maximising shareholder wealth

Rationale: The objective of corporate governance is overall performance, enhanced by good supervision and management, within best practice guidelines. Business is to be conducted in a way that is both ethical and effective from the perspective of all stakeholders – not just shareholders.

8.4 The correct answer is: Strategic importance

Rationale: Corporate governance includes the selection of senior officers (with influence over the future direction of the organisation), and relationships between the organisation and its key stakeholders. It is therefore regarded as being of strategic importance.

8.5 The correct answer is: Domination of the board by a single individual

Rationale: This is a feature of poor corporate governance because it makes way for self-interested decision-making. The others may 'look' like negatives, but are in fact the opposites of three other features of poor corporate governance: lack of independent scrutiny; lack of supervision; and an emphasis on short-term profitability (which can cause pressure to conceal problems or manipulate accounts).

Ways in: You could have got to the answer with logic, with a sound grasp of corporate governance – but it would be worth learning the list of features of poor corporate governance, so you can recognise them in an exam question.

8.6 The correct answer is: The board of directors

Rationale: These are some of the roles fulfilled by the board. The audit committee reviews financial statements, audit procedures, internal controls and risk management. The Public Oversight Board monitors and enforces legal and compliance standards. The nomination committee oversees the process for board appointments.

Pitfalls: You need to be able to distinguish clearly between all the various participants in the corporate governance system.

Ways in: Strategy formulation should have steered you towards the correct answer.

8.7 The correct answer is: (1), (2) and (4) only

Rationale: Professional ethics concern the individual ethical sphere, not the wider sphere of Corporate Social Responsibility which operates at the level of the firm. All of the others are CSR principles: human rights as a component of ethical trading and investment; employee welfare as part of ethical employment; and support for local suppliers as an example of sustainability.

ANSWERS

Pitfalls: The combinations were designed to test if your thinking was limited to internal organisational matters or commercial matters.

8.8   The correct answer is: Corporate social responsibility

Rationale: Employment protection is just one example of an area which is subject to law. Corporate governance is an area which is subject to codes of best practice (and law in some countries). CSR is therefore the area subject to least regulation and most managerial discretion.

8.9   The correct answer is: To provide guidance on the standards of best practice companies should adopt

Rationale: Codes of practice are usually associated with a principles-based approach (rather than a rules-based approach) and so the first two options should have been easily eliminated. The words 'guidance' and 'should adopt' were the key words to lead to the correct option.

8.10 The correct answer is: A remuneration committee made up of independent non-executive directors

Rationale: Only this option fulfils the requirement for full independence of the body that sets directors' remuneration (to avoid directors' awarding themselves unjustifiable rewards!). A nomination committee has the separate task of overseeing board appointments.

8.11 The correct answer is: To set out the directors' analysis of the business, in order to provide investors with a historical and prospective view through the eyes of management.

Rationale: This is the definition used by the Accounting Standards Board. The third option is another corporate governance report that may be required. The first option is just a distractor.

8.12 The correct answer is: (1), (2) and (3)

Rationale: 4 is incorrect and can actually be problematic for non-executive directors. Non-executive directors often have limited time to devote to the role as they are likely to have other time consuming commitments.

9 Section B MTQs

9.1   (a) Paul

| Sales orientation |

Mary

| Product orientation |

Alan

| Production orientation |

Kate

| Marketing orientation |

Adding additional features but without actually researching what customers want is product orientation, which is a variant of production orientation.

(b) Breaking up the market into different groups, which each have common needs, wants and preferences is known as | market segmentation. |

9.2   (a) The correct answers are:

Which business should we be in?	**CORPORATE**		

Should we specialise in a profitable product?		**BUSINESS**	
How best can we market the products?			**OPERATIONAL**
Should we segment the market?		**BUSINESS**	

(1) Corporate strategy is concerned with what types of business the organisation is in.

(2) Business strategy is how an organisation approaches a particular market area.

(3) This relates to a functional decision and therefore is at the operational level.

(4) Business strategy is how an organisation approaches a particular market area.

(b) The correct answers are:

- Managers are able to take a wider view
- Procedures and documentation can be standardised

Managers are able to take a wider view, procedures and documentation can be standardised. The other statements are advantages of decentralisation or delegation.

9.3 (a) Company W

Individualism

Company X

Uncertainty avoidance

Company Y

Masculinity

Company Z

Power distance

(1) This company has a high individualism culture.

(2) This company has a high uncertainty avoidance culture.

(3) This company has a low masculinity culture.

(4) This company has a low power distance culture.

(b) Patterns of greeting styles and business formalities are known as   attitudes

Concrete expressions, such as office premises design, are   artefacts

Attitudes are patterns of collective behaviour such as greeting styles, business formalities, social courtesies and ceremonies.

Artefacts are concrete expressions such as architecture and interior design, dress code and symbols.

9.4 (a) The correct answers are:

Canteen worker		SUPPORT STAFF		
Production worker	OPERATING CORE			
Production manager				MIDDLE LINE
Director			STRATEGIC APEX	

(1) Support staff provide ancillary services.

(2) Production is part of the operating core, taking inputs and converting them into outputs.

(3) Middle managers such as a production manager form the middle line of an organisation.

(4) The board would form the strategic apex of the organisation.

(b) The correct answer is: Technostructure

Machine bureaucracies are characterised by multiple layers of management, formal (often rigid) procedures and standardised production processes, so the technostructure is very important

9.5 (a) The correct answers are:

- Arranging an overdraft - **Treasury**
- Managing foreign currency exposure - **Treasury**
- Recording financial transactions - **Financial accounting**
- Cash budgeting - **Treasury**
- Reporting to shareholders - **Financial accounting**
- Repaying loans - **Treasury**

The treasury department plans and controls the sources and uses of funds by the organisation.

(b) Markets for trading short-term financial instruments are known as money markets .

Money markets are markets for trading short-term financial instruments.

9.6 (a) To define the purpose of the company

To define the values by which the company will perform its daily duties

To identify the stakeholders relevant to the company

To develop a strategy combining these factors

To ensure implementation of this strategy

(b) The correct answer is: Chairing management committee meetings

Chairing management committee meetings is part of the usual responsibilities of the CEO.

10 The role of accounting

10.1 The correct answer is: To provide financial information to users of such information

Rationale: This is the main or overall aim of accounting.

10.2 The correct answer is: Charities and professional bodies do not have to produce financial statements in the same way as businesses.

Rationale: Non-commercial undertakings still prepare annual financial statements, for accountability to their trustees, members or funding bodies.

10.3 The correct answer is: The Management Accountant

Rationale: The Management Accountant provides information for management: cost accounting, budgets and budgetary control and financial management of projects. The Financial Controller is responsible for routine accounting, accounting reports, cashiers' duties and cash control. A Treasurer would be responsible for treasury management: raising and investing funds and cash flow control.

10.4 The correct answer is: Time sheets

Rationale: Time sheets are used to calculate hours worked and overtime, in order to calculate gross pay (before deductions). The system information for management (payroll analysis), information for employees (pay slips) and methods of payment (credit transfer forms), are all outputs.

Pitfalls: It is worth sorting out the inputs, processing and outputs of any financial system.

10.5 The correct answer is: To ensure that all credit notes received are recorded in the general and payables ledger

Rationale: All the other aims relate to the control system relating to receivables and sales.

Pitfalls: You have to get straight in your mind which transactions and controls relate to payables/purchases and which to receivables/sales.

10.6 The correct answer is: A true and fair view of the statement of affairs of the company as at the end of the financial year

Rationale: The first option refers to the statement of profit or loss, not the statement of financial position. The second option refers to audit reports.

Pitfalls: If you were in a hurry, you might have selected the first option immediately you saw the words 'true and fair'. Avoid such mistakes by reading through **all** question options carefully, keeping an open mind.

10.7 The correct answer is: Specialised capabilities

Rationale: An integrated package is expected to do everything, so it may have fewer facilities than specialised modules (especially as it also requires more computer memory). The other options are advantages of integration: ability to update multiple records from one data entry; ability to extract data from all relevant sources to compile specified reports; and less likelihood of discrepancies in different records.

10.8 A module is a program which deals with one particular part of a computerised business accounting system.

Rationale: A suite is a set of several modules. A spreadsheet is a type of program, and a format for displaying and processing data: it is often used to integrate data from accounting modules for decision-support and management information systems.

A database is a collection of data.

10.9 The correct answer is: There is much stronger provision for data security

Rationale: There is no scope for data in manual systems to be affected by cyber-attacks and they are not vulnerable to corruption or loss of data through user error.

10.10 The correct answer is: Automatic correction of all data entered by the operator into the spreadsheet

Rationale: Unfortunately: 'garbage in, garbage out!'…

10.11 The correct answer is: National legislation

Rationale: Mandatory reports to government and shareholders are required under national legislation. Codes of corporate governance are principles-based and voluntary in nature. International and local Accounting Standards do affect the content and presentation of accounts but it is national legislation which dictates the requirements for preparation and filing of accounts

10.12 The correct answer is: A computer-based accounting system will always reject inaccurate financial information input to the system's database

Rationale: 'Garbage in, garbage out'!

10.13 The correct answer is: The analysis of those items where performance differs significantly from standard or budget

Rationale: Exception reporting focuses attention on those items where performance differs significantly from standard or budget.

Pitfalls: The word 'exceptional' was placed in other options as a distractor!

10.14 The correct answer is: This company's computer system does not receive email from customers or suppliers

Rationale: Back-up storage, virus detection software and password protection are basic security requirements of any computer system, regardless of whether they are connected to the Internet. Because this system is not so connected, however, it cannot receive email.

Pitfalls: Make sure you distinguish between intranet (internal network) and Internet (world wide network), and read questions carefully to see which is being discussed.

10.15 Executive Support Systems pool data from internal and external sources and make

information available to senior managers, for strategic, unstructured decision-making.

Rationale: This is the definition of an Executive Support System. It is distinguished from a DSS by supporting decision-making at a higher and less structured level. Expert systems draw on a knowledge base to solve well-defined technical problems.

Pitfalls: 'Management', 'Expert' and 'Decision' were plausible distractors: make sure you can distinguish between the different types of system, and how they contribute to decision-making and problem solving.

10.16 The correct answer is: Data is always in numerical form whereas information is always in text form.

Rationale: Data is any kind of unprocessed information, and information is any kind of processed information.

10.17 Database management system

Rationale: The database management system (DBMS) is the software that builds, manages and provides access to a database. Data storage is carried out in the database itself. The database administrator is a person (not a part of the system) who controls the system. EPOS is a form of data collection and input.

10.18 The correct answer is: Loss or corruption of data is almost always non-deliberate.

Rationale: Data can be lost or corrupted as the result of deliberate actions such as fraud, sabotage, commercial espionage or malicious damage – as well as human error.

The other statements are true: new staff pose a security risk because of the risk of human error (if they are inexperienced or untrained); it is impossible to prevent all threats (important to be realistic!); and smoke detectors are an example of protection from physical risks (in this case, fire).

Pitfalls: Don't forget physical security measures: you may have discounted the fourth option too quickly. Data security also involves protection against fire, flood, interruption of power source and so on.

10.19 Office Automation Systems are designed mainly to increase the $\boxed{\text{productivity}}$ of data

and information workers.

Rationale: Office automation systems (OAS), with functions such as word processing, digital filing, email, schedulers and spreadsheets, are primarily designed to streamline administrative tasks: document management, communication, data management.

10.20 The correct answer is: Managers of the company

Rationale: Managers need most information, at a significant level of detail, to enable them to make planning and control decisions. They have special access to information, because they can arrange to obtain the information they need through the accounting system. Shareholders are entitled to certain information, focused on particular areas of interest (mainly profits). Financial analysts may only have access to public information and reports.

10.21 The correct answer is: The audit committee of the board of directors

Rationale: In order to control the risks of fraud and error, the internal audit department should be separate from the finance department.

10.22 The correct answer is: Information and Communication Technology (ICT) systems are more efficient than manual systems for any task an accountant may have to perform.

Rationale: A quick phone call may be a more efficient way of obtaining or giving information than email, for example. You may have hesitated over the third option because of often-stated warnings about 'garbage in, garbage out'. The risks of input error are the same – but computerised systems reduce the further risk of computation errors.

10.23 The correct answer is: Purchasing/procurement

Rationale: The purchasing or procurement function is responsible for authorising purchases (and suppliers) and approving. The other functions contribute, however: production, by requisitioning only needed items; goods inwards, by checking that what was purchased is what is in fact received; and accounts, by seeking proper documentary evidence and authorisation for payment.

10.24 The correct answer is: The credit control department

Rationale: This should be obvious from the context (debts represent goods bought on credit: hence, credit control) – but make sure that you could define the roles of all the other options, if you needed to!

10.25 The correct answer is: IFAC

Rationale: IFAC is the International Federation of Accountants. It produces an ethical code but it is not part of the regulatory system.

10.26 The correct answer is: IASB

Rationale: International Financial Reporting Standards are issued by the IASB.

10.27 The correct answer is: National legislation

Rationale: Of the choices offered, only national legislation is entirely legally binding, though elements of all of the distractors may be accepted and incorporated in legislation subsequent to the publication of the standards and principles.

ANSWERS

11 Control, security and audit

11.1   The correct answer is: To eliminate the possibility of impacts from poor judgement and human error

Rationale: The other options were identified as aims of internal controls in the Turnbull report. However, the report also states that even a sound system of internal control reduces, but does not eliminate, the possibilities of poorly judged decisions, human error, deliberate circumvention of controls and unforeseeable circumstances. Systems only provide reasonable (not absolute) assurance.

Ways in: If you had to guess, you could probably see that the correct answer is an exaggerated claim. Look out for options that say 'always' or 'never' or 'total', in a similar vein: these are much more likely to be untrue than true, in the complex world of business...

11.2   Some controls are provided automatically by the system and cannot be by-passed, ignored or overridden: for example, having to input a password to enter a computer system. These are classified as ┌ non-discretionary ┐ controls.

Rationale: Non-discretionary controls are as described: as opposed to discretionary controls which are subject to human choice. 'Mandated' is a similar idea, but mandated controls are required by law and imposed by external authorities (as opposed to voluntary controls, chosen by the organisation). Detect controls are controls designed to detect errors once they have happened. Administrative controls are to do with reporting responsibilities, communication channels and other means of implementing policies.

Pitfalls: There is so much terminology in this area: fertile ground for exam questions. Be able to use distinctions within classifications (as in 'discretionary and non-discretionary', or 'prevent, detect, control') as well as across classifications, as in this question.

11.3   The correct answer is: Organisation

Rationale: Organisation in this context means identifying reporting lines, levels of authority and responsibility to ensure that everyone is aware of their control responsibilities. The full mnemonic stands for: Segregation of duties; Physical; Authorisation and approval; Management; Supervision; Organisation; Arithmetical and accounting; and Personnel.

11.4   The correct answer is: Systems for authorising transactions within specified spending limits

Rationale: This is an internal control, rather than an internal check. Internal checks are more about dividing work (so that the work of one person can be independently proved by that of another) and using 'proof measures' to ensure the accuracy of records and calculations.

11.5   The correct answer is: Internal audit is an independent appraisal activity

Rationale: Internal audit is **independent**, but is still part of the internal control system: it is a control which examines and evaluates the adequacy and efficacy of other controls. Internal auditors should report direct to the audit committee of the board of directors (in order to preserve independence). It is **external** audit which is for the benefit of shareholders: internal audit is a service to management.

Ways in: Once you realised that the options were circling round different aspects of the definition of internal audit, and the difference between internal and external audit, you would be better able to sort out which statement was given to you 'straight' – and which were opposites of the true points.

11.6   The correct answer is: Weather

Rationale: This should be straightforward if you think through what the potential threats involve. Lightning strike or electrical storms are a key cause of power supply failures and surges which may effect computer functions.

Fire and accidental damage are also physical threats to data and equipment. Hacking is a non-physical threat involving unauthorised access to data (possibly resulting in data theft or destruction).

11.7   The correct answer is: System recovery procedures

Rationale: System recovery procedures are set in place for activation in the event of breakdown, to get the system up and running again: this is a contingency control, because it plans for a 'worst case scenario'. Password access is an example of a **security** control: protecting data from unauthorised modification, disclosure or destruction of data. Audit trails (showing who has accessed a system and what they have done).

Pitfalls: There is a lot of vocabulary and procedure in this area: make sure that you could answer questions on a variety of different data security controls.

11.8   The correct answer is: The independence of controls from the method of data processing

Rationale: It would be a limitation if controls **depended** on the method of data processing. The others are limitations, because: the costs of control must not outweigh the benefits; there is always potential for both human error and deliberate override of controls by management; and controls are designed to cope with routine transactions, not non-routine transactions.

11.9   The correct answer is: The primary responsibility of external auditors is to investigate financial irregularities and report them to shareholders

Rationale: The primary responsibility of the external auditor is to report to shareholders on whether the client's financial statements are accurate and free from bias ('true and fair'). The other options are true.

11.10   The correct answer is: To identify errors and omissions in financial records

Rationale: Substantive tests 'substantiate' the figures in the accounts. They are used to discover **whether** figures are correct or complete, not **why** they are incorrect or incomplete, or how the figures 'got there'. Establishing whether internal controls are being applied as prescribed is the aim of **compliance** tests.

11.11   The correct answer is: Correct

Rationale: Correct controls are designed to enable the organisation to minimise the effect of errors: in this case, restoring data from the back-ups if the main data store is corrupted. Prevent controls are designed to prevent errors from happening in the first place, and detect controls are designed to detect errors once they have happened.

11.12   In the context of data security controls, ⸢ audit trails ⸣ are records showing who has

accessed a computer system and what operations he or she has performed.

Rationale: Audit trails enable system administrators to maintain security, check transactions (in order to identify errors and fraud), recover lost transactions and monitor the use of network resources. Passwords are access controls and archives are long-term back-up storage: both are good system controls.

Pitfalls: There is lots of terminology in this area: get to grips with all the basic terms and procedures.

11.13   The correct answer is: Operational audit

Rationale: A systems audit is based on the testing and evaluation of internal controls. A probity (or transaction) audit checks account entries to identify errors or omissions which may indicate fraud. A social audit measures the social responsibility or social impacts of the business.

Pitfalls: This is another area of distinctive clusters of terminology: make sure you can identify operational, systems and transactions audits – and the types of tests they use (compliance v substantive).

11.14   The correct answer is: No audit manuals or working papers are available for inspection

Rationale: This may suggest that internal audit work is not properly planned, reviewed or documented: a failure of due professional care. The other options show good status, scope and technical competence.

ANSWERS

12 Identifying and preventing fraud

12.1　The correct answer is: Teeming and lading

Rationale: Collusion is working with another party (eg customers or suppliers) to commit fraud.

Misrepresentation is stating that something is so, when it is not, in order to mislead (eg overstating profits).

12.2　The correct answer is: (1), (2), (3) and (4)

Rationale: Payslips can be deliberately miscalculated to pay extra amounts. Staff may collude with customers to under-record quantities of despatched goods on delivery notes so the customer pays less: conversely, employees may collude with suppliers to pay invoices for larger quantities than were actually delivered. Option (4) may have made you hesitate: it seems such a positive, desirable thing! However, profits in excess of target may be siphoned off, with less scrutiny once targets have been met.

12.3　The correct answer is: It results in the intentional overstatement of profits and net assets

Rationale: One form of fraud is the intentional misrepresentation of the financial position of the business. Bad debt policy may be unenforced deliberately, in order to overstate profits.

12.4　Dishonesty is a ⟦ pre-disposition ⟧ to act in ways which contravene accepted ethical,

social, organisational or legal norms for fair and honest dealing.

Rationale: This is an important distinction in making sense of the three prerequisites for fraud: dishonesty (a willingness to act dishonestly), motivation (an incentive or reason to act dishonestly) and opportunity (an opening to act dishonestly).

12.5　The correct answer is: Increased competition

Rationale: Increased competition is a risk factor (because it may put pressure on managers to manipulate results) – but it is an **external** factor. The others are internal factors which increase risk because they disrupt supervision and control or introduce unknown factors.

Pitfalls: Look carefully at question stems for qualifier key words such as 'internal' and 'external'.

12.6　The correct answer is: Staff not taking their full holiday entitlements

Rationale: This may seem like normal behaviour in a 'workaholic' office culture, but failure to take full holiday entitlement may signal an employee trying to prevent a temporary replacement from uncovering a fraud. The other options are factors in **reducing** risk: lack of segregation enables fraud to go undetected; low staff morale is often a motive for fraud (in retaliation against the firm); and an autocratic management style may prevent questioning.

Pitfalls: Ensure that you know what 'segregation of duties' means: otherwise, it might look like a risk factor (because it sounds like allowing people to work independently and unsupervised, say).

12.7　The correct answer is: Increase in working capital

Rationale: There is a reduction in working capital, which makes it more difficult for the company to operate effectively, potentially resulting in corporate collapse. The other effects should be obvious (remember, we are talking about removal of funds or assets and not overstatement of profits and/or net assets). Reputational damage refers to loss of shareholder and market confidence in the organisation's management when the fraud emerges.

12.8　The correct answer is: Requiring signatures to confirm receipt of goods or services

Rationale: This should be clear from the context, because of the collusion with customers (if you remembered what collusion was). Physical security refers to keeping assets under lock and key: not to be dismissed as a fraud prevention measure! Sequential numbering works because it is easy to spot if documents are missing. Authorisation policies increase checks and accountabilities.

12.9   In a limited company, or plc, it is the ultimate responsibility of $\boxed{\text{the board of directors}}$ to

take reasonable steps to prevent and detect fraud.

Rationale: The directors are responsible for the conduct of the business, the deterrence and detection of fraudulent (and other dishonest) conduct, and the reliable reporting of financial information. The responsibility of the external auditor is only to express an opinion on the financial statements, although audit procedures should have a reasonable expectation of detecting misstatements arising from fraud. The audit committee reviews the organisation's performance in fraud prevention, but also reports to the board.

12.10   The correct answer is: Inability to secure access to data

Rationale: There are plenty of ways of securing access to data, using available software tools: password protection, encryption and so on. (Of course, the firm has to **use** them, but that is a separate issue!) Hackers are unauthorised people breaking into the system. Lack of managerial understanding creates loopholes in controls, and the ability to conceal fraud by technical staff. Integrated systems also help to conceal fraud, by ensuring that alterations to records are consistent: fewer discrepancies to trigger investigation.

12.11   The correct answers are:

- Investors

- Suppliers

Rationale: Investors will be making decisions (and taking risks) on inaccurate information. Suppliers will extend credit without knowing the true financial position of the company. (Staff and customers will eventually be effected if shortfalls in working capital threaten the business ...)

12.12   The correct answer is: Fraud awareness training and recruitment controls.

Rationale: These are measures for fraud prevention and control. A fraud response plan specifically deals with investigating and dealing with the consequences of identified frauds. This includes taking immediate steps to secure the security of records that will be investigated and launching an investigation into the method and extent of fraud.

12.13   The correct answer is: Limitation control

Rationale: Limit controls limit opportunity for fraud: another example is limiting access to the computer network by means of passwords. Segregation of duties means ensuring that functions which **together** facilitate fraud are performed by **different** individuals: eg separating the cheque signing function from the authorisation of payments. Appropriate documentation involves recording, authorising and tracking transactions through purchase requisitions, orders, invoices and so on.

12.14   The correct answer is: Performance-based rewards for managers reduce the risk of fraud.

Rationale: Performance-based rewards increase pressures and motivation for managers to manipulate results.

Ways in: A good approach for these sorts of question is to work systematically through the options to eliminate those which are clearly true. That way, even if you are left with an option you are not sure about (because performance-related pay for managers is such a popular strategy, say), it is the best option you've got.

12.15 $\boxed{\text{Money laundering}}$ constitutes any financial transactions whose purpose is to conceal the

origins of the proceeds of criminal activity.

Rationale: The statement is the definition of money laundering.

12.16   The correct answer is: Placement

Rationale: The order is placement, layering and integration.

13 Financial technology (Fintech)

13.1　The correct answer is: Big data

Rationale: A company that uses big data for competitive advantage streams vast volumes of data from many internal and external sources, and applies data analytics to obtain value from the data.

13.2　The correct answer is: Velocity

Rationale: Velocity concerns the speed of data and is therefore connected to the ability to stream large amounts of data into an organisation's systems in real time. If velocity was not quick enough, the data would be subject to a time-lag which might undermine its usefulness.

13.3　The correct answer is: Risk management

Rationale: Data analytics on big data can assist with the identification, quantification and management of business risk. It is not used in connection with the other options.

13.4　 Open data is a source of big data that originates from public sector data (for example transport, government financial and public service data).

Rationale: Open data originates from the public sector data (for example transport, government financial and public service data). Processed data originates from existing databases of business and other organisations. Machine-generated data originates from fixed and mobile sensors, as well as computer and website logs.

13.5　The correct answer is: Users of cloud accounting software are completely reliant on the provider of the software to ensure their data is secure and to take backups of it

Rationale: Users of cloud accounting software are completely reliant on the provider of the software to ensure their data is secure and to take backups of it. The other options are disadvantages of traditional accounting software.

13.6　The correct answer is: Distributed ledger (Blockchain)

Rationale: Distributed ledger technology allows people who do not know each other to trust a shared record of events.

13.7　The correct answer is: Downloading bank transactions into the accounting system

Rationale: Automation allows certain routine procedures to be undertaken without the input of a human (such as the automatic download of bank transactions). The other options are all areas of work that require human input or artificial intelligence.

13.8　The correct answer is: Posting transactions to nominal codes

Rationale: Artificial intelligence allows a system to learn certain basic tasks and perform them in future (such as identifying transactions and posting them to appropriate nominal codes). The other options are all areas of work that require human input or simple automation.

13.9　Distributed ledgers reduce the need for auditors to verify the ownership of assets because they have a source of information that they can trust.

Rationale: Distributed ledgers give auditors reassurance about the ownership of assets. They do not reduce the need for an audit opinion or to check for material misstatement.

14 Section C MTQs

14.1 (a) The correct answers are:

Assessing how effectively management is running the company			**SHARE-HOLDERS**	
To advise clients				**FINANCIAL ANALYSTS**
To assess tax payable by the company		**TAX AUTHORI-TIES**		
To assess the ability of the company to pay its debts	**SUPPLIERS**			

(1) Suppliers will want to know whether the company is able to pay its debts.

(2) Tax authorities want to assess whether tax paid is adequate for the level of profits.

(3) Shareholders want to assess the effectiveness of management in performing its stewardship function.

(4) Financial analysts need information to advise investors whether to invest or not.

(b) The correct answer is: False

Charities and public sector organisations also need to prepare accounts.

(c) The statement of financial position must give a true and fair view of the company at the end of the financial year.

True and fair is usually taken to mean accurate and not misleading.

14.2 (a) The correct answers are:

- Balancing of accounting entries - **Non-disc.**
- Authorisation of non-current asset purchase - **Disc.**
- Password access to the system - **Non-disc.**
- Review of the audit trail - **Disc.**

Balancing of accounting entries

This control is built in to the system.

Authorisation of non-current asset purchase

This control can be bypassed so is discretionary.

Password access to the system

This control is built in to the system.

Review of the audit trail

This control can be bypassed so is discretionary.

(b) A systems audit is testing and evaluating internal controls of an organisation.

Operational audits can be concerned with any sphere of a company's activities and a transactions audit aims to detect fraud.

(c) The correct answer is: False

The existence of the controls is not enough. The controls also need to be applied properly and honestly in order for them to be effective.

14.3 (a) The correct answers are:

- Processing is faster
- Corrections can be made quicker

Information is more accessible in a computerised system and the risk of errors is reduced rather than eradicated.

(b) A ⬚ module ⬚ is a program that deals with a particular part of the accounting system.

This is the definition of a module.

(c) The correct answer is: False

A database should be evolve both in the short term and also the long term.

14.4 (a) The correct answers are:

- Door locks
- Intruder alarms

These controls are designed to restrict physical access.

(b) The correct answer is: Input control

These are all examples of input controls.

(c) ⬚ Contingency ⬚ controls help an organisation recover in the event of a disaster.

14.5 (a) Which of the following offences has been committed by Stella? ⬚ Failure to report ⬚

Which of the following offences has been committed by James? ⬚ Tipping off ⬚

By not reporting suspicions of fraud, Stella is committing an offence.

By informing the financial controller, James is tipping off the client and may prejudice the investigation.

(b) Which of the following phases of money laundering is being undertaken by Elyse?

⬚ Layering ⬚

Which of the following phases of money laundering is being undertaken by Laura?

⬚ Placement ⬚

Layering involves the transfer of monies from business to business or place to place to conceal the original source.

Placement is the initial disposal of the proceeds of criminal activity into apparently legitimate business activity or property.

14.6 (a) The correct answer is: Use of control totals

Internal checks are checks on day-to-day transactions, where the work of one person is proved independently, or is complementary to the work of another. A control total is a total of any sort, used by comparing it with another total that ought to be the same. The other options in the question are features of the overall internal control system.

(b) The correct answers are:

- Work relates to the financial statements, and the financial records that underlie them - **External**
- Designed to add value and improve operations - **Internal**
- Enables an opinion to be expressed on the financial statements - **External**
- Report is to those charged with governance - **Internal**
- Work relates to the operations of the organisation - **Internal**
- Independent of the company and its management - **External**

15 Leading and managing

15.1 Leaders may be distinguished from managers by the fact that they do not depend on

position power in the organisation.

Rationale: Position power is legitimate organisational authority, by virtue of a position in the organisation hierarchy: managers depend largely on it for their influence. Leaders are often required to exercise informal, interpersonal forms of influence, such as person power (charisma, inspiration) and expert power (valued knowledge). Physical power (intimidation) should be used by neither managers nor leaders!

Pitfalls: the classifications of power are a rich source of related terminology, and hence a potential source both of confusion – and of exam questions!

15.2 The correct answer is: FW Taylor

Rationale: Frederick Taylor is associated with scientific management. The other writers are associated with the human relations school, focusing on the role of 'higher order' needs (such as challenge and interest in the work) in human motivation.

Ways in: You could halve your options by realising that Maslow and Herzberg belong to the same school: therefore the 'odd one out' must be one of the other two.

15.3 The correct answer is: Country club

Rationale: The 'country club' is low-task, high-people focus and 1.9 on Blake and Mouton's managerial grid. This describes Monica. Impoverished is 1.1 (both low), task management is 9.1 (all about the task), and dampened pendulum is 5.5 (swinging between the two extremes).

15.4 The correct answer is: (1), (2) and (3)

Rationale: Psychologically distant managers (PDMs) maintain distance from their subordinates and they prefer formal procedures rather than informal ones, for example, a formal consultation method.

Ways in: Hopefully you were able to rule out the fourth statement and therefore option D. Psychologically close managers are closer to their subordinates. If you remembered that PDMs prefer formal procedures then you may have been able to work out that statements 1, 2 and 3 were correct.

15.5 The correct answer is: Authority

Rationale: The essence of delegation is that the superior gives the subordinate part of his or her own authority. Power is not conferred by the organisation, so it cannot be delegated: it must be possessed. The most important thing to note is that responsibility is not delegated: the superior makes the subordinate responsible to him for the authority he has delegated, but he remains responsible for it to his own boss.

Pitfalls: It is easy to confuse these concepts, which is why they would make an excellent exam question.

15.6 The correct answer is: Multi-skilled teamworking

Rationale: Skilling was an important aspect of scientific management – but multi-skilled team working wasn't. Taylor's approach to job design was to break jobs down into single, simple tasks which were given to an individual as a whole (specialised, repetitive) job for an individual. The other options are key techniques.

15.7 The correct answer is: Awareness of the importance of group dynamics and worker attitudes as an influence on productivity

Rationale: The second option is not a central concern of human relations: rather, this could apply to the scientific management school. The third option is a contribution of the contingency school.

The fourth option has not yet been provided by any school of management or motivation theory: apart from anything else, business success depends on factors other than the productivity of the workers.

15.8   The correct answer is: Democratic

Rationale: Democratic is a 'joins' style: decision is more or less by vote or consensus. Consultative means that the leader takes subordinate views into account, but still makes the decision. Autocratic is basically a 'tells' style and persuasive is a 'sells' style.

15.9   The correct answer is: Monitor

Rationale: The monitor role involves scanning the environment and gathering information from a network of contacts. As spokesperson, the manager can then provide information on behalf of the department or organisation to interested parties. As disseminator, (s)he can also spread relevant information to team members. The role of leader means hiring, firing and training staff.

Pitfalls: The other options all information roles, so the distinction between them is quite fine. However, questions have been set at this level of detail, so such models are worth learning.

15.10 | Supervision | is the role at the interface between the operational core (non-managerial workers) and management.

Rationale: This is the key definition of the supervisory role: it is between non-managerial and managerial, acting as an information filter and overlap (since supervisors both do operational work and fulfil some managerial functions at a low level). Middle line and junior management are higher, since they are already managerial positions.

15.11   The correct answer is: It is most popular among subordinates

Rationale: A consultative style is the most popular among subordinates, although a 'sells' style is perceived to be most used by leaders – and a 'tells' style encourages the highest productivity in many circumstances.

15.12   The correct answer is: Authority

Rationale: Responsibility is the duty to perform an action. Power is the ability to perform an action (and in particular, to influence others). Influence is a process by which a person can direct or modify the behaviour of another person.

Pitfalls: These are fine distinctions in meaning – but they underpin the idea of management and leadership and are an excellent source of potential exam questions.

15.13   The correct answer is: Figurehead

Rationale: Interpersonal roles are based on the manager's formal authority: they include the roles of figurehead, leader and liaison. Informational roles are based on the manager's position in internal and external information networks: they include monitor, spokesperson and disseminator. Decisional roles relate to the work of the manager's department: entrepreneur, disturbance handler, resource allocator and negotiator.

15.14   The correct answer is: Contingency theories

Rationale: Contingency theories are based on the belief that there is no 'one best way' of leading but that effective leaders adapt their behaviour to changing variables. Adair's model sees the leadership process in a context made up of the task needs, individuals' needs and group needs.

15.15   The correct answers are:

- Adair's leadership model focuses on what leaders do and not what they are - **False**
- The Ashridge leadership model proposes a democratic approach to leadership - **True**

Rationale: This is just textbook knowledge. You must ensure that you understand the main principles associated with the management theories in the study text.

15.16　The correct answer is: Action-centred leadership

Rationale: This is a description of John Adair's action-centred leadership model. Contingency theory is more general: indeed, Adair's model is within the contingency school of thought. The managerial grid is based on two dimensions: concern for task and concern for people. Dispersed leadership (Heifetz) is the idea that individuals at all organisational levels can exert a 'leadership influence'.

15.17　| Organising | is the managerial function concerned with establishing a structure of tasks; grouping and assigning them to appropriate units; and establishing lines of information and reporting to support performance.

Rationale: Planning is about determining objectives and how to reach them. Controlling is measuring and adjusting activities in line with plans.

Ways in: even if you didn't recognise the description of organising, you could probably have eliminated the other options.

15.18　The correct answer is: Motivating

Rationale: Fayol's five functions of management are: planning, organising, commanding, co-ordinating and controlling. It is assumed that subordinates will carry out a command whether motivated or not.

15.19　The correct answer is: Developing people

Rationale: Drucker grouped the work of the manager into five categories, the fifth being developing people. The other options are from Mintzberg's managerial role types.

15.20　The correct answer is: Bennis

Rationale: Heifetz wrote on dispersed leadership, Fielder carried out research on the notion of leadership and Blake and Mouton published the managerial grid.

15.21　The correct answer is: Heifetz

Rationale: This question is a test of whether candidates can recognise the essential features of leadership theories and attribute them to the relevant writer. Kotter's theory is concerned with the leader's responsibilities in coping with changes, and focuses on differences between 'leadership' and 'management'. Adair's work relates to the effectiveness of leaders in achieving a balance between achieving the task, maintaining the team and developing individuals. Mintzberg considers the roles of leaders. It is Heifetz who proposed that leaders can emerge informally in his theory of dispersed leadership.

16 Recruitment and selection

16.1　The correct answer is: Screening application forms

Rationale: Screening means sorting through application forms received, in order to separate out candidates which are clearly ineligible for the vacancy, immediately worth short-listing and so on. It is selection because it is part of the process of measuring candidates against requirements, and selecting those who are most suitable. Recruitment is the process of defining requirements and reaching potential applicants.

16.2　The correct answer is: Job description

Rationale: This is job description rather than job analysis, because a job description is the statement produced from a process of job analysis. This is job description rather than personnel specification, because it addresses the requirements of the **job**, rather than the qualities of the ideal job holder or person. Job advertisement is just a distractor.

Pitfalls: The difference between job description and personnel specification has cropped up frequently in exams over the years. There is potential for confusion: remember that one describes the 'job', the other the 'person' ...

16.3   The correct answer is: Motivation

Rationale: 'Motivation' is a heading in an alternative method of person specification (the Five Point Pattern of Personality, by J Munro Fraser). Rodger's Seven Points are: physical make-up, attainments (qualifications), general intelligence, special aptitudes, interests, disposition (temperament) and circumstances.

16.4   The correct answer is: Devolve recruitment and selection to line managers

Rationale: The current trend is to devolve recruitment and selection (among other HRM activities) increasingly to line managers, who handle recruitment within their own departments.

16.5   The correct answer is: Tests are generally less accurate predictors of success than interviews

Rationale: All the other criticisms about the reliability of selection tests are valid – and yet tests are **still** more reliable than interviews at predicting performance in the job!

16.6   The correct answer is: Leading

Rationale: A leading question pushes the interviewee to give a certain answer. (In this case, it is obvious that the interviewer expects the interviewee to agree.) An open question requires self-expression; a closed question invites a one word either/or answer, and a problem-solving question presents candidates with a situation and asks them to say how they would deal with it.

Pitfalls: This is an easy aspect of interviewing technique to set questions on: make sure you can identify all types of questions.

16.7   The correct answer is: Questions tend to be more varied and more random

Rationale: This is a disadvantage because there may not be a clear interview strategy, and candidates may have trouble switching from one topic to another. The first option is an advantage, because it reduces individual bias, and saves time in sharing assessments (eg compared to a series of one-to-one interviews). The second option is an advantage, because a single interviewer may not be able to spot candidate weaknesses in technical areas. The fourth option is an advantage, because personal rapport may lead to favourable bias on the part of an interviewer.

16.8   The correct answer is: A tendency for people to make an initial judgement based on first impressions, and then letting this colour their later perceptions.

Rationale: These are all different types of bias and errors of judgement in interviewing. The first option is halo effect. The second option is contagious bias. The third option is stereotyping. The fourth option is projection.

Ways in: Stereotyping is probably the most recognisable of the options, so you could at least narrow your options by ruling the third out option.

16.9   Selection tests which focus on aptitude, intelligence and personality factors are called

psychometric   tests.

Rationale: Proficiency tests focus on current ability to perform tasks. 'Standardised' is a desirable quality of any type of test, meaning that it is applicable to a representative sample of the population being tested. 'Sensitive' is another desirable quality meaning that the test can discriminate between different candidates.

16.10   The correct answer is: A series of tests, interviews and activities undergone by a group of candidates over several days

Rationale: Assessment centres are group assessments, usually used for higher-level positions, because of the time and costs involved in exploring candidates' personalities and skills in depth.

Pitfalls: Don't fall for the common trap of thinking that an assessment 'centre' is a place!

16.11 The correct answer is: At least two employer references are desirable

Rationale: Two employer references provide necessary factual information and comparison of views (to minimise bias). The other options are untrue: references are highly subjective and/or deliberately limited and personal references are selected to be supportive (you can choose your friends in a way you can't choose your employers!).

16.12 The correct answer is: Employee flexibility

Rationale: Job descriptions can be narrow and restrictive, giving people a limited sense of what is their 'job' and what isn't. This can create demarcation lines which prevent people from flexibly switching tasks, or working effectively in multi-skilled teams. The other options are all potential uses of job descriptions, because they clearly state all the elements of a job: for calculating their value to the organisation (job evaluation), identifying gaps in job holders' ability (training needs analysis) and preparing selection criteria (recruitment).

16.13 The correct answer is: Local newspapers

Rationale: A professional journal would not be read by the target audience. National newspapers will be too expensive, given that most of the audience will not be the firm's target group: low level positions are more likely to attract local applicants.

Pitfalls: If asked about choice of advertisement media, you need to think about cost and audience targeting together.

16.14 The correct answer is: Innovation

Rationale: Succession planning develops managers in order to ensure managerial continuity over time – and internal promotion is a key way of grooming managers for higher positions. Induction time would be shorter, because an internal promotee is already familiar with the organisation's culture, structures, systems and personnel. Innovation is **not** necessarily supported by internal promotion, because it does not bring 'new blood' into the organisation.

16.15 The correct answer is: Getting as much information as possible about the applicant

Rationale: 'Maximum' information is not the point of interviews: squeezing as many questions as possible into the time allowed can restrict the flow of communication and put unnecessary pressure on the candidate, while a lengthy open-ended interview will be costly. The **relevance** of the information for selection is more important.

16.16 The correct answer is: The organisation has complex cultural, business and technical selection criteria for its staff, but is considering using a consultancy for the first time, because it requires new people urgently in order to exploit an opportunity

Rationale: The key factors here are the urgency, and the fact that the consultants do not know the organisation: there is not enough time to give the consultants an adequate understanding of the complex recruitment needs.

In the first option, consultants would bring a 'fresh eye' and avoid bringing the same old types of people into the organisation.

In the second option, consultants would provide expertise and resources to handle large-scale recruitment, which the organisation lacks in-house.

In the third option, the organisation can be confident that use of consultants would not be resented and resisted.

Ways in: It helps if you have a checklist in your head of reasons to outsource recruitment: 'new blood', resources/expertise and internal support would certainly be on that list. 'Lead time to brief consultants on the needs of the organisation' would be on the list of reasons **not** to use consultants ...

16.17 Competences are capacities that lead to behaviours that meet job demands within the

parameters of the organisational environment.

Rationale: Attributes are simply 'characteristics' of any kind. Skills are learned behaviours, rather than capacities.

BPP
LEARNING
MEDIA

16.18 The correct answer is: To identify a vacancy

Rationale: This should have been fairly straightforward. It would be quite difficult to write a job description or a person specification if a vacancy had not first been identified.

17 Diversity and equal opportunities

17.1 The correct answer is: (1), (2), (3) and (4)

Rationale: As well as compliance with relevant legislation, these are the main arguments for having an equal opportunities policy. It is good HR practice to attract and retain the best people for the job, regardless of race or gender.

17.2 The correct answer is: To provide that women have the right to equal pay to work of equal value to that of men

Rationale: This does **not** imply that the woman has to be in the same job. Job evaluation is recommended as a way of establishing relative values of jobs, but is not compulsory. Equal Pay deals only with sexual discrimination – not race or other grounds.

17.3 The correct answers are:

- Taking active steps to encourage people from disadvantaged groups to apply for jobs and training is classed as positive discrimination. - **False**
- Diversity in the workplace means implementing an equal opportunities policy. - **False**

Rationale: Positive discrimination refers to actions being taken which give preference to a protected person, regardless of genuine suitability and qualification for the job. Statement 1 is not positive discrimination as the steps are only taken to encourage people to apply. It does not say that they will necessarily be accepted.

Diversity goes further than equal opportunities. The ways in which people meaningfully differ in the work place include not only race and ethnicity, age and gender but personality, preferred working style, individual needs and goals and so on.

17.4 The correct answer is: Harassment

Rationale: Harassment is the use of threatening, intimidating, offensive or abusive language or behaviour focused on the race, religious belief, sex or sexual orientation of another person. This sounds like victimisation, but victimisation is a separate form of discrimination, involving penalising someone because they are involved in a claim of discrimination against an employer.

17.5 The correct answer is: Better understanding of target market segments

Rationale: A business can better understand (and meet) the needs of market segments if it employs representatives of those segments: this is a business benefit, because it enhances customer loyalty, sales revenue, profitability etc. The first option is a legal/moral benefit (and addresses equal opportunities rather than diversity). The second option is a benefit to employees in a diverse organisation. The fourth option is not true of diversity, which requires significant management investment and less 'standardised' HR solutions.

17.6 The correct answer is: Employers must adjust working arrangements or the physical features of premises to remove any disadvantage to disabled people

Rationale: The duty is to make 'reasonable' adjustments. The other statements are true.

17.7 The correct answer is: Setting age limits or ranges in an employment advertisement

Rationale: Now that age discrimination legislation is in force, this would be direct discrimination (akin to saying 'blue-eyed, English-speaking people only need apply'). The other options may well be construed as **indirect** discrimination.

17.8 The correct answer is: The organisation has laid itself open to a claim of indirect sexual discrimination, but such a claim would not be successful

Rationale: The organisation has laid itself open to a claim of indirect discrimination, because if the selection decision had been made on the basis of a question asked of a woman but **not** of men, it may have been construed as such. The claim would not succeed because the organisation would be able to justify the apparently discriminatory conditions on non-discriminatory (job-relevant) grounds.

Pitfalls: You need to get to grips with the basics of how this works, and recognise examples when you see them.

17.9   The concept of | managing diversity | is based on the belief that the dimensions of

individual difference on which organisations currently focus are crude and performance-

irrelevant, and that an organisation should reflect the range of differences within its

customer and labour markets.

Rationale: Equal opportunity is a narrower concept based on eradicating discrimination based on the crude dimensions of individual difference. The other option is just a distractor.

17.10   The correct answer is: Selecting a certain number of people from ethnic minorities for jobs, regardless of job-relevant selection criteria

Rationale: Positive discrimination (treating a minority group 'unfairly' well) is not permitted, except in relation to training provision. 'Quotas' are positive discrimination, because selection decisions cannot be justified on non-discriminatory grounds: 'targets' are 'positive action' – because they lead organisations to encourage under-represented groups to apply for jobs, and make non-discrimination a performance measure for selectors.

18 Individuals, groups and teams

18.1   The correct answer is: Members passively accept work decisions

Rationale: Members of an effectively functioning group will take an active interest in decisions affecting their work. The first option is healthy, particularly in avoiding problems that occur when groups seek consensus at all costs (eg 'group think'). The second option is healthy, as it unites and stimulates the group. The fourth option can be a sign that the group is supporting the performance of its members – not just that they are focusing on their own performance at the expense of the group.

Pitfalls: If you were trying to go by 'common sense' instead of knowledge, you might think that intra-team disagreement and inter-team competition were negatives: not so. There are no 'trick' questions, but questions can be designed to separate those who have studied from those who are guessing!

18.2   The correct answer is: Encourage the members to modify their personalities

Rationale: Personality is a relatively stable and distinctive concept: it is very difficult (if not impossible) to change personality, and the attempt has radical effects! The other options are constructive approaches to handling personality clashes in a team.

18.3   The correct answer is: Storming

Rationale: This is typical of 'storming' behaviour. Forming would be more tentative: just getting to know one another. Norming would be further along in the process of settling into shared values and behaviours.

Pitfalls: Don't assume that 'storming' is all about conflict! If you did this, you might have mistaken this description for norming, say.

Ways in: Underline some key words in the micro-scenario: 'debating', 'factions', 'disagree' ...

18.4 | Attitudes | are mental states (made up of thoughts, feelings and intentions) which influence

an individual's response to all objects and situations with which they are related.

Rationale: This is the definition of attitudes. Personality traits are relatively stable, enduring qualities of an individual's personality (eg 'impulsiveness'). Perceptions are how people 'see' things, according to how the brain selects and organises information. Emotional intelligence is a concept popularised by Daniel Goleman to describe awareness of, and ability to manage, one's own emotions and those of others. None of these concepts is explicitly mentioned in the syllabus – but you are required to know something about the 'characteristics of individual behaviour', so it is worth getting to grips with some of the basics.

Ways in: Perceptions are about thinking, emotions are about feeling – and the question asked for something that combines thinking, feeling and intention.

18.5 The correct answer is: Crisis decision-making

Rationale: Teams are not the best vehicle for crisis decision-making, because group decision-making takes longer, and decisions may protect the team at the expense of the right (possible tough) solution. Teams are, however, great for decision-making where the hearing of different viewpoints is beneficial. They are also great for ideas generation (think of group brainstorming) and coordination (teams are often cross-functional). You might have hesitated over the fourth option, but it is important to realise that distance is now no obstacle to team working (think of virtual teams, connected by IT and communications links).

Pitfalls: Don't forget 'virtual' teams in your thinking.

18.6 The correct answer is: Blocking

Rationale: Blocking (or difficulty stating) is where members put obstacles in the way of proposals: this may be a positive contribution in circumstances where the proposals are risky or unrealistic – but it is probably contributing to the problem here. Bringing-in is encouraging the contribution of others; summarising, drawing together passages of discussion; testing understanding, checking whether points have been understood. They are generally supportive behaviours, which could be used to get the team back into constructive discussion.

18.7 The correct answer is: Members are as alike as possible

Rationale: 'Compatibility' is not the same as 'homogeneity': teams need diversity, in order to have a mix and balance of contribution and roles. The other options correspond to team identity, and shared objective: two of the key tools of team building.

18.8 The correct answer is: Completer – finisher

Rationale: The key words in the question were 'keen eye for detail', 'always meets deadlines' and 'reluctant to involve others'. These phrases are typical characteristics of a completer-finisher.

18.9 The correct answer is: Identity

Rationale: The definition of a group is, basically, 'any collection of people who **perceive** themselves to be a group' (Handy). Identity means that there are acknowledged boundaries to a group, which define who is 'in' and who is 'out', 'us' and 'them'. Groups **may** have a defined purpose, but not always. Conformity can be an attribute of groups or crowds.

Pitfalls: Note that this wasn't a question about the difference between a group and a team – although this too would make a good exam question...

18.10 The correct answer is: A mix and balance of team roles

Rationale: This should be straightforward if you have understood the Belbin model. A healthy team has a mix and balance of roles. However, members can adopt more than one role, or switch roles as required: there need not be nine members with fixed roles. Belbin argues that it is the **process** roles (how people behave, contribute and interact with others), rather than the functional roles (technical skills and operational knowledge) that impact on team functioning – although functional roles are still important for getting the task done!

18.11 The correct answer is: Adjourning

Rationale: Adjourning is where the group sees itself as having fulfilled its purpose, and there is a process of disconnecting from the task and group – because there will have to be a renegotiation of aims and roles for the new task. Dorming is where a group grows complacent about performance. Norming is a much earlier stage in the cycle, where the group reaches agreement about work methods, roles and behaviours.

Pitfalls: Dorming and adjourning are all late stages of group development, and can be confused if you are not clear about them. Although 'forming, storming, norming and performing' is better known, these additional stages are part of Tuckman's model.

18.12 The correct answer is: Encouraging members to express disagreements

Rationale: Competition with other groups enhances solidarity, and competition within a group destroys it, so the first and second option are the opposite of solidarity-enhancing. The fourth option would lead to 'group think': inability to confront problems, lack of criticism of poor decisions, false consensus. It may create high solidarity, but not healthy solidarity.

18.13 The correct answer is: Multi-skilled team

Rationale: A multi-skilled team is one which brings together versatile individuals who can perform any of the group's tasks. Multi-disciplinary (or multi-functional) teams bring together individuals with **different** skills and specialisms, so that their skills can be pooled or exchanged.

Self-managed teams are given discretion to plan their own task sharing and work methods, within defined task objectives: there is no suggestion that this is the case here. A virtual team is a geographically dispersed team, connected by information and communication technology (ICT) links.

18.14 The correct answer is: Shaper

Rationale: The Shaper is the 'dynamo' of the team: one of the forms of leadership in Belbin's model. The Plant is the ideas person and creative problem-solver. The Co-ordinator is the chairperson, clarifying goals, delegating, promoting decision-making. The Implementer is the person who turns ideas into practical actions.

Pitfalls: There are several 'leader' roles in Belbin's model: you need to distinguish between them. The Plant is an ideas leader; Resource investigator an entrepreneur; Co-ordinator a task organiser; and the Shaper an interpersonal leader.

18.15 The correct answer is: Shutting out

Rationale: You may have hesitated between the third and fourth options. However blocking is putting obstacles in the way of a proposal without offering any alternatives; whereas shutting-out is interrupting or overriding others and taking over.

18.16 The correct answer is: Performing

Rationale: The team is executing its task and the team briefing is dealing with progress to date.

19 Motivating individuals and groups

19.1 The correct answer is: The work

Rationale: Intrinsic rewards are 'part of' the work itself: extrinsic rewards are 'external' to the work itself.

Pitfalls: Potential confusion between intrinsic and extrinsic: a classic exam test!

19.2 The correct answer is: Need for affiliation

Rationale: Affiliation is actually a category in another need model by David McClelland. The other options are Maslow's (although freedom of inquiry and expression overarches the hierarchy itself).

19.3   The correct answer is: (4) only

Rationale: In Herzberg's theory, only training is a 'motivator factor'.

The others are all 'hygiene' factors: if they are inadequate, employees will be dissatisfied, but even if they are got right, they will not provide lasting satisfaction or motivation.

Herzberg argued that satisfaction comes only from the job.

Pitfalls: Herzberg is often examined, and students frequently get the basics of the theory wrong! Make sure you can sort the motivator factors from the hygiene factors.

19.4   The correct answer is: Goals

Rationale: Goals are things people choose to pursue: each individual will have their own goals, which may vary with time, circumstances and other factors. The idea of innate (in-born, instinctive) needs is that they are biological or psychological imperatives, common to all people. (This is what makes it possible to have need theories with discussion of only a few innate needs.) Satisfaction arises when a goal is achieved.

19.5   The correct answer is: Valence would be around 0, expectancy high, motivation low

Rationale: Willy's expectancy (expectation that by working hard he will be given the team leadership) is high, but valence (importance to Willy of becoming a team leader) is neutral, because he has both positive and negative feelings about it. Since Motivation = E × V, if V is 0, motivation is also 0.

Pitfalls: Make sure you get valence and expectancy the right way round, and that you recognise why Willy's valence is 0.

Ways in: Work through the equation, calculating your own values for V and E …

19.6   The correct answer is: Motivator factor

Rationale: Herzberg used the other three terms to describe the same set of factors: the ones that maintain morale but do not positively motivate (maintenance); prevent dissatisfaction but do not promote satisfaction, in the same way that hygiene prevents ill-health but does not promote well-being (hygiene); and that relate to the environment of work rather than to the work itself (environmental). The opposite set of factors is 'motivator' factors in the work itself, which – according to Herzberg – positively create satisfaction and motivation to superior performance.

Pitfalls: An exam question may refer to hygiene factors by any one of its three names, so it is worth using this question to check that you know them all!

19.7   The five core dimensions which contribute to job satisfaction are skill variety, task identity,

task significance, | autonomy | and feedback.

Rationale: Autonomy is a degree of freedom or discretion in the job: the removal of restrictive controls.

Ways in: You may have spotted that all the core dimensions are all intrinsic to the job itself: they are all what Herzberg would call 'motivator' factors. You could then eliminate some of the options that are clearly extrinsic to the job, or 'hygiene' factors …

19.8   The correct answer is: Everyone is allowed to participate equally

Rationale: Participation will only work if the individual has the ability and information to participate effectively (the principle of 'capacity'): otherwise, they will feel frustrated and under pressure. You may have hesitated over the fourth option, but this is necessary for people to take participation seriously (the principle of 'consistency').

19.9   The correct answer is: Theory X

Rationale: Theory X is the managerial assumption that most people dislike work and responsibility and will avoid them if possible they have to be coerced and controlled to work adequately – hence the kinds of management measures described. Theory Y is the managerial assumption that people can be motivated to accept challenge and responsibility and contribute willingly to the firm – resulting in a quite different management style!

Pitfalls: You really do need to know which way round X and Y are! (If it helps, think of X as a 'cross' against workers' names …)

19.10　The correct answer is: Immediacy of reward following results

Rationale: The other options are essential for an individual to work out how much effort will be required, and whether it will be worth it for the rewards expected (due to consistency) to be available. However, 'immediacy' is not necessarily required: people may have a high tolerance for 'delayed gratification', and be willing to wait for rewards as long as they have a reasonable expectation that they will eventually accrue. (As a student, for example, you may be working sacrificially hard now, in order to gain qualifications that will benefit your career in several years' time.)

19.11　The correct answer is: Its effect on team motivation

Rationale: Team members may work for individual rewards, rather than contributing to the group, especially since there is a problem offering rewards for less measurable criteria such as team-work.

The first option is clearly a benefit.

The second option is a benefit of PRP because it relates rewards directly to business objectives.

You may have hesitated over the third option but this is a benefit because PRP is a way of rewarding employees when there is no other way to do so (eg because they have reached the top of the salary/wage range their position is eligible for).

19.12　The correct answer is: It replaces monetary rewards

Rationale: Job enrichment cannot offer management a cheap way of motivating employees: even those who want enriched jobs will expected to be rewarded with more than job satisfaction. The other options have been found in practice to be benefits of job enrichment.

19.13　The correct answer is: Self-actualisation

Rationale: According to Maslow, self-actualisation is the final 'need' to be satisfied. It is the fulfilment of personal potential. Maslow claims that this can rarely be satisfied.

Ways in: It might be worth memorising the triangular diagram and perhaps adding pictures to help you remember.

Pitfalls: You may have hesitated over the first option but this was just a fictitious distracter. Esteem needs and physiological needs are lower down the hierarchy.

19.14　The correct answer is: Job content

Rationale: Job evaluation focuses on job content, to measure the relative value of jobs, compared to each other, **not** their worth in money terms. Actual pay levels are set with reference to the other options, among others.

19.15　The correct answer is: The strength of an individual's preference for a given outcome

Rationale: The first option is valence (V). The third option refers to 'expectancy' (E). The second option is 'force of motivation (F): the product of valence and expectancy. Hence the equation: $F = V \times E$.

19.16　The correct answer is: Job enlargement

Rationale: Eva's new tasks are of the same skill level and responsibility as her original task, so her job has been horizontally enlarged rather than vertically enlarged (which would be job enrichment). If she had gone from just packing one shift, to just stamping on the next shift (and so on), this would have been job rotation.

Pitfalls: Any area like this where students frequently confuse similar terminology is ripe for testing. Read, think and check your answers carefully, to avoid careless errors!

ANSWERS

19.17 The correct answer is: Micro-division of labour

Rationale: Micro-division of labour (or job simplification) is breaking down jobs into their smallest possible components, and having one person carry out one component. Division of labour is specialisation, but not to this extent. Job enlargement implies greater task variety, and empowerment, greater task significance and responsibility.

19.18 The correct answer is: Integration

Rationale: The correct answer is implied in the scenario, in that the manager is urging team members to put their feelings aside for the benefit of the team. In other words, Javed is seeking greater integration in relation to their goals and objectives.

20 Training and development

20.1 The correct answer is: Theorist

Rationale: The Theorist seeks to understand basic principles and to take an intellectual, 'hands off' approach prior to trying things. Pragmatists are the opposite. You may have hesitated over the first option, but Reflectors learn by thinking things through, rather than necessarily by applying theoretical concepts.

Pitfalls: This is an area ripe for exam questions, because of the clarity of the style classifications. Make sure you can identify the label to go with a description and vice versa.

Ways in: You could probably rule out Pragmatist quite quickly, because of Sara's dislike of 'hands on' methods.

20.2 The correct answer is: A scientific approach to problem-solving, in order to minimise risk and error

Rationale: The scientific approach to problem-solving **is** a characteristic of learning organisation, but this involves experimentation and learning by testing ideas and making mistakes. Learning organisations have a high tolerance for risk, and regard errors as learning opportunities.

Ways in: If you don't recognise the concept or model, don't give up and guess: think through the options and how they relate to each other. A question phrased 'which is **not**...?' suggests that you are looking for the 'odd one out'. If you look at the options, you should find three that are compatible with each other – leaving one that isn't.

20.3 The correct answer is: Training can be an effective solution to some performance problems

Rationale: This is a positive and realistic view of the benefits and limitations of training: not **all** performance problems are amenable to training, and may need other sorts of intervention (discipline, counselling, equipment repair, job re-design, motivation and so on). The first option would fail to involve trainees and line managers, who are key stakeholders in training. The second option would limit training provision, ignoring its significant benefits. The third option would fail to design training programmes appropriately for specific training needs and learner style preferences.

20.4 | Training | is 'the planned and systematic modification of behaviour through learning events, programmes and instruction which enable individuals to achieve the level of knowledge, skills and competence to carry out their work effectively'.

Rationale: Conditioning may have sounded familiar if you only read as far as 'modification of behaviour', but it involves specific repetition-and-reward techniques. Education is the gradual acquisition of knowledge, by learning and instruction, often leading to qualifications.

Pitfalls: This kind of related terminology lends itself to exam questions. Training, education and development all involve 'learning', but the learning experiences are of different types, and with different overall aims.

20.5 The correct answer is: Experiential

Rationale: The learning cycle is experiential learning or 'learning by doing'. 'Action learning' sounds similar, but is actually a specific learning method by which managers are brought together as a problem-solving group to discuss real work issues. Programmed learning is highly structured learning, which doesn't apply here. Reflection is a way of thinking about what you have learnt.

20.6 The correct answer is: Enhanced employability of staff members

Rationale: 'Employability' refers to an individual's having a portfolio of skills and experience that are valuable in the labour market, thus enhancing his or her mobility (and ability to get a job outside the present employer). This is a double-edged sword for the organisation: it is socially responsible and fosters employee satisfaction but may also cause a skill drain to other organisations. You should be able to see how training contributes to the other options, and why they are benefits for the organisation.

Pitfalls: Look out for qualifier keywords like 'for an organisation' (that is, **not** 'for the individual'). Think carefully through 'which is the exception?' questions, too. Logically, an option may be an exception for more than one reason: in this case, because it isn't a benefit (but a drawback) **or** because it isn't a benefit to the **organisation** (but a benefit to the individual). In a well designed question, you should get the same answer either way!

20.7 The correct answer is: Methods (2), (3) and (4) only

Rationale: Day release is 'off-the-job', because the learning comes from the employee's attending a college or training centre one day per week. The other methods are all 'on the job'.

Pitfalls: Note the variety of 'on the job' methods: don't forget to include job rotation (which you might otherwise connect with job design and Herzberg) and temporary promotion (which you might not think of as training).

20.8 The correct answer is: Application of learned skills to the job

Rationale: On-the-job approaches support 'transfer of learning': skills are learned in the actual context in which they will be applied – so application is seamless. The first two options are advantages of **off**-the-job training: the learners don't have the distraction of other work duties, and errors while learning are less likely to have real consequences. You may have hesitated over the third option, but there is a risk that by learning on the job, people will pick up 'bad habits' and short-cuts – rather than best practice.

20.9 The correct answer is: Level 3: job behaviour

Rationale: Level 1 measures how employees rated the training. Level 2 measures how much they learned: what they know or can do that they didn't do before. However, for a manager concerned with departmental productivity, the important thing is whether the trainees **applied** what they learned effectively to the job: Level 3. Level 5 is the impact of training on the wider 'good' of the organisation and its stakeholders: this kind of information is usually only available (and worth the cost of gathering and analysing it) at senior management level.

20.10 Personal development is a process whereby employees are offered a wide range of

developmental opportunities, rather than focusing on skills required in the current job.

Rationale: Management relates specifically to management effectiveness and succession; career to planning opportunities for new challenges and learning through career moves (whether vertical or lateral).

20.11 The correct answer is: On-the-job coaching by his supervisor

Rationale: A Pragmatist likes to learn in 'hands-on' ways that have a direct link to real, practical problems – so on-the-job practice is ideal. The second option would suit an Activist – a similar style, enjoying practical, active, participative learning, but without the need to see a work-related 'payoff'. The third option would suit a Reflector, since a journal offers opportunity for learning through reflection. And the fourth option would suit a Theorist, with a preference for structured intellectual study.

Pitfalls: The pairs of 'hands off' and 'hands on' styles are quite similar: don't confuse them. It may help to relate each style to a different stage of Kolb's learning cycle, to make them more distinct. The Pragmatist focuses on the job; the Reflector reflects on what happened; the Theorist seeks to understand it; and the Activist plans to try something new.

20.12 The correct answer is: Increased employee satisfaction

Rationale: Employee satisfaction would not be regarded as a quantifiable benefit – unless it could be correlated directly with figures such as reduced absenteeism and labour turnover (although it would be difficult to relate this specifically to training, as opposed to other effects).

Pitfalls: Watch out for qualifier keywords in the question like 'quantitative' or 'qualitative' (benefits, characteristics). Always read questions carefully!

20.13 The correct answer is: 1 is the definition of development and 2 is the definition of training

Rationale: It is important to separate development, training and education in your mind for this syllabus. Development is the growth of a person's potential. Training is a planned learning event. Education is knowledge that is acquired gradually by learning or instruction.

20.14 The correct answer is: A set of competence standards for your job or department

Rationale: A formal training needs analysis involves systematic study (at the level of the individual, job or department) of the required level of competence, the present/actual level of competence and any gap between them. The other options are all ways in which learning needs may 'emerge' in the course of work: the first option, through monitoring developments in your field; the second option as a 'critical incident' and the fourth option as on-going performance feedback.

20.15 | E-learning | is learning through a network of computers or the internet (but not stand-alone CD-Rom or tuition software), so that learning support is available from online tutors, moderators and discussion groups.

Rationale: It is the networked aspect that makes e-learning different from computer based training (CBT) (using stand-alone computers). Blended learning involves learning using a combination of different methods and technologies: this would be the correct option if the learning support was available from face-to-face tuition, say.

Pitfalls: Learning technologies is fertile territory for exam questions, because there are so many closely-related methods and terms (coaching, mentoring etc).

Ways in: Just about anything with an 'e-' in front of it, these days, is about the internet – not stand-alone computers.

20.16 The correct answer is: (2), (4), (1), (3)

Rationale: This is Kolb's learning cycle which is a 'learning by doing' approach. It puts the learner in an active problem-solving role and encourages them to formulate and commit themselves to their own learning objectives.

Ways in: Simplified, this learning by doing approach involves:

(1) Act

(2) Analyse action

(3) Suggest principles

(4) Apply principles

(5) Act ... and so on

20.17 The correct answer is: To identify present level of competence

Rationale: This can then be used to plan for the other options.

21 Performance appraisal

21.1 The correct answer is: Job evaluation

Rationale: Job evaluation is a method of measuring the value of a job, **not** the performance of the person holding the job. The other options are key applications of performance appraisal. (Succession planning is a form of promotion or potential review, aimed at identifying future managers.)

Pitfalls: This is a common source of confusion (akin to the difference between job descriptions and person specifications in recruitment).

21.2 The correct answer is: Guided assessment

Rationale: Overall assessment is narrative comment without the guidance on how the terms should be applied. Grading uses rating scales (definitions of performance on each characteristic from 1-5, say). Behavioural incident methods compare specific behaviours against typical behaviour in each job.

21.3 The correct answer is: They should be easily achievable

Rationale: Achievable (which is part of the SMART objectives framework) is different from 'easily achievable': one of the key points of performance measures is that they should be motivational, which means that they should be at least a little bit challenging.

21.4 The correct answer is: Tell and listen

Rationale: This manager tells in the first part and listens in the second part of the interview, taking on a dual role as critic and counsellor – and not assuming that all performance problems are the fault of the employee himself. Tell and sell would be more one-sided ('selling' simply being gaining acceptance of the evaluation and improvement plan). Problem-solving is even more of a collaborative, proactive process, with the manager in the role of coach. Sell and listen is not an appropriate method.

21.5 The correct answer is: 360-degree feedback

Rationale: 360-degree is, by definition, a 'rounded' view of an individual's performance from the appraisee, colleagues, superiors, subordinates and relevant business contacts. Self appraisal is likely to be biased by self-perception; peer appraisal by team relationships; and upward appraisal by subordinates' fear of reprisals.

21.6 Performance management is 'a process to establish a shared understanding about what is to be achieved, and an approach to managing and developing people in order to achieve it'.

Rationale: This is the definition of performance management. It differs from performance appraisal in its emphasis on collaboration, objective-setting and on-going management.

21.7 The correct answer is: (1), (2), (3) and (4) only

Rationale: These are all valid criteria. The fifth criteria would be relevance not results.

21.8 Multi-source feedback is the name given to gathering of appraisals from the individual, superiors, subordinates, peers and co-workers and customers.

Rationale: Multi-source feedback is another term for 360-degree feedback or appraisal. Management by objectives and performance management are both approaches to collaborative objective-setting, on-going development and periodic review.

21.9 The correct answer is: There is an implied link between assessment and reward

Rationale: This is a double edged sword: a link between assessment and reward may motivate employees to take appraisal seriously, but can also make it threatening if they fear that they haven't done well. Moreover, there are other factors in setting rewards – and if there isn't a real connection between a positive appraisal and a meaningful reward, the 'implication' that there is will only undermine the appraisal system. The other options are clearly positive.

21.10 The correct answer is: Appraisal is seen as an opportunity to raise workplace problems and issues

Rationale: The other options were identified as barriers to effective appraisal by Lockett: 'appraisal as unfinished business' (distracting from future-focused improvement planning); 'appraisal as bureaucracy' (a mere form-filling exercise); and 'appraisal as an annual event' (where on-going performance management is required). Lockett also identified 'appraisal as confrontation' as a barrier, but this is not what is implied by the correct answer, which reflects a genuine, job-relevant, problem-solving approach.

21.11 The correct answer is: Bonuses awarded

Rationale: Although appraisals can be used to measure the extent to which an employee is deserving of a bonus, it cannot be used to measure the effectiveness of the appraisal scheme itself. Funds may not be available for bonuses but this does not mean that the appraisal system is ineffective. Appraisals must be carried out with serious intent and managers must be committed to the system. The system should be fair and reasonably objective.

21.12 The correct answer is: Individual objectives are related to the objectives of the whole organisation

Rationale: This is an advantage because it gives the individual a greater sense of meaning and contribution to the organisation.

It is also an advantage to the organisation – as are all the other options. You may have hesitated over the first option. This would certainly be an advantage to appraisees identified for promotion – but not everyone.

21.13 The correct answer is: Results-oriented

Rationale: This involves setting specific targets and standards of performance, and measuring performance against them.

Behavioural incident focuses on job behaviours; rating scales are the same as grading; and guided assessment is narrative comment on defined characteristics.

22 Section D MTQs

22.1 (a) Peter

Implementer

Gloria

Shaper

Shirley

Specialist

Matthew

Monitor-Evaluator

These all relate to the descriptions of Belbin's team roles.

(b) Victimisation occurs when an individual is penalised for giving information in a discrimination claim against an employer.

Victimisation occurs when an individual is penalised for giving information in a discrimination claim against an employer.

(c) The correct answer is: True

Note that this is not the same thing as positive discrimination.

22.2 (a) The correct answers are:

- A feeling of achievement - **Intrinsic reward**
- A promise of additional time off for meeting a target - **Incentive**
- Working conditions - **Extrinsic reward**
- Salary - **Extrinsic reward**

Intrinsic rewards arise from the performance of the work.

An incentive is a promise or offer of a reward.

Extrinsic rewards are separate from the job itself and dependent on the decisions of others.

(b) The correct answers are:

- Giving an employee freedom to decide how the job should be done
- Encouraging employee participation in planning decisions of superiors

Transferring an employee from one job to another is job rotation. Increasing the number of tasks an employee participates in is job enlargement. Dividing a job up into a small number of sequential tasks is job simplification.

22.3 (a) The correct answers are:

Theorists	SHAUN			
Reflectors		LOUISE		
Activists				TONY
Pragmatists			SUSAN	

These all relate to the classifications of Honey and Mumford.

(b) The correct answers are:

- Computer-based training
- College courses

The other options are all on the job training methods.

22.4 (a) The correct answers are:

Management development		HELEN		
Personal Development	GEORGE			
Professional development			JOSH	
Career development				LEIGH

(1) Personal development can help to foster employee job satisfaction, commitment and loyalty.

(2) This may include the development of management/leadership skills or management education such as an MBA.

(3) This is an example of continuing professional development (CPD). CPD is based on the belief that a professional qualification is the basis for a career lifetime of development.

(4) The trend for delayered organisations reduces opportunities for promotion, so opportunities are planned for sideways or lateral transfers.

(b) The correct answers are:

- There should be clear objectives
- There should be timely feedback

For training to be effective there should be timely feedback and also clear objectives for the training.

Training does not need to be on or off the job to be effective, it can be either. Training does not need to be expensive to be useful.

22.5 (a) The correct answers are:

Guided Assessment			COMPANY Y	
Grading		COMPANY X		
Behavioural-incident method				COMPANY Z
Results-oriented scheme	COMPANY W			

(1) This scheme is based on the results achieved by the sales staff.

(2) Each manager is graded on their performance.

(3) This is a guided assessment method.

(4) This method concentrates on employee behaviour measured against typical behaviour in each job.

(b) The correct answer is: Problem-solving

This is a problem solving approach.

(c) The correct answer is: True

This is one of the objectives of performance appraisal.

22.6 (a) The correct answer is: Negative power

Negative power is the use of disruptive behaviour to stop things from happening.

(b) The correct answers are:

- Individuals at all levels can exert a leadership influence - **Heifetz**
- There are 'psychologically close' and 'psychologically distant' managers - **Fiedler**
- The manager 'does things right' while the leader 'does the right thing' - **Bennis**

Heifetz: theory of dispersed leadership

Fiedler: contingency theory; people become leaders partly because of their own attributes and partly because of their situation

Bennis: put forward specific differences between managers and leaders

23 Personal effectiveness and communication

23.1 The correct answer is: Diagonal

Rationale: The communication here is both upwards and 'sideways'.

23.2 The correct answer is: Personal development planning

Rationale: Personal development planning is something the individual does for his or her own improvement and learning, although a coach, mentor or counsellor may facilitate this process. The other options are all types of 'developmental relationships': a coach helps a trainee for a brief period to work on job-relevant skills; a mentor helps a less experienced person over the long term to work on more general personal development issues; and a counsellor helps an individual to work through emotional or social issues or problems.

Pitfalls: These are distinct roles: make sure you can identify them correctly.

23.3 The correct answer is: An assertive style of communication

Rationale: An assertive style of communication will help in time management, because it enables you to say 'no' (appropriately) to interruptions and unscheduled demands.

23.4 The correct answer is: The wheel

Rationale: The wheel has a central figure who acts as a hub for all messages between members. The circle involves a message going from one person to another. The 'Y' involves a message going from person to person up a chain, until it reaches someone who is in contact with more than one person. And all-channel involves everyone sending messages to everyone else.

Ways in: If you can visualise the situation, it helps: you could then eliminate the circle and all-channel, at least.

23.5 The correct answer is: Mobile communications

Rationale: A mobile phone enables both colleagues and customers to reach you when you are out of the office. It also enables you to call the office eg to check inventory availability of items, place immediate orders and so on. (If you had a laptop, this would be even better: you could have direct connection with office systems.) The first two options all involve linked computer systems, so are not relevant.

23.6 The correct answer is: Security

Rationale: Security is a key vulnerability of email: there is no guarantee of privacy (and a risk of accidentally sending the message to the wrong person). The other options are significant strengths, however. If you hesitated over the fourth option, think about how email can be used for memos/reports/letters, and how many formats (visual, audio) can be 'attached' to email messages.

23.7 Counselling is essentially a/an non-directive role.

Rationale: Counselling is facilitating others through the process of defining and exploring their own issues and coming up with their own solutions: this is relatively non-directive. Advising is a relatively directive role: offering information and recommendations on the best course of action to take. Counselling is often **not** directly task-related: it is often about helping employees to formulate learning goals or to cope with work (or non-work) problems.

23.8 The correct answer is: Accurate

Rationale: The grapevine is a 'rumour mill': information is often inaccurate and exaggerated.

Communication is, however, fast, selective (in that information is not randomly passed on to everyone) and up-to-date (information is often more current than in the formal system).

ANSWERS

23.9 The correct answer is: Exception reporting

Rationale: Exception reporting may improve the quality of upward communication (making it more selective), but it does not encourage it: if anything, it may create a culture in which staff don't 'bother' their superiors with information. The other options are all ways of encouraging upward flow of information and ideas – which otherwise tends to be rare in organisations.

23.10 The correct answer is: Sender, Coded message, Decoded message, Receiver, Feedback

Rationale: The sender encodes the message and transmits it through a medium to the receiver who decodes it into information. The answer cannot be A since you need to have a message to feedback on before you provide the feedback.

Ways in: It might help you to picture the radio signal diagram in your mind.

23.11 The correct answer is: Team meetings

Rationale: Notice boards are unsuitable for upward communication, and organisation manuals and team briefings are for downward communication.

Pitfalls: You needed to be aware of the nature of a team briefing, which is for information and instructions to be given (downward) to a team.

23.12 The correct answer is: Distortion

Rationale: Noise is the **other** main type of communication problem: interferences in the environment in which communication takes place, affecting the clarity, accuracy or arrival of the message. Redundancy is a **positive** principle in this context: you can use more than one form of communication, so that if one message does not get through (perhaps because of noise or distortion), another may. Feedback is an essential part of the communication cycle: it is the response which indicates to the sender whether the message has been correctly received.

23.13 The correct answer is: Wheel

Rationale: The wheel was the fastest and the Y was the second fasted in Leavitt's experiment. The chain was the slowest. The reason was the fact that messages came through and were distributed from a central source.

23.14 The correct answer is: Developing the individual by helping to build on skills and overcome weaknesses

Rationale: If you got this answer incorrect then remember the importance of having a clear understanding of the key definitions within the syllabus. For example, coaching is not one-way so the second option could immediately be eliminated. It is important to look for key words (clues) to the right answer.

23.15 The correct answer is: People pay less attention to non-verbal cues than to what is being said

Rationale: Research shows that people pay **more** attention to non-verbal cues in interpreting what someone means than they do to the words themselves. The other statements are true.

Pitfalls: You may have wrongly selected the third option if you associated non-verbal communication too narrowly as 'body language': be aware of the full range of non-verbal signals that can be given or received.

23.16 The correct answer is: Measurable

Rationale: SMART is 'Specific, Measurable, Attainable, Relevant and Time-bounded', although versions differ. The first and third options are both very plausible – and also qualities of effective goals – but you wouldn't want to replace 'measurable', which is essential (otherwise, how will you know when you've reached your goal?).

23.17 The correct answer is: Failed to meet deadlines

Rationale: You may have considered failing to communicate, but you are not given enough information in the scenario to assume that this is the case.

23.18 The correct answer is: Setting up a competence framework

Rationale: A competence framework sets out what an employee should be able to do and ought to know.

23.19 The correct answer is: A dispute focuses attention on individual contributions

Rationale: Focusing attention on an individual's contribution may be constructive, if it brings the employees involved to realise what each contributes.

24 Section E MTQs

24.1 (a) The correct answers are:

- The task will satisfy a key customer
- The task will add value to the organisation

These are two of the conditions of an important task. The other is that the potential consequences of failure are long-term, difficult to reverse, far reaching and costly.

(b) The correct answers are:

- A meeting without a clear objective will always give value to everyone attending for the time taken. - **False**
- Time management can be improved by setting aside times when an individual is not contactable by others. - **True**

Meetings without objectives can be a waste of time for all those attending.

Constant interruptions from others can prevent work being completed. Setting aside time for these tasks will improve time management.

24.2 (a) The correct answers are:

Denial				LEONA
Compromise	**TREVOR**			
Dominance			**MICHAEL**	
Integration / Collaboration		**JOSS**		

(1) Compromise involves bargaining, negotiating and conciliating.

(2) Integration/collaboration involves emphasis being put on the task and individual esteem being subordinate to the needs of the group.

(3) Dominance is the application of power or influence to settle the conflict.

(4) Ignoring the issue is known as denial.

(b) The correct answers are:

- Compromises result in all parties being satisfied - **False**
- A win-win situation is rare, but is the best solution to conflict resolution - **True**
- A lose-lose situation is not possible - **False**
- Win-lose situations can result in damaged relationships within the team - **True**

Even positive compromises only result in half-satisfied needs.

Win-win situations can result in mutual respect and co-operation.

Compromise comes into the category.

If one team member gets what they want at the expense of another, relationships within the team may break down.

ANSWERS

24.3 (a) The correct answers are:

- Completed questionnaires for market research - **Data**
- Company website page - **Information**
- Calculations showing whether an investment is profitable - **Information**
- An individual employee's test score - **Data**
- Variance reports for a department manager - **Information**
- The average employee assessment grade for a company - **Information**

Data: This is raw material to be processed.

Information: This has been processed and then presented.

(b) The correct answer is: Strategic

Strategic information will help senior managers with long-term planning.

24.4 (a) The correct answer is: Timing

The email has been sent too close to the date of the meeting, when the financial controller could have sent it much earlier. The medium, clarity and recipients of the email are all suitable for the communication.

(b) The correct answers are:

- Information is not divulged randomly
- It can bypass secretive management
- It relates to internal politics

The grapevine operates inside the place of work, the grapevine is most active when the formal communication network is active and informal communication is more current than formal information.

24.5 (a) The correct answers are:

- Slang is used in task instructions
- An email sent to all employees using IT jargon

Slang or jargon could create misunderstanding if the recipient of the communication is unaware of the meaning.

(b) $\boxed{\text{A grievance}}$ occurs when an individual thinks that they have been wrongly treated by a colleague or supervisor.

This is the definition of a grievance.

(c) The correct answer is: Distortion

This is the definition of distortion.

24.6 (a) One of the most important things is for Susan to establish priorities with Peggy. This will enable her to delegate some of her routine work to enable her to make some time for the project.

(1) Establishing priorities with Peggy

(2) Delegation of routine tasks

(3) Identification of information sources within the business

(4) Sequencing of interviews with relevant staff

(5) Collation of information

(6) Report writing

(b) The correct answer is: Helping John to prepare for his upcoming appraisal

This option would appear to apply more closely to a mentoring role.

25 Ethical considerations

25.1 Managers are said to have a [Fiduciary] responsibility (or duty of faithful service) in

respect of the entities whose purposes they serve.

Rationale: 'Fiduciary' means 'of trust'. Although this is a terminology question, it addresses the important point that all managers (and organisations) are accountable to some external entity and purpose.

25.2 The correct answer is: Utilitarianism

Rationale: Utilitarianism is based on 'usefulness': the greatest good of the greatest number. Deontology is an alternative approach based on absolute moral principles (or categorical imperatives): what is morally 'right' in a situation. Virtue ethics is a belief in pursuing positive moral qualities, which flow out into behaviour.

25.3 The correct answer is: It constitutes grease money.

Rationale: Grease money refers to payments for benefits to which the company is legally entitled – just to 'oil the wheels'. Bribery is payment for benefits to which the company is **not** legally entitled – to 'bend the rules'! In either case, this is unethical (and in some situations, illegal) – regardless of the legitimacy of the claim or the purposes to which the payment is (supposedly) put.

Pitfalls: Know the difference between extortion, bribery, grease money, gifts and hospitality.

25.4 The correct answer is: Integrity based

Rationale: The emphasis on managerial responsibility is a feature of the integrity or values-based approach to ethics management. A concern for the law alone is a compliance based approach. The third and fourth options are examples of responsibilities.

25.5 Farrah works in the sales tax section of the accounts department of BCD Co. When the

finance director is on holiday, Farrah notices that BCD Co has not been paying the correct

quarterly amounts to the authorities. Farrah had suspected this for some time and decides

to contact the authorities to tell them about the fraud. This disclosure is known as [Whistle

blowing]

Rationale: Corporate conscience is irrelevant, and confidentiality breach is incorrect, since whistle-blowing gives some protection to employees from being in breach of confidentiality.

25.6 The correct answer is: (1), (2), (3), (4) and (5)

Rationale: These are all potential ethical issues. Materials used impacts on product safety and eco-friendliness (eg for recycling). Quality is a safety and customer satisfaction issues. Advertising poses issues of truth and non-manipulation. You may have hesitated over supplier labour practices, but this is a key area of ethical sourcing. It can cause significant damage to corporate reputations. Packaging raises issues of safety/perishability, eco-friendliness and truthful product labelling.

25.7 Reliability, responsibility [timeliness] , courtesy and respect are the personal qualities

expected of an accountant.

Rationale: Accountability and social responsibility are classed as professional qualities, not personal qualities.

ANSWERS

Ambition is a personal quality – but is not considered essential in a professional ethics context: it can even pose ethical dilemmas ...

Pitfalls: You need to read the question stems carefully to pick up fine distinctions such as 'personal' and 'professional'.

25.8   The correct answer is: Independence in appearance

Rationale: Independence in appearance means avoiding situations that could cause a reasonable observer to question your objectivity. In the scenario, this is a risk – while independence of mind (free from actual partiality) isn't. The pure distractors were plausible because of the possibility of raising questions (scepticism) with your superiors (accountability) – but irrelevant.

25.9   The correct answer is: Employability training

Rationale: Employability training helps employees to get other employment but it is not an ethical objective.

25.10   The correct answer is: The law

Rationale: The saying is: 'the law is a floor'. By meeting non-legal regulations (including the rules of your workplace) you should meet a higher standard of behaviour than the legal requirements. Ethical behaviour is a higher moral standard, based on society's expectations and principles.

25.11   The correct answer is: Fairness

Rationale: This is a definition of fairness.

25.12   The correct answer is: Telling the truth and not misleading stakeholders

Rationale: The first option is a definition of openness, the third is responsibility and the fourth is accountability.

25.13   The correct answer is: Integrity

Rationale: The statement is the definition of integrity made by the UK Nolan Committee on Standards in Public Life.

25.14   The correct answer is: Organisational self-interest

Rationale: Organisational self-interest is a threat to independence and a source of conflict of interest. The other options are different varieties of ethical systems.

25.15   The correct answer is: Self-interest

Rationale: A firm or a member of an assurance team should not accept gifts or hospitality unless the value is clearly insignificant. In this case, it is likely that the cost of corporate hospitality at major sporting events will be significant.

25.16   The correct answer is: Intimidation

Rationale: This is a case of intimidation. You may have been tempted to pick self-interest but the threat of legal proceedings makes this intimidation.

25.17   The correct answer is: An ACCA member is an officer of the client company but does not deal with the client's affairs

Rationale: The fact that the ACCA member does not deal with the client's affairs is a safeguard against a conflict of interest.

25.18   The correct answer is: Confidentiality

Rationale: The issue for you is confidentiality, as the accounts are likely to contain sensitive information and should definitely not be left lying around. You may have wondered about unprofessional behaviour but this would apply to your supervisor rather than you.

25.19   The correct answer is: The ethics appropriate for a given situation will depend on the conditions at the time

Rationale: The first option refers to absolutism and the second refers to egoism.

25.20 The correct answer is: It takes no account of changing norms in society

Rationale: The first and third options are criticisms of relativism and the fourth option refers to egoism.

25.21 The correct answer is: The duties of the decision taker

Rationale: The virtues of a person are those characteristics regarded by society as desirable, and may result in an observer arriving at the conclusion that the individual will take good or bad decisions. A duty-based perspective considers whether a decision or action will be compliant with the perceived responsibilities of a person or organisation, which in turn may rely on consistency with the law, codes of practice or generally accepted standards. This is the deontological approach.

The consequentialist approach considers right and wrong from the viewpoint of an action or decision bringing about an end result that is right or wrong. This is called the teleological approach.

26 Section F MTQs

26.1 (a) The correct answers are:

- It leads to a philosophy of anything goes
- It is based on a fundamental contradiction

It is argued that relativism leads to a philosophy of anything goes and the statement that all statements are relative is an absolute (therefore non-relative) statement.

(b) The correct answers are:

- Social responsibility action is likely to have an adverse effect on shareholders' interests in the short term - **True**
- An environmental audit involves assessing the opportunities and threats to an organisation - **False**
- Only governments are concerned with social responsibility - **False**
- Guaranteeing employees a minimum 'living wage' is an example of social responsibility - **True**

Social responsibility costs money and goes against the idea of maximising shareholder wealth.

An environmental audit monitors things such as legal compliance with environment regulations or emissions levels.

As can be seen in many examples, a number of companies take socially responsible actions.

This is an example of a company being socially responsible.

26.2 (a) The correct answers are:

- The teleological view of ethics is based on duty - **False**
- Bribery can sometimes be legal - **False**
- Virtue ethics suggests that managers should incorporate values such as fairness and loyalty into their decision-making - **True**
- An accountant's ethical behaviour serves to protect the public interest - **True**

This is the deontological view. Teleology is based on consequences.

Bribery involves payment for services that the organisation is not legally entitled to.

Virtue ethics suggest managers should incorporate such virtues into their daily behaviour.

This is a key reason why accountants should behave ethically.

ANSWERS

(b) The correct answers are:

- It takes no account of evolving norms
- Whatever source is used, human interpretation will lead to different views

It takes no account of evolving norms, whatever source is used, human interpretation will lead to different views.

Absolutism takes no account of 'advances' in morality and if human interpretation leads to different views there cannot be universal agreement.

26.3 (a) The correct answers are:

- Reliability
- Courtesy
- Respect
- Timeliness

The personal qualities that an accountant should demonstrate are reliability, responsibility, courtesy, respect and timeliness.

(b) The correct answers are:

- Integrity
- Objectivity

The fundamental principles are integrity, confidentiality, objectivity, professional behaviour and professional competence and due care

26.4 (a) The correct answers are:

Familiarity threat		COMPANY X		
Advocacy threat	COMPANY W			
Self-review threat				COMPANY Z
Self-interest threat			COMPANY Y	

YRT Co is threatening its independence by taking the client's position in the legal case.

Since the audit partner has a long-term relationship with the audit client, there is a familiarity threat.

A self-interest threat exists if there are close personal relationships between the client and the audit team.

Where the external auditor helps to prepare the financial statements, there is a clear self-review threat.

(b) The correct answer is: Litigation against the external auditor by an audit client

Litigation gives rise to a threat of intimidation. The others give rise to self-interest threats.

(c) Ethics are a set of | moral principles | that guide behaviour.

Ethics are a moral rather than legal or regulatory issue, although professional ethics are particularly important.

26.5 (a) The correct answers are:

- Self-interest threat
- Intimidation threat

Self-interest threat, Intimidation threat

Because it is important for JKL Co to retain this client, due to significance of the revenue, there is a self-interest threat here. The client is also looking to intimidate the auditors over the fee negotiations.

(b) The correct answers are:

- When dealing with ethical dilemmas ACCA students must follow ACCA's code of conduct. - **True**
- Professional ethics should not be followed at the expense of contractual obligations. - **False**
- There is a public expectation that accountants will act ethically. - **True**
- A prospective audit firm quoting a significantly lower fee for assurance work than the current auditors charge does not raise a threat of a conflict of interest. - **False**

ACCA students and members must always follow ACCA's code of conduct.

Professional ethics should be followed even if this is at the expense of a contractual obligation.

The public expects all professionals to act in an ethical manner.

This process is known as lowballing and raises a significant self-interest threat, particularly if the firm want to offer more profitable non-audit services as well.

26.6 (a) The correct answers are:

- Decisions of this stakeholder may be influenced by ethical considerations - **Customers**
- Standards of behaviour expected of this stakeholder should be communicated to them - **Employees**
- This stakeholder may need reassurance that the organisation will act as a 'good citizen' - **Local communitie**

For example, customer purchases may be influenced by ethical considerations.

Employees need to know what is expected of them.

Local communities may need reassurance that the organisation will act as a 'good citizen'.

(b) The correct answer is: Effective education and training for all staff

The most effective way to ensure standards are maintained is to instil the standards into the company culture. Staff training is the only way to ensure that standards are communicated, and that staff understand the implications of any violation.

ANSWERS

27 Mixed Bank 1

27.1 The correct answer is: Isolated from its external environment

Rationale: The difference between an open and a closed system is very basic, and depends on the relationship the system has with its environment. A system being closed to protect from unauthorised access merely refers to the system's security arrangements. Incapability of further technical enhancement refers to a stage in the system's life cycle.

27.2 The correct answer is: Indirect discrimination

Rationale: This is indirect discrimination because most part time employees are women. If it were direct discrimination then the advert would actually state that women had less favourable terms.

27.3 The correct answer is: To record financial information

Rationale: This is its basic, original role and is still the best way to describe its part in the modern business organisation.

27.4 The correct answer is: Improves the motivation of junior managers

Rationale: While the other options may arise in a decentralised organisation, they are not necessarily features that are specifically associated with decentralisation.

27.5 The correct answer is: There is little similarity between team members' work

Rationale: Where there is little similarity in work, subordinates will not be able to help each other, and will rely more heavily on their managers.

Where the work is routine, or the team very experienced, team members will require less support so a wider span may be appropriate. the wider the geographical dispersion, the narrower the span.

27.6 The correct answer is: Independence of the non-executive directors

Rationale: This will be examined in the internal position audit of the company rather than the environmental analysis which looks at matters external to the company.

27.7 The correct answer is: Managing the prompt payment of suppliers

Rationale: The purchasing manager will be concerned with all aspects of supplier management (eg discussing prices, discounts, delivery lead times, specifications, chasing late deliveries, sanctioning payments).

27.8 The correct answer is: (2), (3) and (4) only

Rationale: The other statement describes the adhocracy, which is complex and disorderly and does not rely on standardisation to co-ordinate its activities. It also relies on the expertise of its members, but not through standardised skills.

27.9 The correct answer is: (1) and (4) only

Rationale: Customisation should not stop the company from being able to buy 'add-ons' to the basic package. In fact they are sometimes used to give the package more flexibility to suit particular needs. Dependence on the supplier for maintenance is also a disadvantage of ready-made packages.

27.10 The correct answer is: Variable costs

Rationale: In the short run, firms will continue to supply customers provided that they cover variable costs. They will incur fixed costs whether they produce any output or not. Therefore provided revenues cover variable costs and therefore make a contribution towards fixed costs, it is beneficial for the firm to continue producing.

27.11 The correct answer is: Dual authority

Rationale: Dual authority may lead to conflict between the managers involved.

The advantages of such a structure are:

- Greater flexibility
- Improved communication
- Motivating employees

27.12 The correct answer is: The board of directors

Rationale: As with all company-specific matters it is the directors who are primarily responsible for the implementation of procedures, which follow best practice with regard to the current corporate governance advice.

27.13 The correct answer is: Shareholders are accountable to auditors

Rationale: All the other statements are true. Both directors and auditors are agents of the shareholders and their primary duties relate to them.

27.14 The correct answer is: To examine and express an opinion on the company's periodic financial statements

Rationale: This is a Companies Act requirement. The other responses are specific director responsibilities.

27.15 The correct answer is: An audit trail

Rationale: An audit trail shows who has accessed a system and the operations performed.

27.16 The correct answer is: (2), (3) and (4) only

Rationale: It should be **accurate** – in the sense of correct for the purpose. Inaccurate information is of little use for strategic, tactical or operational purposes. **Authoritative** means that the source of the information should be reliable. It must also be **relevant to** the user's needs. Information that is not needed for a decision should be omitted, no matter how 'interesting' it might be. If the information is **comprehensive**, it may be more wide ranging than it needs to be. It needs to be complete ie include everything that is needed.

27.17 The correct answer is: External auditors need to assess the work of internal audit first

Rationale: Although some of the procedures that internal audit undertake are very similar to those undertaken by the external auditors, the whole basis and reasoning of their work is fundamentally different.

27.18 The correct answer is: (1), (3) and (4) only

Rationale: Capital costs, which are capitalised and then depreciated, include installation, hardware purchase and software purchase costs. Routine system maintenance costs are revenue items which are expensed as incurred.

27.19 The correct answer is: Shareholders

Rationale: It is very important that external auditors are independent of the company's management.

27.20 Receipts must be [banked] promptly

The record of receipts must be [complete]

The loss of receipts through theft or accident must be [prevented]

Rationale: In any business controls over cash receipts are fundamental if the company is to keep a healthy cash position.

27.21 The correct answer is: Dishonesty, motivation and opportunity

Rationale: If one or more of them can be eliminated, the risk of fraud is reduced.

27.22 The correct answer is: A higher than normal risk audit

Rationale: The instances given are all examples of inherent risk or control risks and therefore they would be indicative of higher risk audit.

Certain of the factors combined, such as a poor internal control environment coupled with a dominant chief executive, might raise the auditors' suspicions of fraud, but not necessarily. However, they would all increase the overall risk of the audit.

27.23 The correct answer is: (1), (3) and (4) only

Rationale: Data and information captured from internal sources come from transaction systems, such as the payroll system and the sales ledger, or is communicated formally or informally, as in a decision taken at a meeting.

Although the type of information is circulated within the organisation, it is captured from outside. For example, the source of the market information is the market itself, which is clearly external to the organisation.

28 Mixed Bank 2

28.1 The correct answer is: (2), (3) and (4) only

Rationale: Fayol wrote that to manage is to forecast and plan, to organise, to command, to co-ordinate and to control. Commanding is the exercise of centralised authority and leadership. Co-ordinating involves harmonising the activities of all groups towards the common objective. Controlling is measuring performance and accounting for deviations from plans. Writers after Fayol substituted functions such as motivating and consulting for commanding.

28.2 The correct answer is: Organisational design will be determined by a number of factors all of which depend on the others

Rationale: These factors include elements such as the company's objectives, the environment, the staff, the culture, the management style, the tasks carried out, the structure and the technology used.

28.3 The correct answer is: Planning and control

Rationale: The five categories are setting objectives, organising the work, motivation, the job of measurement and developing people. Planning and control are included within setting objectives and measurement. Drucker gave more emphasis to the 'human resource' aspects of management than writers on classical management theory such as Fayol.

28.4 The correct answer is: Position power

Rationale: Position power or legitimate power is conferred by the authority linked to a formal position within the organisation structure.

28.5 The correct answer is: Benevolent authoritative, participative, exploitative authoritative, democratic

Rationale: These are Likert's four management styles.

28.6 The correct answer is: Storming

Rationale: This is the storming stage, as identified by Tuckman. During this stage, conflict can be quite open. Objectives and procedures are challenged and risks are taken. However, there is a considerable amount of enthusiasm within the group and new ideas emerge. So too do political conflicts, as leadership of the group becomes an issue. This appears to be the situation described in the question.

28.7 The correct answer is: (2) and (3)

Rationale: Job analysis involves finding out what are the task, skill and knowledge requirements of a job. This information is then output in the form of a job description (tasks, duties, objectives and standards of a job) and a person specification (reworking of the job description in terms of the kind of person needed to perform the job).

A human resource plan is a much broader statement of the future skill requirements of the organisation as a whole, and how they will be met (by recruitment, training, retention and so on).

A performance appraisal analyses how a job holder **does** the job – not the nature of the job itself.

28.8 The correct answer is: Shaper

Rationale: All of Belbin's roles are important to the effective functioning of a team. You should familiarise yourself with all nine roles.

- Plant
- Shaper
- Resource investigator
- Monitor evaluator
- Company worker
- Completer finisher
- Team worker
- Chairman
- Specialist

28.9 The correct answer is: Attacker

Rationale: The shaper is a leader role, where the role holder spurs the team to action. The plant provides the creative thinking in the team, while the finisher's actions are directed to the completion of the task.

Attacking is a type of group behaviour identified by Rackham & Morgan.

28.10 The correct answer is: All four

Rationale: A team is a number of people with complementary skills who are committed to a common purpose for which they hold themselves basically accountable. This is a control mechanism which improves work organisation by using knowledge from a broad range of perspectives to evaluate decision options.

28.11 The correct answer is: Forming, storming, norming, performing

Rationale: Forming is the stage where the team comes together. Storming happens next; the group re-assesses its targets and (hopefully) trust between group members develops. Norming is a period of settling down, when the group established norms and procedures for doing their work. Performing then occurs; the team sets to work to execute its task and the difficulties of development no longer hinder it.

28.12 The correct answer is: Herzberg

Rationale: Herzberg found that people's behaviour in the workplace was affected by more than their physical and social needs; the content of the work itself had an effect on motivation and performance.

28.13 The correct answer is: (1), (2) and (4)

Rationale: Bruce's course would have covered many approaches to resolving problems. The negotiation techniques you should have identified include trying to develop options that would result in mutual gain; defining the problems carefully and looking for a wide variety of possible solutions. Evaluating progress towards objectives and creating a trusting supportive atmosphere in the group will enhance the project team's performance but would not be considered negotiation techniques.

28.14 The correct answer is: (1), (2) and (4)

Rationale: The feature is an advantage associated with other types of communication. Complex ideas that require deeper consideration are probably best communicated in written form, or perhaps in a presentation. Holding a meeting is the main communication technique for allowing multiple options to be expressed. However, an effective chairperson is needed if all sides are to be heard.

28.15 The correct answer is: (1) and (2) only

Rationale: Hygiene factors are extrinsic or environmental factors (salary and job security), while motivator factors are to do with the satisfactions of the work: challenging work is clear in this category – and recognition could be in either.

28.16 The correct answer is: (2), (3) and (4) only

Rationale: Colloquialisms should only be used in informal conversation and jargon should be avoided, although it may be used where it is an excellent form of shorthand and unique to the particular organisation, provided it remains comprehensible and is understood by all parties. Acronyms can be used freely as long as they are explained.

28.17 The correct answer is: (1), (3) and (4) only

Rationale: Complex images can be included as an attachment to an email and there is no limitation on their transmission.

28.18 Subjects for discussion 5

Minutes of previous meeting 2

Date of next meeting 6

Any other business 1

Apologies for absence 4

Matters arising 3

Rationale: The sequence of items on an agenda is apologies for absence, approving the minutes of the previous meeting, matters arising out of the minutes, the main items of business on the agenda (subjects for discussion), any other business (items not on the agenda) and finally deciding the date of the next meeting.

28.19 The correct answer is: (1), (2) and (3) only

Rationale: Peers or co-workers could be members of a team or people receiving or providing services.

Customers can be a useful source, especially for sales staff. Knowing what customers think of you helps to improve your technique.

When individuals carry out their own self-evaluation, it is a major input to the appraisal process because they can identify the areas of competence that are relevant to the job and their own relative strengths.

28.20 The correct answer is: Upward

Rationale: There is a current trend towards this more progressive appraisal system where subordinates appraise their superiors.

Potential problems with this method may include:

- Fear of reprisal
- Vindictiveness
- Unwillingness of superior to respond to feedback

28.21 The correct answer is: Deal with grievances

Rationale: Grievances should be dealt with by a formal mechanism separate from the appraisal process. If a grievance arises during appraisal it should be dealt with using the normal grievance procedure.

28.22 The correct answer is: Accounts payable clerk

Rationale: It is unlikely that the accounts payable clerk will be asked. The others will all come in contact with the sales manager and therefore potentially could be asked to assist with completing the appraisal forms required by 360 degree feedback process.

28.23 The correct answer is: Enabling accounting

Rationale: Enabling accounting is a made up term here, and sounds like a rather dubious practice for a business. Accounting should be a well-controlled and regulated process.

The other options are all characteristics of a learning organisation.

28.24 The correct answer is: (1), (2) and (4) only

Rationale: The advantages of upward appraisal are that the subordinates feel more involved, managers receive objective feedback and can therefore improve their performance.

29 Mixed Bank 3

29.1 The correct answer is: PEST

Rationale: PEST (Political, Economic, Social and Technological) are the environmental factors that affect an organisation. Sometimes two more factors, ecological and legal are added. PERT is a tool used in project management. SWOT is used to analyse the internal and external environment, so not just the external environment.

29.2 The correct answers are:

- Designing systems
- Standardising work

29.3 The correct answer is: The number of employees reporting to one manager

Rationale: This is the definition of span of control.

29.4 The correct answer is: The directors of the company

Rationale: The role of the internal auditor requires independence from other employees, therefore they should report to the directors. Some companies have an audit committee which is a sub committee of the board of directors, and the internal auditors report to the audit committee. If there is no audit committee then the auditors should report directly to the board of directors.

29.5 The correct answers are:

- Arithmetic
- Physical

Rationale: SPAMSOAP stands for: Segregation of duties, Physical, Authorisation and approval, Management, Supervision, Organisation, Arithmetical and accounting and Personnel.

29.6 The correct answers are:

- Sales invoicing
- Payroll

Rationale: Inventory valuation would be performed by the management accountant. Project appraisal would be performed by the financial manager.

29.7 The correct answer is: Hersey and Blanchard

29.8 The correct answer is: All team members have different skills and specialisms which they pool

29.9 The correct answers are:

- Maslow's hierarchy of needs
- Herzberg's two factor theory

Maslow's hierarchy of needs and Herzberg's two factor theory.

29.10 The correct answers are:

- Mentoring by a colleague
- Secondments to other departments

Mentoring by a colleague and secondments to other departments.

Rationale: They these types of training take place in a work environment.

29.11 The correct answer is: Diagonal

Rationale: The manager is in a different function and also below the director.

ANSWERS

29.12 The correct answer is: Prefers to think things through first

29.13 'An organisation is a social arrangement which pursues collective ⬚goals⬚ , which controls

its own performance and which has a boundary separating it from its environment.'

Rationale: Collective goals or aims are a feature of organisations.

29.14 The correct answers are:

- Strategic apex
- Support staff

Strategic apex, support staff

Rationale: The others are distractors! Make sure you do know these technical terms as your exam could include a similar question.

29.15 The correct answer is: All of the above

Rationale: All of these are examples of weaknesses in financial controls.

29.16 The correct answer is: The Management Accountant

Rationale: The Management Accountant provides information for management: cost accounting, budgets and budgetary control and financial management of projects.

29.17 The correct answer is: Purchasing/procurement

Rationale: The purchasing or procurement function is responsible for authorising purchases (and suppliers) and approving.

29.18 The correct answer is: Teeming and lading

29.19 The correct answer is: (1), (2) and (4) only

29.20 A ⬚module⬚ is a program which deals with one particular part of a computerised business

accounting system.

Rationale: A suite is a set of several modules. A spreadsheet is a type of program, and a format for displaying and processing data: it is often used to integrate data from accounting modules for decision-support and management information systems.

29.21 The correct answer is: Legitimate power

Rationale: This is also known as 'position' power.

29.22 The correct answer is: Identity

Rationale: The definition of a group is, basically, 'any collection of people who perceive themselves to be a group' (Handy). Identity means that there are acknowledged boundaries to a group, which define who is 'in' and who is 'out', 'us' and 'them'.

29.23 The correct answer is: Specialist

29.24 The correct answer is: Safety needs

Rationale: Safety needs is one of the needs in Maslow's hierarchy.

30 Mixed Bank 4

30.1 The correct answer is: Output control

Rationale: Output control. Ouchi assumed that output control was part of market control, where it is possible to price output of a system effectively and where there is external competition as a reference.

30.2 The correct answer is: Five pop fans

Rationale: Five pop fans. They are a random collection of people.

They have no common purpose, or common leader and they do not see themselves as having a common identity.

30.3 The correct answer is: Passive acceptance of work decisions

Rationale: Passive acceptance of work decisions. Members of an effectively functioning group will take an active interest in decisions affecting their work, rather than passively accepting them.

30.4 The correct answer is: Position power

Rationale: Position power. A leader is someone who does not have to rely on position power alone.

30.5 The correct answers are:

- Doesn't trust staff to carry out delegated tasks
- Wants to control all activities under his or her responsibility

Rationale: These suggest a lack of trust by the manager toward staff. The other reasons are likely to lead to reduced delegation in themselves.

30.6 The correct answers are:

- Look for a wide variety of possible solutions
- Define the problem carefully
- Try to develop objectives resulting in mutual gains

Rationale: Evaluating progress towards objectives will enhance team performance but would not be considered a negotiation technique. Monitoring others is not negotiation.

30.7 The correct answer is: Allocating scarce resources

Rationale: Allocating scarce resources. This could be concerned with people as a resource but is not people-centred.

30.8 The correct answer is: To take reasonable care of themselves

Rationale: To take reasonable care of themselves. Although there is an employer duty of care towards employees, this does not cover employee negligence or stupidity.

30.9 The correct answers are:

- Shareholders
- Customers

Rationale: These are groups outside the organisation's boundary, in its environment. The others are within the boundary and belong to the organisation system.

30.10 The correct answers are:

- Suspension without pay
- Dismissal

Rationale: Suspension without pay or demotion. Dismissal is a course of action an employer can take although not provided for specifically in the employee's contract of employment.

30.11 The correct answer is: Task

Rationale: The matrix structure requires a culture that reacts quickly to change and focuses on particular projects or tasks as dictated by the needs of the business. A task culture will suit this best as it focuses an achievement of the task above all else, and is very flexible and reactive to changes in the environment.

30.12 The correct answers are:

- Handy
- Schein

Rationale: This quote is variously attributed to Schein and Handy.

An organisation's culture is exclusive, shared and gives its participants a sense of community.

ANSWERS

30.13 The correct answers are:

- Suppliers
- Customers

Rationale: The other options are internal stakeholders.

30.14 The correct answer is: Ensuring the organisation pursues its objectives and serves the needs of its owners and stakeholders

Rationale: The second option describes the 'operating core'. The third option is the 'middle line'.

30.15 The correct answers are:

- Planning and preparing budgets
- Appraisal of capital investment projects

30.16 The correct answer is: Sales ledger and receipts

Rationale: Teeming and lading is the theft of cheque receipts. Setting subsequent receipts against the outstanding debt conceals the theft.

30.17 The correct answer is: Dishonesty, opportunity, motivation

Rationale: All three are essential: dishonesty, opportunity and motivation.

30.18 The correct answer is: Systems

30.19 The correct answer is: Person culture

30.20 The correct answer is: Low concern for people and low concern for the task

Rationale: This option is the worst of both worlds.

30.21 The correct answer is: Highly-strung, outgoing and dynamic and committed to the task

Rationale: The shaper thrives on pressure.

30.22 The correct answer is: Encoded message, medium, decoded message

30.23 The correct answer is: Consistency

Rationale: Consistency was found to be more important to subordinates than any particular style.

30.24 The correct answers are:

- Reporting lines
- Job content

Salary and hours of work will be in the employment contract.

31 Mixed Bank 5

31.1 The correct answers are:

- They can be used by non-specialists
- They provide more consistent processing than manual systems

Rationale: They can be used by non-specialists, they provide more consistent processing than manual systems. In fact it may be more difficult to see where a mistake has been made.

31.2 The correct answer is: Employment protection

Rationale: The other areas are dealt with by a combination of best practice, codes and some legislation.

31.3 The correct answer is: Falls

Rationale: Because chips are a complementary product to fish, a rise in the price of fish will lead to a fall in the demand for chips.

31.4   The correct answers are:

- Reporting to shareholders
- Giving an opinion on financial statements

Reporting to shareholders, giving an opinion on financial statements.

Rationale: The other options are the responsibility of the internal auditor, and ultimately of management.

31.5   The correct answers are:

- Wastage rates
- Labour utilisation figures

31.6   The correct answer is: There is a formal process for decision-making

31.7   The correct answer is: Herzberg

31.8   The correct answer is: Power associated with physical force or punishment

Rationale: Coercion means compelling someone to do something.

31.9   The correct answers are:

- Managing team performance
- Organising the work of others

Managing team performance, organising the work of others

Rationale: The other options will generally be carried out by higher levels of management.

31.10   The correct answer is: Work sampling

Rationale: Work sampling (via portfolios of work or trial periods, say) have the highest reliability (followed closely by cognitive selection tests). Personality testing and assessment centres (group selection exercises) are slightly less reliable. Interviews, ironically, have a very low predictive power – at about the same level as reference checking.

31.11   The concept of managing diversity is based on the belief that the types of individual

difference which are protected by anti-discrimination legislation are crude and irrelevant to

successful performance, and that an organisation can benefit from embracing all kinds of

difference.

Rationale: Equal opportunity is a narrower concept, based on securing non-discrimination on the basis of those 'crude' dimensions of individual difference (sex, age, disability and so on). Diversification is from an organisational strategy involving widening its range of products/markets.

31.12   The correct answer is: Concrete experience, observation and reflection, abstract conceptualisation, active experimentation

Rationale: This may also be worded as: have an experience, review the experience, conclude from the experience and plan the next steps.

31.13   The correct answer is: Scalar chain

Rationale: The scalar chain is the downward flow of delegated authority in an organisation and the need for reports to flow back 'up': it is often a source of slow communication and rigidity (eg in bureaucracies). Horizontal structure allows the flow of information and decisions across functional (vertical) boundaries: it is a key approach to flexibility. The 'Shamrock' is a form of numerical flexibility, where a firm has a core staff and a various peripheral 'leaves' which it can draw on as the demand for labour fluctuates.

31.14   The correct answer is: Taking and circulating minutes of the meeting

Rationale: Minute-taking is one of the roles of the secretary, who essentially provides administrative support to the committee. The first option is the role of the chair, while the second and fourth options may be imposed on the committee by the authorities to which it reports.

31.15 The correct answer is: Zeus

Rationale: Apollo is associated with role culture; Athena with task culture; Dionysus with person culture.

31.16 The correct answer is: (1), (2), (3), (4) and (5)

Rationale: The founder influences culture through founding values; history/experience through creating expectations and stories; recruitment and selection by choosing people who will 'fit' (or change) the culture; industry by having its own culture; and labour turnover by allowing people who don't 'fit in' to 'get out'.

31.17 The correct answer is: Boundary

Rationale: Boundaries are the rules that restrict management's freedom of action: they include legislation, regulation and contractual agreements. Responsibilities are obligations which a company voluntarily undertakes. The primary economic objective relates to optimal resource-conversion (eg profitability). Non-economic, social objectives modify management behaviour in line with stakeholder expectations.

31.18 The correct answer is: Encourages consistent application of rules

Rationale: A framework approach sets out principles and guidelines, rather than detailed rules to cover every specific situation. This leads to listed advantages – but not to consistent application, since there is a high degree of discretion in applying guidelines to different cases.

31.19 The correct answer is: Members do not challenge or criticise

Rationale: Failure to challenge or criticise is not a positive thing, in this context, but a symptom of poor communications: the 'building block' would be developing a climate in which people can speak their minds, constructively. The other options describe positive building blocks in the areas of membership, review and control and objectives. (The terminology of 'building blocks' and 'blockages' is drawn from a model by Woodcock, but it is not essential to know this.)

31.20 The correct answer is: Time available to devote to the role

Rationale: This is a major problem for non-executive directors, because they are likely to have other commitments. You should have had to think through the other options, however. Some of the advantages of non-executive directors are that they offer a comfort factor for third parties such as investors and suppliers; they have a wider perspective and (hopefully) no vested interest; and they have a combination of knowledge/expertise and detachment.

31.21 The correct answers are:

- Using local suppliers
- Minimising energy consumption

Using local suppliers, minimising energy consumption

Rationale: Using local suppliers is part of the government's sustainability strategy, as it develops and preserves local business, employment and communities. Minimising energy consumption conserves resources. The other two options are not directly related to sustainability goals.

31.22 Macro-economics is the study of the aggregated effects of the decisions of individual economic units (such as households or businesses).

Rationale: Macro-economics looks at a complete national economy or economic system: factors such as economic activity and growth, inflation, unemployment and the balance of payments. The other options are pure distractors, drawn from other disciplines.

31.23 The correct answer is: (1), (2) and (3)

Rationale: These are three of the ways that government can directly affect the economic structure, according to Porter. Demand is affected as the government is a major customer.

Governments can affect capacity expansion, for example, by using taxation policies to encourage investment in equipment. Government can introduce regulations and controls within an industry which may affect growth and profits and may therefore affect competition.

31.24 The correct answer is: A reasonable prospect of detecting irregular statements or records

Rationale: It is important for students to be realistic about what the external auditing function can achieve. (In other words, common sense should help to answer this type of question.)

32 Mixed Bank 6

32.1 The correct answer is: Shareholders

Rationale: The shareholders are the owners, as they provide the capital for the business.

32.2 The correct answer is: Analysts such as accountants and workplanners, whose objective is to effect standardisation in the organisation

Rationale: This is the definition of the 'technostructure' in Mintzberg's components of structure.

32.3 The correct answers are:

- Outsourcing production of the product to low-cost countries
- Consolidating purchases of the components and sourcing from a single supplier to reduce sourcing costs

Outsourcing production of the product to low-cost countries, consolidating purchases of the components and sourcing from a single supplier to reduce sourcing costs

Rationale: Secure continuity of supply and quality are Z's priorities. Long-term partnership helps secure both, while having a small number of suppliers avoids the risk of supplier failure.

32.4 The correct answer is: Tactical management

Rationale: This is the definition of tactical management, carried out by middle management. Strategic management is at a higher level of establishing corporate direction and policy: carried out by senior management. Operational management is at a lower level of implementing the tactical plans: carried out by supervisors and operatives.

32.5 Corporate governance is the system by which organisations are directed and controlled by their senior officers.

Rationale: Strategic management is a process which may or may not be carried out in a given organisation. Executive directorship and internal controls are elements of corporate governance.

32.6 The correct answer is: It takes a higher proportion of income in tax as income rises.

Rationale: This is the definition of a progressive tax (such as income tax in general).

The first option is a 'regressive' tax (such as road tax) which is the same for all people.

The second option is a 'proportional tax' (such as Schedule E income tax within a limited range of income).

32.7 The correct answer is: Dismissal because the employee is pregnant

Rationale: The first three are circumstances defined as redundancy.

Dismissal on the grounds of pregnancy is automatically considered to be unfair dismissal.

32.8 The correct answers are:

Ability to maintain and repay loans		FINANCIERS		
Potential social contributions and impacts				PUBLIC
Management stewardship	SHARE-HOLDERS			
Attainment of performance objectives			EMPLOYEES	

Rationale: This should be straightforward if you work through the options.

32.9 The correct answer is: Extranet

Rationale: Researchers may connect to this network via the internet (world wide web), and the university may have an intranet for its own lecturers and students. An extranet, however, is an intranet that is accessible to authorised 'outsiders', using a valid username and password.

32.10 The correct answer is: It maximises the attractiveness of the job and organisation to potential applicants

Rationale: Job advertisements must be positive, but they should also be honest, in order to manage applicants' (and future employees') expectations. The second and fourth options should be obvious. You may have hesitated over the first option, but advertisements should encourage unsuitable applicants to rule themselves out before applying (and wasting the organisation's time).

32.11 The correct answers are:

Recruitment reference checking			DISHON-ESTY
Disciplinary codes	MOTIVATION		
Internal checks and controls		OPPORTU-NITY	

Rationale: Motivation is the incentive to behave dishonestly: one part of this equation is the risks, and whether they are worth the rewards – so strong disciplinary penalties for fraud are a disincentive. Opportunity is having an opening for fraud: internal checks and controls (such as segregation of duties and authorisations) limit those openings. Dishonesty is a pre-disposition or tendency to behave unethically: it needs to be spotted early – ideally before a person joins the organisation!

32.12 The correct answer is: Data management

Rationale: The database concept encourages management to regard data as an organisational resource, which needs to be properly managed. However, there are problems of data security and privacy, due to the potential for unauthorised access and sharing. If the organisation develops its own system from scratch, initial development costs will be high.

32.13 | Hawthorne | Studies is the name given to experimental social research initiated by Elton

Mayo, which identified the influence exercised by social needs and informal groups in the

workplace, and gave rise to the human relations school of management.

Rationale: Hawthorne studies. These were carried out at the Hawthorne Plant of Western Electric. The Ashridge studies are a study in leadership styles (tells, sells, consults, joins). Hofstede's model describes dimensions of difference in national cultures.

32.14 The correct answer is: To monitor PEST factors

Rationale: Political, Economic, Socio-cultural and Technological (PEST) factors are the external factors which may impact on the organisation. SWOT (strengths, weaknesses, opportunities and threats) incorporate data from the environmental scan, by analysing PEST factors that present opportunities and threats: however, the name given to this process is corporate appraisal. The third option would be called competitive intelligence.

32.15 The correct answer is: Financial reporting

Rationale: IASs are standards for financial reporting: the preparation of financial statements and accounts. They are used as bases and benchmarks for companies and national standard-setting systems.

32.16 The correct answer is: Keep informed

Rationale: Local nature appreciation groups would have high interest (due to potential environmental impacts) but relatively low power: because of their high interest, though, they might be able to band together or lobby to increase their power. So a 'keep informed' strategy is appropriate to segment B.

32.17 The correct answer is: A strategy for investigating and dealing with the consequences of suspected or identified fraud

Rationale: Fraud response relates specifically to investigation and damage minimisation (not prevention), including: actions that will be taken to protect the security of records that will be required for identification; protection of vulnerable assets; investigation procedures; and crisis management. Implementing this plan would be the responsibility of a fraud officer.

32.18 The correct answer is: Public services

Rationale: A growing economy is more easily able to provide welfare services without creating a heavy tax burden on the community. Growth has potential adverse effects for employment, where some sections of the population are unable to adapt to demands for new skills. It also has potential adverse effects for the environment, in terms of resource usage, pollution, emissions etc.

32.19 The correct answers are:

- Focuses on people
- Innovates

Focuses on people, innovates

Rationale: The other options are managerial attributes.

32.20 The correct answer is: Deterrence

Rationale: Deterrence is an approach which seeks to minimise threats due to deliberate action, by creating penalties to 'put people off' attempting the action.

Correction is an approach to ensure that vulnerabilities are dealt with when found. Detection is an approach to identifying vulnerabilities and attacks (eg keeping a log of patient records accessed or removed).

Threat avoidance means eliminating a threat (eg by changing the system so no unauthorised access is possible).

32.21 The correct answers are:

Assessment interview		B	
Follow up action			C
Criteria for assessment	A		

Rationale: This should be straightforward if you think systematically through the process.

BPP LEARNING MEDIA

ANSWERS

32.22 The correct answer is: Social

> **Rationale:** In the PEST model, social factors include demographics: the study of population structures and characteristics. Birth and mortality rates affect population numbers, distribution (if they are unequal in different areas) and age structure (lower birth and mortality rates creates an ageing population).

32.23 In the context of rewarding team performance, team-based rewards and bonuses are more effective if individual team members' contributions and work patterns are | interdependent |

> **Rationale:** Interdependence of team members is important, because no-one feels they could earn higher rewards on their own: everyone's contribution is necessary, and everyone 'pulls their weight'.

33 Mixed Bank 7

33.1 The correct answer is: Statutory deductions from pay

> **Rationale:** Non-statutory deductions (such as pension contributions) should be authorised, to prevent money being 'siphoned' off via non-existent deductions. However, statutory deductions are non-discretionary: they cannot not be authorised!

33.2 The correct answers are:

- Expert power
- Negative power

> **Rationale:** The production mixer has expert power, because he has knowledge that is recognised and valued by the rest of the staff. The shop-floor staff exercise negative power: the power to disrupt operations. Neither have position power (organisational authority), nor (as far as we know) personal power, or charisma.

33.3 The correct answers are:

Jemima			PLANT
Frank	MONITOR-EVALUATOR		

> **Rationale:** In Belbin's model, the Plant is the ideas person; the Monitor-Evaluator the discerning critic; and the Team worker the diplomatic relationship-builder.

33.4 The correct answer is: Outsourcing carries commercial and reputational risks.

> **Rationale:** There are several risks associated with outsourcing: being locked in to an unsatisfactory relationship; losing in-house assets and knowledge; sharing confidential information; and 'reputational' risk (if the supplier gives poor service, or is found to be unethical in its practices, say). The other statements are untrue: an organisation should **not** outsource its 'core competences' (areas of unique and non-replicable competitive advantage); outsourcing often creates economies of scale (taking advantage of the larger dedicated resources of the contractor); and outsourcing still incurs significant costs, including internal costs of managing the relationship.

33.5 The correct answer is: Process theory

> **Rationale:** Process theories explore the process by which individuals come to value, select and explore goals: in other words, **how** people become motivated. Content theories (including Maslow's hierarchy of needs and Herzberg's two-factor theory) explore the needs that motivate people to act in certain ways: in other words, **what** motivates people.

33.6 The correct answer is: Introducing reporting by exception

> **Rationale:** Reporting by exception means only reporting to managers when there is a deviation from plan. The first and third options would increase information flow. The fourth

option would not address the problem: information overload is about excessive complexity as well as volume!

33.7   The correct answer is: The balance in a manager's leadership style between concern for the task and concern for people and relationships

Rationale: This is straightforward, if you recall the managerial grid. It does not represent a continuum because it assumes that the two things are compatible: they can both be high or low at the same time. The grid can be used in appraisal, to focus attention on the manager's approach, but does not indicate 'success' or effectiveness.

33.8   The correct answers are:

- Closed

- Probing

Closed, probing

Rationale: Closed questions pin the candidate down to either/or options. Probing questions push for an answer where a candidate is being vague. Open questions wouldn't work here, because they give the candidate space to answer in any way (s)he wishes. You may have hesitated over leading questions, but these would encourage the candidate to give a **particular** reply, suggested by the interviewer – not to pin down what the **candidate** meant.

33.9   The correct answer is: Instrumental orientation

Rationale: An instrumental orientation accounts for why some people take jobs offering high monetary rewards rather than intrinsic interest or job satisfaction (up to a certain point). Job enrichment is a form of job design which more or less assumes the **opposite**: that people seek intrinsic satisfactions in work itself. Theory Y is irrelevant, relating to McGregor's Theory X and Theory Y.

33.10   The correct answer is: An approach to appraisal interviewing

Rationale: 'Tell and listen' is one of Maier's three approaches to appraisal interviewing: 'tell and sell' and 'problem-solving' are the other two approaches.

33.11   The correct answer is: A gap between current performance and required performance is a learning gap which requires training.

Rationale: A gap between current 'competence' and required 'competence' may be amenable to learning or training. A gap between current 'performance' and required 'performance', however, may be caused by other problems to do with supervision, systems, resources, motivation and other factors. The other options are true.

33.12   The correct answers are:

- Award of a departmental prize for your performance

- Receiving praise on an achievement from your work team

Rationale: Esteem needs are for recognition and respect from others. The other options relate to self-actualisation and social need.

33.13   The correct answer is: Dorming

Rationale: This is the definition of dorming. Forming is a 'getting to know each other' stage; norming the development of agreed ways of behaving; and storming a stage of conflict and testing.

33.14   The correct answer is: 1(i), 2(v), 3(ii), 4(iv), 5(iii)

Rationale: This should be straightforward, if you work through the options carefully. A person specification is prepared **from** a job description. Testing follows interviewing, as a more rigorous form of selection. Reference checking comes last, as it only applies to candidates who are potentially going to be offered a job.

BPP
LEARNING
MEDIA

33.15 One of the distinctions between coaching and mentoring is that a ⎡mentor⎤ is not usually

the immediate superior of the person being helped.

Rationale: A coach is often the trainee's immediate superior: indeed, coaching is accepted as a style of management/leadership. A mentor is **not** usually the immediate superior of the protégé, so that there can be open, confidential discussion of work and non-work issues.

33.16 The correct answer is: Cognitive psychology

Rationale: Cognitive psychology argues that the human mind uses feedback information on the results of past behaviour to make rational decisions about whether to maintain successful behaviours or modify unsuccessful behaviours, according to the outcomes we want. Behaviourist psychology focuses on the relationship between stimuli and responses: we are 'conditioned' to respond in ways that are repeatedly positively reinforced (rewarded) and to avoid behaviours that are repeatedly negatively reinforced (punished). The third option is not a learning theory, and the fourth is a particular learning model (by Honey & Mumford) not relevant here.

33.17 The correct answers are:

- The auditor's mandatory authority
- The auditor's own professionalism

The auditor's mandatory authority, the auditor's own professionalism

Rationale: The third element in the auditor's independence is the responsibility structure – which does **not** mean freedom from accountability. The internal auditor is accountable to the highest executive level in the organisation (preferably the audit committee of the board of directors). The auditor's involvement in the activities being appraised is the opposite of independence: internal auditors should not install new procedures or systems, or engage in activities, which they will later have to appraise – as this might (or might be seen to) compromise their independence.

33.18 The correct answer is: The organisation is looking to introduce a culture of innovation for the first time

Rationale: Cultural change is a good reason to seek 'new blood' in management, rather than promote people who are used to thinking in familiar ways. The first and third options argue for internal promotion as a matter of policy and staff retention and as a way of preserving culture.

33.19 The correct answer is: Level of risk for acquiring new skills

Rationale: Off-the-job training allows people to make mistakes in learning, without the costs and consequences of making the same mistakes on the job. However, formal courses may **not** always be directly relevant to the circumstances of the job and workplace, and it may not be easy to 'transfer learning' from the classroom to the job, for various reasons. Meanwhile, formal courses take people away from work. You could think of the other options as advantages of on-the-job training.

33.20 ⎡Victimisation⎤ occurs when a person is penalised for giving information or taking action is

pursuit of a claim of discrimination.

Rationale: Remember that direct discrimination is less favourable treatment of a protected group. Indirect discrimination is when requirements cannot be justified on non-discriminatory grounds.

33.21 The correct answer is: Monitoring numbers and performance of ethnic minority staff

Rationale: This is likely to be a sensitive issue. How do you identify job applicants' ethnic origins without potentially causing offence or suspicion? How do you apply particular performance monitoring to ethnic minority staff without seeming to discriminate? All the other options are much more straightforward!

33.22 The correct answer is: Considering whether directors act on internal audit information

Rationale: The first three options are internal checks to an internal control system. External auditors will need to check that directors and management act on any internal audit recommendations.

33.23 The correct answer is: 1(iii), 2(iv), 3(ii), 4(v), 5(i)

Rationale: The lowest level is how trainees feel about the training: this is an inexact measure of results. Level 2 is trainee learning, measuring what the trainees have learned (what they know or can do at the end of the course, compared to pre-training tests): the likely focus of trainers. Level 3 is changes in job behaviour, which measures whether learning has been **applied** successfully to the job: the likely focus of departmental managers. Level 4 is whether these changes result in measurable performance gains for the organisation: the likely focus of senior management's cost-benefit analysis of training. Level 5 (which many organisations never reach) is evaluating impacts on 'wider' goals such as greater social responsibility.

33.24 The correct answers are:

- Card entry systems
- Personal identification numbers

Card entry systems, personal identification numbers

Rationale: Physical access controls are basically 'lock and key' systems – basic though that may sound! Card entry and PIN systems are ways of identifying yourself (by swipe card and keypad entry respectively) in order to gain authorised entry to an area or storage device. Logical access systems are non-physical access controls, involving password-protected access to data in the system. Back-ups are not access controls at all: they are integrity and/or contingency controls.

33.25 The correct answer is: False

Rationale: Connected stakeholders include shareholders, customers, suppliers and financiers. Don't confuse this with internal stakeholders which include employees and management.

Mock Exams

Foundation in Accountancy/ACCA

Business Technology (BT/FBT)

Mock Exam 1

Specimen Exam

Questions	
Time allowed	2 hours
This exam is divided into two sections: Section A – ALL 46 questions are compulsory and MUST be attempted Section B – ALL SIX questions are compulsory and MUST be attempted	

DO NOT OPEN THIS EXAM UNTIL YOU ARE READY TO START UNDER EXAMINATION CONDITIONS

Section A

ALL 46 questions are compulsory and MUST be attempted

1 The major purpose of the International Accounting Standards Board (IASB) is to ensure consistency in _____ _____.

Required

Which two words complete the sentence above?

○ Financial control

○ Corporate reporting

○ External auditing

(1 mark)

2 The leadership style that least acknowledges the contribution that subordinates have to make is:

○ Authoritarian

○ Autocratic

○ Assertive

(1 mark)

3 In relation to the management of conflict, which of the following approaches will maximise the prospect of consensus?

○ Acceptance

○ Negotiation

○ Avoidance

○ Assertiveness

(2 marks)

4 Darragh has been appointed to the management team of a professional football club.

His role includes coaching, mentoring and counselling young players who have just signed contracts with the club for the first time.

Required

Will the following activities be related to his role as coach, mentor or counsellor?

	Coaching	Mentoring	Counselling
Identifying each player's key skills and encouraging them to develop new skills	○	○	○
Helping the players to anticipate opponents' reactions	○	○	○
Advising the players on addressing personal issues, such as managing their finances	○	○	○
Helping the young players to settle in during their first week	○	○	○

(2 marks)

5   In order to ensure that the policies of an organisation are consistent with the public interest, on which of the following should the directors of a company focus?

○   The long-term welfare of the shareholders

○   Compliance with legal requirements and codes of governance

○   The collective well-being of stakeholders

(1 mark)

6   Martin is an experienced and fully trained shipbuilder, based in a western European city. Due to significant economic change in supply and demand conditions for shipbuilding in Martin's own country, the shipyard he worked for has closed and he was made redundant. There was no other local demand for his skills within his own region and he would have to move to another country to obtain a similar employment, and could only find similar work locally through undertaking at least a year's retraining in a related engineering field.

Required

Which of the following describes the type of unemployment that Martin has been affected by?

○   Structural unemployment

○   Cyclical unemployment

○   Frictional unemployment

○   Marginal unemployment

(2 marks)

7   Which of the following is the main function of marketing?

○   To maximise sales volume

○   To identify and anticipate customer needs

○   To persuade potential consumers to convert latent demand into expenditure

○   To identify suitable outlets for goods and services supplied

(2 marks)

8   Which **TWO** of the following are the consequences of a listed company failing to file its accounts?

☐   Investigation of its financial affairs by a government department or agency

☐   Imposition of a fine by the government's company registration body

☐   Refusal of the external auditor to sign the financial accounts

☐   Suspension of dealings in securities by the stock exchange

(2 marks)

9   The overall average age of a population in a country is directly dependent on two demographic factors: Birth rate and death rate.

Required

Assuming equal rates of change, will each of the following lead to an overall ageing of the population?

	Yes	No
Increasing death rate	○	○
Decreasing birth rate	○	○

(2 marks)

10   Gils is conducting an appraisal interview with his assistant Jill. He initially feeds back to Jill areas of strengths and weaknesses of performance but then invites Jill to talk about the job, her aspirations, expectations and problems.

He adopts a non-judgemental approach and offers suggestions and guidance.

Required

This is an example of which approach to performance appraisal?

O Tell and sell approach

O Tell and listen approach

O Problem solving approach

O 360 degree approach

(2 marks)

11 What is the primary responsibility of the external auditor?

O To verify all the financial transactions and supporting documentation of the client

O To ensure that the client's financial statements are reasonably accurate and free from bias

O To report all financial irregularities to the shareholders of the client

O To ensure that all the client's financial statements are prepared and submitted to the relevant authorities on time

(2 marks)

12 Which **TWO** of the following are examples of tactical information?

☐ Annual forecasts of revenues and costs for a department

☐ Product development plans for the next 2 – 3 years

☐ Targets agreed by key managers at their performance appraisal interviews

(1 mark)

13 Wasim is the Customer Services Manager in a large leisure park.

The forthcoming weekend is going to be the busiest of the year, as it is a public holiday.

Wasim has to cope with several absentees, leaving him short-staffed in public areas of the park.

His manager has told him that he expects him to catch up with some administrative reports that were due last week. Wasim also has to arrange for six new staff to be trained, who will be arriving imminently.

Required

In order to manage his workload most effectively, what should Wasim do?

O Prioritise the tasks in relation to the most important business outcomes

O Deal with the reports that the manager insists be prepared

O Train the new recruits

O Carry out some of the work that the absentees would normally do

(2 marks)

14 In order to discharge their duties ethically, finance directors must ensure that the information published by their organisations provides a complete and precise view of the position of the business, without concealing negative aspects that may distort the reader's perception of its position.

Required

This duty describes which of the following ethical principles?

O Probity

O Honesty

O Independence

O Objectivity

(2 marks)

15 Which of the following is a purpose of the International Federation of Accountants?

    ○ Agreement of legally binding financial reporting standards across all member accountancy organisations

    ○ Prevention of international financial crimes, such as money laundering and insider dealing

    ○ Promotion of ethical standards in all member organisations

    ○ Development of universally applicable detailed rules to deter inappropriate behaviours

                  (2 marks)

16 The following government policies can be used to expand or slow down economic activity.

Required

Are each of the following consistent with a government's policy objective to expand the level of economic activity?

	Yes	No
An increase in taxation	○	○
An increase in public expenditure	○	○

                   (2 marks)

17 Neill works as the procurement manager of JL Company, a large services company.

Required

Information provided by Neill is most relevant to which of the following elements of the marketing mix?

    ○ Physical evidence

    ○ Distribution (or place)

    ○ Price

    ○ Processes

                   (2 marks)

18 In relation to employee selection, which type of testing assesses the depth of knowledge of a candidate and the candidate's ability to apply that knowledge?

    ○ Intelligence testing

    ○ Competence testing

    ○ Psychometric testing

                   (1 mark)

19 Malachi has been asked by his manager to analyse the financial accounts of ABC Company, which is bidding for a contract offered by Malachi's company in the near future. The two financial statements which he will be using as his sources are the statement of financial position and the statement of profit or loss.

Required

From which financial statements will Malachi obtain the following information?

	Statement of financial position	Statement of profit or loss
The equity of the company	○	○
Operating costs as a percentage of turnover	○	○

	Statement of financial position	Statement of profit or loss
Long-term borrowings	O	O
Liquidity	O	O

(2 marks)

20 Linh owns a busy restaurant. She has had complaints from regular customers about diners failing to control their noisy and unruly children, which is spoiling their dining experiences.

Required

Which of the following courses of action would be regarded as a pluralist solution to this problem?

O Setting aside a separate section of the restaurant for families with children

O Not accepting bookings from families with children

O Advising customers that the restaurant is a family restaurant before they book

O Taking no action, assuming that those who complain will always be a minority   (2 marks)

21 Which of the following is data protection legislation primarily designed to protect?

O All private individuals and corporate entities on whom only regulated data is held

O All private individuals on whom only regulated data is held

O All private individuals on whom any data is held

(1 mark)

22 Which of the following is an example of the system used by a company to record sales and purchases?

O A transaction processing system

O A management information system

O An office automation system

O A decision support system   (2 marks)

23 Which **TWO** of the following are examples of connected stakeholders?

☐ Manager

☐ Customer

☐ Executive Director

☐ Supplier   (2 marks)

24 In an economic environment of high price inflation, those who owe money will gain and those who are owed money will lose.

Required

Is this statement true or false?

O True

O False

(1 mark)

25 Role playing exercises using video recording and playback would be most effective for which type of training?

○ Development of selling skills

○ Regulation and compliance

○ Dissemination of technical knowledge

○ Introduction of new processes or procedures

(2 marks)

26 Renata has attended a leadership development course in which she experienced a self-analysis exercise using the Blake and Mouton managerial grid. The course leader informed her that the results suggested that Renata demonstrated a 9·1 leadership style.

Required

Which **TWO** conclusions may be drawn in relation to Renata's leadership style?

☐ She maximises the involvement of her team

☐ She demonstrates little concern for people in the team

☐ She balances the needs of the team with the need to complete the task

☐ She is highly focused on achieving the objectives of the team

(2 marks)

27 The implementation of a budgetary control system in a large organisation would be the responsibility of the internal auditor.

Required

Is this statement true or false?

○ True

○ False

(1 mark)

28 Which **TWO** of the following are roles of an external auditor?

☐ Confirming that the financial accounts present a true and fair view

☐ Confirming that there are appropriate policies for preventing and detecting fraud

☐ Confirming that the financial accounts have been prepared in accordance with legal requirements

(1 mark)

29 Professional accountants must demonstrate integrity at all times.

Required

Which of the following describes the meaning of integrity?

○ Applying consistently high moral values

○ Maintaining a neutral and unbiased view on all business decisions

○ Provide timely and accurate information free from errors

(1 mark)

30 Which **TWO** of the following are characteristics of a public limited company but not a co-operative?

☐ Maximising the excess of income over expenditure not a primary objective

☐ Members can vote according to the number of shares owned

☐ Shares can be bought and sold through personal transactions of the members

☐ All members are invited to attend the annual general meeting and participate in decisions at the meeting

(2 marks)

31 A company has advertised for staff who must be at least 1·88 metres tall and have been in continuous full-time employment for at least five years.

Required

Which of the following is the legal term for this practice?

O Direct discrimination

O Indirect discrimination

O Victimisation

O Implied discrimination

(2 marks)

32 Which of the following statements is correct in relation to monetary rewards in accordance with Herzberg's two-factor theory?

O Pay increases are a powerful long-term motivator

O Inadequate monetary rewards are a powerful dissatisfier

O Monetary rewards are more important than non-monetary rewards

O Pay can never be used as a motivator

(2 marks)

33 In a higher education teaching organisation an academic faculty is organised into courses and departments, where teaching staff report both to course programme managers and to subject specialists, depending on which course they teach and upon their particular subject specialism.

Required

According to Charles Handy's four cultural stereotypes, which of the following describes the above type of organisational structure?

O Role

O Task

O Power

O Person

(2 marks)

34 Which pattern of communication is the quickest way to send a message?

O The circle

O The chain

O The Y

O The wheel

(2 marks)

35 Kelly is discussing a business problem with Pawel on the telephone.

Required

Who will be involved in 'encoding' the communication that takes place?

O Kelly

O Pawel

O Kelly and Pawel

(1 mark)

36 Which of the following types of new legislation would provide greater employment opportunities in large companies?

○ New laws on health and safety

○ New laws to prevent discrimination in the workplace

○ New laws making it more difficult to dismiss employees unfairly

○ New laws on higher compensation for employer breaches of employment contracts

(2 marks)

37 What is the responsibility of a Public Oversight Board?

○ The establishment of detailed rules on internal audit procedures

○ The commissioning of financial reporting standards

○ The creation of legislation relating to accounting standards

○ The monitoring and enforcement of legal and compliance standards

(2 marks)

38 Adrian is the manager of a call centre.

Consultants have advised him that by reorganising his teams to complete highly specific tasks the call centre will be able to increase the throughput of work significantly, as well as increasing the number of sales calls made to the public.

The reorganisation proposals are unpopular with many workers, who feel that their jobs will become tedious and repetitive.

Required

The proposal to reorganise the work of the call centre utilises principles put forward by which school of management thought?

○ The administrative school

○ The empirical school

○ The scientific school

(1 mark)

39 The aggregate level of demand in the economy is made up of government expenditure, _____, _____ and net gains from international trade.

Required

Which **TWO** of the following correctly complete the sentence above?

☐ Savings

☐ Taxation

☐ Investment

☐ Consumption

(2 marks)

40 In the context of marketing, the 'four Ps' are price, promotion, _____ and _____.

Required

Which **TWO** words correctly complete the above sentence?

☐ Product

☐ Positioning

☐ Place

(1 mark)

41 Which of the following is an advantage of decentralisation?

○ Risk reduction in relation to operational decision-making

○ More accountability at lower levels

○ Consistency of decision-making across the organisation

(1 mark)

42 FKT Company is considering the introduction of a code of ethics following media criticism of its selling practices.

Required

Which of the following is most important when deciding on the content of the proposed code?

○ The minimum acceptable standards of behaviour and conduct of employees

○ The legal requirements affecting the sales of core products and services

○ The main issues of concern to customers who have made complaints

○ The generally accepted standards by other companies operating in the same sector

(2 marks)

43 Ahmed is preparing his personal development plan. He is concerned about how others see him.

Required

In order to analyse this aspect of his personal development plan further, Ahmed should consider which **TWO** of the following?

☐ Strengths

☐ Opportunities

☐ Weaknesses

(1 mark)

44 Jackie leads an established team of six. In the last month, two have left to pursue alternative jobs and one has commenced maternity leave. Three new staff members have joined Jackie's team.

Required

Which of Tuckman's group stages will now occur?

○ Norming

○ Forming

○ Performing

○ Storming

(2 marks)

45 In the context of fraud, 'teeming and lading' is likely to occur in which area of operation?

○ Sales

○ Quality control

○ Advertising and promotion

○ Despatch

(2 marks)

46 Which of the following statements is true in relation to the average revenue function of a business in a perfect market?

○ It is diagonal

○ It is horizontal

○ It is vertical

(1 mark)

Section B

ALL SIX questions are compulsory and MUST be attempted

47   Here are four short references to the function of management:

(1)   There are essentially five functions of management that apply to any organisation.

(2)   Individual and group behaviour at work is a major factor in productivity.

(3)   Management is the development of a true science of work.

(4)   The manager of a business has one basic function – economic performance.

Required

(a)   Select the correct reference for each writer.

Peter Drucker	▼
Elton Mayo	▼
Henry Mintzberg	▼
F W Taylor	▼

Pull down list

- None of the references
- Reference A
- Reference B
- Reference C
- Reference D

(2 marks)

(b)   From the list below identify **TWO** of Henri Fayol's functions of management.

☐   Planning

☐   Organising

☐   Managing

☐   Monitoring

☐   Motivating

(2 marks)

(Total = 4 marks)

---

48   (a)   XYZ company installed a computer system to handle its main accounting functions including accounts receivable, accounts payable and payroll.

Management have a number of concerns about access to the system and are considering a number of controls to overcome these concerns.

Required

Is each of the following a general control or an application control?

	General Control	Application Control
Locking the computer room to prevent access to non-employees.	○	○
Limiting access to the payroll system by making it password protected.	○	○
Taking backup of data files each evening and holding backup copies off-premises.	○	○
Providing basic IT training to the entire staff to prevent errors in using the system.	○	○

(2 marks)

(b) The company has considerable cash collections on a regular basis. The cashier receives the cash, records it and then banks it at the end of each day. Since a single person is responsible for access to cash, the financial director is concerned that fraud and error may occur in cash handling and recording. He proposes use of appropriate internal controls to prevent any such errors or misappropriations.

Required

The following sentences describe internal controls which could be used to prevent fraud and errors. Select the correct internal control to complete each sentence.

Fraud and errors in handling cash can be prevented through [▼] since no one individual could record and process a complete transaction.

Even if such a measure were introduced, the possibility exists that staff could act together to perpetrate fraud and bypass this control.

This can be prevented through [▼] as it would ensure awareness of the heavy sanctions to be imposed in cases of dishonesty.

Pull down list

- Authorisation limits
- Induction and training
- Internal audit
- Segregation of duties

(2 marks)

(Total = 4 marks)

---

49 There are a number of ways of developing staff on a one-to-one basis within organisations. Each has its own strengths and weaknesses and is appropriate in different work situations.

Required

(a) Examples of types of development include coaching, mentoring, counselling and appraising. For each type of development below, which work situation is most appropriate?

	Coaching	Mentoring	Counselling	Appraising
An interview to help another person to identify and work through a problem.	○	○	○	○
A long term relationship in which a more experienced person encourages an individual's personal and career development.	○	○	○	○
An approach whereby a trainee is put under the guidance of an experienced employee who shows the trainee how to perform tasks.	○	○	○	○
An interview, the aim of which is to review performance and identify training and development needs.	○	○	○	○

(2 marks)

(b) An organisation uses mentoring as a form of one-to-one personal development. Which **TWO** of the following are benefits of this approach?

☐ Determine remuneration

☐ Decide promotions

☐ Career and personal development

☐ Resolve a grievance

☐ Demonstrating how to perform

☐ Using experienced staff for training

☐ Providing a role model for an employee

(2 marks)

(Total = 4 marks)

50 Sport-4-Kidz is a charitable organisation that operates a sports centre in a large city.

The land on which the playing fields and facilities are located is held on behalf of the charity by Donna and Dietmar, the two trustees. Donna and Dietmar simply hold the land on behalf of Sport-4-Kidz and play no role in running the charity. They are rarely contacted by the management of the charity. However, they are the only people who are able to enter into contracts in relation to the land and its use.

Sport-4-Kidz is managed and operated by a management committee. The committee has decided on a major expansion of facilities by building a new sports hall. The committee has the power to legally bind the charity in all matters other than the land. Their decisions are overseen by the government charity regulator, which generally sanctions the charity's decisions except in relation to financial reporting.

The management committee is negotiating with four building companies.

The proposed expansion of the facilities has angered the local residents, many of whom are concerned about heavy building site traffic and the danger posed to their children. Many believe that the design of the new sports hall is ugly and insensitive. Three well-respected local politicians serve on the residents' committee.

Required

(a) For each of the following, indicate whether they are internal, connected or external stakeholders.

	Internal	External	Connected
Donna and Dietmar	○	○	○
Local residents	○	○	○
Members of the management committee	○	○	○
The four building companies	○	○	○

(2 marks)

(b) Complete the following table about Sport-4-Kidz stakeholders, with reference to Mendelow's grid.

Stakeholder	Stakeholder category	Communication strategy
Building companies	(1) ▼	(2) ▼
Local residents	(1) ▼	(2) ▼

Pull down list 1

- High power, High interest
- High power, Low interest
- Low power, High interest
- Low power, Low interest

Pull down list 2

- Kept informed
- Kept satisfied
- Treated as key player

(2 marks)

(Total = 4 marks)

51   (a) Select **FOUR** words which are fundamental principles of ethical behaviour from the IFAC (IESBA) and ACCA codes of ethics.

- ☐ Integrity
- ☐ Trustworthiness
- ☐ Professional behaviour
- ☐ Respectfulness
- ☐ Honesty
- ☐ Expertise
- ☐ Confidentiality
- ☐ Objectivity

(2 marks)

(b) Select **FOUR** factors in the list below, which distinguish a profession from an occupation.

☐ Acting in the public interest

☐ Highly skilled

☐ Ethical codes of conduct

☐ Governance by association

☐ Highly valued services

☐ Training requirement

☐ Process of certification

☐ Qualification by examination

(2 marks)

(Total = 4 marks)

---

52   Company A is an accountancy professional body which has a tall structure and a high level of centralisation. The span of control is very narrow.

Subordinates have minimal latitude for self-determination or to influence decision-making and mainly concentrate on carrying out highly prescribed and defined roles.

Company B is a financial services company which gives a wide ranging role to its traders and promotes cultural values such as assertiveness, risk appetite, and encourages a high degree of competition between employees.

The employees are usually young and unmarried and work and socialise together for long hours at a frantic pace.

Company C is a research and development company where the business is divisionalised by product. Staff work very flexibly and often need to communicate laterally to achieve objectives through ad hoc projects and collaboration.

There are no formal rules about reporting structures, or about set starting or finishing times. Staff are rewarded on the basis of creativity and innovation.

Company D is a family company which is highly controlled by the owners and the CEO is the main shareholder.

There is a very low staff turnover, but employees are expected to be very loyal to the company and are often required to work long hours and carry out tasks outside their normal range of duties.

Relationships between employees and managers are very informal and close, and the rights of employees and their overall interests are strongly defended by the owners when challenged.

Required

For each of the four companies above, select the cultural dimension concerned and the level at which the company is demonstrating this cultural dimension.

	Dimension	Level
Company A	(1) ▼	(2) ▼
Company B	(1) ▼	(2) ▼
Company C	(1) ▼	(2) ▼
Company D	(1) ▼	(2) ▼

Pull down list 1

- Individualism
- Masculinity
- Power distance
- Uncertainty avoidance

Pull down list 2

- High
- Low

(Total = 4 marks)

Answers

DO NOT TURN THIS PAGE UNTIL YOU HAVE
COMPLETED THE MOCK EXAM

Section A

1   The correct answer is: Corporate reporting

The IASB seeks to promote consistency in corporate reporting by creating internationally accepted financial reporting standards.

2   The correct answer is: Autocratic

This is the least participative of the styles in the Ashridge model.

3   The correct answer is: Negotiation

Negotiation gives the best opportunity for the two sides in a conflict to converge their positions. The other options either involve backing down, forcing a position, potentially increasing conflict, or leaving the issue unresolved.

4   The correct answers are:

- Identifying each player's key skills and encouraging them to develop new skills - **Coaching**
- Helping the players to anticipate opponents' reactions - **Coaching**
- Advising the players on addressing personal issues, such as managing their finances - **Counselling**
- Helping the young players to settle in during their first week - **Mentoring**

Mentors usually help staff on broader work related development, including orientation and induction.

Coaches work on developing specific skills of the job itself, while counsellors work with people on a personal level, perhaps if they are having non-work related or emotional problems.

5   The correct answer is: The collective well-being of stakeholders

By considering the collective well-being of all stakeholders an organisation will make decisions that are in the public interest.

6   The correct answer is: Structural unemployment

Because of the particular circumstances of the scenario where someone is made redundant from an industry in decline where skills cannot be easily transferred, where re-training might take a long time or where work is not available in the short term within a reasonable geographic proximity, this is classed as structural unemployment.

7   The correct answer is: To identify and anticipate customer needs

The basic principle that underlies marketing is that it is a management process that identifies and anticipates customer needs.

The other distracters in the question refer to specific activities undertaken by a sales or promotion function.

8   The correct answers are:

- Imposition of a fine by the government's company registration body
- Suspension of dealings in securities by the stock exchange

The normal sanctions in such a case is that fines are imposed on companies by the registration body of the company and, where listed, the company may be delisted by the stock exchange authorities.

Although the option wasn't included, sanctions against responsible directors may also be imposed.

9   The correct answers are:

- Increasing death rate - **Yes**
- Decreasing birth rate - **No**

The ageing population trend is caused by a decreasing birth rate and a decreasing mortality rate.

10   The correct answer is: Tell and listen approach

The 'tell and listen' approach encourages input from the individual, promoting participation in the process by the appraisee.

11   The correct answer is: To ensure that the client's financial statements are reasonably accurate and free from bias

The external auditor has to ensure that the financial statements of the organisation truly reflect the activities of the business in the relevant accounting period. This assessment should be independent and therefore free from subjectivity on the part of the management of the client organisation.

12   The correct answers are:

- Annual forecasts of revenues and costs for a department
- Targets agreed by key managers at their performance appraisal interviews

Tactical information is medium term in nature and so does not include the long term product development plans, but does include annual forecasts and targets from performance appraisals.

13   The correct answer is: Prioritise the tasks in relation to the most important business outcomes

An employee with a range of tasks or objectives to achieve and pressures to achieve them to set deadlines, should always prioritise tasks in accordance to business importance. Deciding on other criteria such as pressure applied by colleagues, whether someone is absent or not or simply because a task is urgent may damage wider business objectives.

14   The correct answer is: Objectivity

A professional accountant acting in accordance with the fundamental ethical principles is demonstrating objectivity when they give a complete and precise view, which by implication means that negative aspects should not be concealed or positive aspects accentuated.

15   The correct answer is: Promotion of ethical standards in all member organisations

IFAC has no legal powers against businesses, nor does it set financial reporting standards. It is an accounting association member body which promotes educational and ethical standards of behaviour amongst its member bodies, through a code of ethics and behaviour, but does not prescribe detailed rules on this.

16   The correct answers are:

- An increase in taxation - **No**
- An increase in public expenditure - **Yes**

Increasing taxation leaves individuals with less disposable income for expenditure within the economy thereby slowing economic activity. The same effect is caused by a reduction in government expenditure. Therefore economic activity can be stimulated by reducing taxation and increasing government expenditure.

17   The correct answer is: Price

Information on purchase costs of finished goods or raw materials is important in establishing the price of a product. In terms of the marketing mix, this information is most relevant to the price element as prices should be set at least to cover cost and give an acceptable level of profit.

18 The correct answer is: Competence testing

Competence testing is most appropriate when testing a specific skill.

19 The correct answers are:

- The equity of the company - **Statement of financial position**
- Operating costs as a percentage of turnover - **Statement of profit or loss**
- Long-term borrowings - **Statement of financial position**
- Liquidity - **Statement of financial position**

These answers correctly match the information required to the particular financial statement in which they are to be found.

20 The correct answer is: Setting aside a separate section of the restaurant for families with children

The pluralist solution is to cater for the needs of more than one stakeholder group without seriously compromising the interests of any individual group. Therefore setting aside a special area for families with children while having an adults only section would achieve this. The other options involve adversely affecting the rights of one or other group of stakeholders in some way.

21 The correct answer is: All private individuals on whom only regulated data is held

Data protection legislation applies only to regulated data and is designed to protect the interests of private individuals only.

22 The correct answer is: A transaction processing system

A transaction processing system records a company's transactions, such as its sales and purchases.

An office automation system automates certain business processes.

A management information system processes information held by a business to help support management decisions. A decision-support system would *analyse* information.

23 The correct answers are:

- Customer
- Supplier

Customers and suppliers deal closely on a transactional basis with the organisation, but they are not internal stakeholders like managers and executive directors.

24 The correct answer is: True

In a period of high price inflation the value of money is reduced over time, so those who owe money are better off and those who are owed money lose out.

25 The correct answer is: Development of selling skills

Role playing exercises are most effectively used for skills development, including sales training. Other common business applications include effective selection interviewing and performance appraisal interviewing.

26 The correct answers are:

- She demonstrates little concern for people in the team
- She is highly focused on achieving the objectives of the team

ANSWERS

The Blake and Mouton managerial grid enables leadership styles to be categorised on a nine point scale with reference to concern for production and concern for people. Renata is therefore highly concerned with the task and much less interested in her team as individuals.

27 The correct answer is: False

Internal auditors are responsible for monitoring the effectiveness of systems, not implementing them.

28 The correct answers are:

- Confirming that the financial accounts present a true and fair view
- Confirming that the financial accounts have been prepared in accordance with legal requirements

External auditors are responsible for ensuring that the financial statements show a true and fair view and that they comply with legal requirements. Directors are responsible for ensuring that systems are in place to prevent and detect fraud.

29 The correct answer is: Applying consistently high moral values

Integrity is often described as being honest and applying morality to decisions. Accuracy relates to professional competence and being neutral does not indicate morality.

30 The correct answers are:

- Members can vote according to the number of shares owned
- Shares can be bought and sold through personal transactions of the members

Only shareholders have voting power related to the number of shares that they own. Members of a co-operative organisation can vote but will only have one vote. Co-operatives may be owned by members, but ownership stakes cannot be exchanged between members unless the members belong to limited companies.

31 The correct answer is: Indirect discrimination

To discriminate against someone on the grounds of characteristics which are predominately associated with their sex, gender, nationality or religion is illegal.

As women are generally shorter than men, to restrict admission on the basis of height, indirectly discriminates against women. The other options are either direct discrimination, or other illegal and undesirable employment practices.

32 The correct answer is: Inadequate monetary rewards are a powerful dissatisfier

According to Herzberg, money is a hygiene factor (or dissatisfier).

Although it is a powerful short-term motivator, it is questionable whether each individual increase in monetary reward will have a major long-term effect.

According to Herzberg, 'A reward once given becomes a right'.

33 The correct answer is: Task

The task culture is appropriate where organisations can accommodate the flexibility required to adjust management and team structures to address the tasks that must be fulfilled.

This is very common in large consultancy firms.

34 The correct answer is: The wheel

The wheel facilitates transmission of the message directly to all receivers and therefore transmits most quickly.

35 The correct answer is: Kelly and Pawel

In a two-way communication link, both parties need to encode messages and both have to decode them in order for the communication to be understood.

36 The correct answer is: New laws to prevent discrimination in the workplace

Equal opportunity policies widen opportunity and enlarge the potential pool of employees to recruit from. The other options either indirectly or directly reduce the potential for staff turnover and therefore limit the number of job vacancies available at any point in time.

37 The correct answer is: The monitoring and enforcement of legal and compliance standards

The primary aim of a public oversight board is to eliminate or minimise any actual or potential breaches of legislative requirements and to ensure compliance with regulations applicable to organisations within their terms of reference.

38 The correct answer is: The scientific school

Maximising efficiency in production (as in the scenario) is a feature of scientific management.

39 The correct answers are:

- Investment
- Consumption

The components of effective demand in the economy are consumer spending, investment by enterprises, central and local government expenditure and the net gains from international trade.

40 The correct answers are:

- Product
- Place

The four Ps are Price, Promotion, Product and Place.

41 The correct answer is: More accountability at lower levels

Decentralisation involves having greater authority and power at lower levels of the organisation and accountability goes with this power.

42 The correct answer is: The minimum acceptable standards of behaviour and conduct of employees

Compliance with legal requirements may not eliminate unethical behaviour. The issues of concern to those who complain may not be fully representative of issues of concern to customers in general.

Other companies in the sector may not be concerned about ethical behaviour.

43 The correct answers are:

- Strengths
- Weaknesses

Using SWOT analysis, the strengths and weaknesses are the relevant points as these are internal to the individual and these are the factors that would influence the opinions of others.

44 The correct answer is: Forming

As new members have just joined the group, essentially the group is reforming which is the start of a new group development process.

The other options are all later stages in group development as identified by Tuckman.

BPP
LEARNING
MEDIA

ANSWERS

45 The correct answer is: Sales

Teeming and lading involves the theft of cash and is a type of fraud that is carried out by manipulating transactions. There would be most potential for this fraud within the sales department where cash may be received and remitted.

46 The correct answer is: It is horizontal

The demand curve in a perfect market is horizontal, because they can sell as much as they want at the prevailing market price and nothing at all at a higher price.

Section B

47 (a) Peter Drucker | Reference D |

Elton Mayo | Reference B |

Henry Mintzberg | None of the references |

F W Taylor | Reference C |

Drucker emphasised the economic objective of managers in business.

Mayo investigated individual and group behaviour at work, as a factor in productivity.

Mintzberg described managerial roles, arguing that management is a disjointed, non-systematic activity.

Taylor pioneered the scientific management movement and sought the most efficient methods.

(b) The correct answers are:

- Planning
- Organising

Fayol classified five functions of management: Planning, Organising, Commanding, Co-ordinating and Controlling.

48 (a) The correct answers are:

- Locking the computer room to prevent access to non-employees. - **General Control**
- Limiting access to the payroll system by making it password protected. - **General Control**
- Taking backup of data files each evening and holding backup copies off-premises. - **General Control**
- Providing basic IT training to the entire staff to prevent errors in using the system. - **Application Control**

General controls relate to the environment in which the application is operated.

Application controls are controls that prevent, detect and correct errors.

(b) Fraud and errors in handling cash can be prevented through | Segregation of duties | since no one individual could record and process a complete transaction.

Even if such a measure were introduced, the possibility exists that staff could act together to perpetrate fraud and bypass this control.

This can be prevented through | Induction and training | as it would ensure awareness of the heavy sanctions to be imposed in cases of dishonesty.

Segregation of duties would prevent one individual recording and processing a complete transaction.

Induction and training would make staff aware of sanctions in cases of dishonesty.

49 (a) The correct answers are:

- An interview to help another person to identify and work through a problem. - **Counselling**
- A long term relationship in which a more experienced person encourages an individual's personal and career development. - **Mentoring**
- An approach whereby a trainee is put under the guidance of an experienced employee who shows the trainee how to perform tasks. - **Coaching**
- An interview, the aim of which is to review performance and identify training and development needs. - **Appraising**

Coaching involves a trainee being put under the guidance of an experienced employee.

Mentoring is a long-term relationship where a more experienced person encourages career and personal development.

Counselling is an interpersonal interview to help an individual identify and work through a problem.

Appraisals are part of performance management and can be used to establish areas for improvement and training and development needs.

(b) The correct answers are:

- Career and personal development
- Providing a role model for an employee

Mentoring is a long-term relationship where a more experienced person encourages career and personal development and can also be a role model.

50 (a) The correct answers are:

- Donna and Dietmar - **Connected**
- Local residents - **Internal**
- Members of the management committee - **Connected**
- The four building companies - **External**

Donna and Dietmar are connected stakeholders as they are trustees of the charity.

The management committee are internal to the charity as they can legally bind the charity.

The building companies are in negotiation with the management committee and therefore are connected stakeholders.

Local residents will always be external stakeholders.

(b)

Stakeholder	Stakeholder category	Communication strategy
Building companies	Low power, High interest	Kept informed
Local residents	High power, High interest	Treated as key player

Residents have high interest due to the anticipated effects of the development, but due to the involvement of the local politicians they also have high power.

Stakeholders with high power and high interest should be treated as key players.

The building companies have high interest in the decision to award the building contract.

Stakeholders with low power and high interest should be kept informed.

51 (a) The correct answers are:

- Integrity
- Professional behaviour
- Confidentiality
- Objectivity

The fundamental principles are Integrity, Confidentiality, Objectivity, Professional behaviour and Professional competence and due care.

(b) The correct answers are:

- Acting in the public interest
- Ethical codes of conduct

- Governance by association
- Process of certification

These qualities distinguish a profession from an occupation.

	Dimension	Level
Company A	Power distance	High
Company B	Masculinity	High
Company C	Uncertainty avoidance	Low
Company D	Individualism	Low

High power distance cultures accept greater centralisation, a top-down chain of command and closer supervision.

High masculinity cultures clearly differentiate gender roles. Masculine values of assertiveness, competition, decisiveness and material success are dominant.

Low uncertainty avoidance cultures respect flexibility and creativity. They have less task structure and written rules. There is more tolerance of risk, dissent, conflict and deviation from norms.

Low individualism cultures emphasise interdependence, reciprocal obligation and social acceptability. The organisation is seen as a family.

Foundation in Accountancy/ACCA

Business Technology (BT/FBT)

Mock Exam 2

Questions	
Time allowed	2 hours
This exam is divided into two sections: Section A – ALL 46 questions are compulsory and MUST be attempted Section B – ALL SIX questions are compulsory and MUST be attempted	

DO NOT OPEN THIS EXAM UNTIL YOU ARE READY TO START
UNDER EXAMINATION CONDITIONS

BPP
LEARNING
MEDIA

Section A

ALL 46 questions are compulsory and MUST be attempted

1 Consider the following:

   (1) Private companies can raise share capital by advertising to the general public.

   (2) Private companies can raise share capital from venture capitalists.

   Required

   Are these statements true or false?

   O Statement 1 is true and statement 2 is false

   O Statement 1 is false and statement 2 is true

   O Both statements are true

   O Both statements are false

   (2 marks)

2 Nysslit Lerner plc, an organisation of some 400 employees, has an average span of control of three, throughout its structure. From this, which of the following inferences might one make?

   O The work is systematic and routine

   O The level of complexity in the work is high

   O The organisation is flat

   (1 mark)

3 Which of the following is part of the research and development function of a business?

   O The analysis of survey data on consumer behaviour, produced under contract by an independent market research company

   O Creating new products and improving existing ones

   O Contracting independent advertising agencies to promote the products being sold by the company

   (1 mark)

4 Which of the following members of the finance function would be responsible for deciding how much credit should be given to customers?

   O The financial manager

   O The financial accountant

   O The management accountant

   (1 mark)

5 Mrs Grey likes swimming and playing badminton as part of her exercise routine.

   She has a budget of up to $25 to spend each week on getting fit. Each trip to the swimming pool costs $3, and each badminton session costs $4.

Number of trips	Marginal utility of swimming	Marginal utility of badminton
1	90	100
2	80	90

Number of trips	Marginal utility of swimming	Marginal utility of badminton
3	70	80
4	60	70
5	50	60

Required

Swimming trips

(1) ▼

Badminton sessions

(2) ▼

Pull down list 1

- 1
- 2
- 3
- 4

Pull down list 2

- 3
- 4
- 5

(2 marks)

6 You have received a letter from an estate agent, requesting financial information about one of your clients, who is applying to rent a property.

The information is needed as soon as possible, by fax or e-mail, or the client will lose approval.

Required

Which of the following ethical principles, identified in the ACCA code of ethics, is raised by the decision of whether, when and how to respond to this request?

- O Objectivity
- O Technical competence
- O Confidentiality
- O Professional behaviour

(2 marks)

7 A large, well-established construction company organises itself on a project basis, using temporary matrix and project team structures.

Required

What cultural type is most likely to fit this organisation?

- O Role culture
- O Power culture
- O Task culture

(1 mark)

8 Which of the following options sets out the required procedures for all of the various functions of a business?

○ An accounting manual

○ A function policy

○ A management information manual

○ A policy manual

(2 marks)

9 Which of the following is a purpose of a job evaluation?

○ Identifying individuals' training and development needs

○ Evaluating the organisation's recruitment and selection procedures

○ Improving upward communication

○ Demonstrating compliance with equal pay legislation

(2 marks)

10 Which of the following is an external stakeholder?

○ Professional body

○ Customer

○ Bank of the organisation

(1 mark)

11 Helen, Jack, Sue and Joe work in the finance department of Y Co which has separate financial accounting and management accounting functions.

Helen works on inventory valuation, budgetary control and variance analysis.

Jack deals with sales invoicing and debt collection.

Sue deals with quarterly sales tax returns and corporation tax and Joe carries out risk assessments and assists in project planning.

Required

Which member of the department would report to the management accountant?

○ Helen

○ Jack

○ Sue

○ Joe

(2 marks)

12 Homer and Marge work for similar companies but at Marge's company a mechanistic system of management exists, in contrast to the organic approach at Homer's firm.

They are discussing some of the characteristics of each system, which are outlined below.

Required

Which **TWO** would Marge recognise from her workplace?

☐ Managers are responsible for co-ordinating tasks

☐ Insistence on loyalty to the organisation

☐ Job description are less precise, it is harder to 'pass the buck'.

☐ Flexibility in job roles

(2 marks)

13 Individuals may conform with the norms and customs of a group without real commitment.

Required

Which of the following terms describes such behaviour?

O Compliance

O Counter-conformity

O Internalisation

O Identification

(2 marks)

14 Which of the following is a negative contribution of the audit committee, in a corporate governance framework?

O A lack of independence in reviewing the proposed approach of the external auditors

O Acting as a barrier between the main (executive) board and the external auditors

O Not allowing a forum to raise issues of concern

(1 mark)

15 Which of the following is a feature of ineffective delegation by a manager?

O Specifying performance levels and the results expected of the subordinate

O Obtaining the subordinate's agreement with the task and expected results

O Ensuring that all the subordinate's decisions are confirmed or authorised by the superior

O Ensuring that the subordinate reports the results of their decisions to the superior

(2 marks)

16 In the context of fraud, which of the following statements is **FALSE**?

O Deliberate manipulation of depreciation figures is difficult because of its cash flow effects.

O Fraudulently understating expenses will inflate the reported profit figure.

O Selling goods to friends (with a promise of buying them back at a later date) is potentially fraudulent.

O Employees within or outside the payroll department can perpetrate payroll fraud.

(2 marks)

17 If you are a team leader, seeking to evaluate the effectiveness of your team, which of the following criteria should you use?

Criteria:

(1) Contribution to organisational objectives

(2) Fulfilment of group task objectives

(3) Satisfaction of the development needs of members

O Criterion (2) only

O Criteria (1) and (2) only

O Criteria (2) and (3) only

O Criteria (1), (2) and (3)

(2 marks)

18 In the context of motivation theory, what are Douglas McGregor's Theory X and Theory Y?

O Extreme types of managers

O Extreme sets of assumptions that managers may have about workers

O Extreme types of employees

(1 mark)

19 In the context of interpersonal skills for counselling, _____ is the skill of seeing an issue from the other person's point of view and reflecting your understanding back to the other person.

Required

Which of the following terms correctly completes this sentence?

○ Rapport-building

○ Active listening

(1 mark)

20 Which one of the following is **NOT** an offence relating to money laundering?

○ Concealing the proceeds of criminal activity

○ Tipping off

○ Dealing in price affected securities

○ Failing to report suspicion of money laundering

(2 marks)

21 Anna, Barry, Charles, Dilip and Elaine all work in the same department and form a communication network within the department. When there is information to be communicated, Charles is given this information. He then communicates this to Barry, Dilip and Elaine. Barry will then communicate this information to Anna.

Required

Which of the following patterns of group communication is being used here?

○ Wheel

○ Chain

○ Circle

○ Y

(2 marks)

22 Lockett suggested a number of barriers to effective performance appraisal, including 'appraisal as unfinished business'. What is meant by this phrase?

○ Appraisal interviews are subject to interruption or left incomplete

○ The manager is embarrassed by the need to give feedback and set challenging targets, and leaves the interview with unresolved issues.

○ Appraisal is used as a wrapping up of the unresolved performance issues of the past year, rather than focusing on future improvement and problem-solving

○ Appraisal is seen as a sort of show-down, in which unresolved conflicts can be brought into the open

(2 marks)

23 Which word or phrase correctly completes this definition?

In the context of work planning, a [▼] has a defined beginning and end and is

carried out to meet established goals within cost, schedule and quality objectives.

Pull down list

• Contingency plan

• Project

• Strategy

(1 mark)

24 The management of RST Co recently held a meeting regarding its financial results for the last year.

It has been suggested in the media that RST Co makes excessive profits.

In order to combat this the management have decided to deliberately understate its financial performance for the last year.

Required

Which of the following is a potential consequence of RST, fraudulently understating its results?

○ Excessive distribution of profits to shareholders

○ Restricted access to loan finance

○ Unrealistic expectations in the financial markets

○ Potential shortfalls in working capital   **(2 marks)**

25 The price elasticity of demand (PED) of good A is negative, its income elasticity of demand (IED) is positive and its cross elasticity of demand (XED) with respect to good X is negative.

What is the nature of good A?

○ A good bought for purposes of ostentation, complementary to X

○ An inferior good, substitute for X

○ A normal good, complementary to X   **(1 mark)**

26 In the context of Tuckman's model of team development, which of the following sequences of stages is correct?

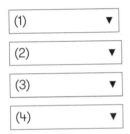

(1) ▼

(2) ▼

(3) ▼

(4) ▼

Pull down list 1

- Forming
- Norming
- Performing
- Storming

Pull down list 2

- Forming
- Norming
- Performing
- Storming

Pull down list 3

- Forming
- Norming
- Performing
- Storming

Pull down list 4

- Forming
- Norming
- Performing
- Storming

(2 marks)

27 In the regulatory system surrounding financial accounting, which body has as a key objective the development of a single set of enforceable global accounting standards?

○ The Accounting Standards Board

○ The International Accounting Standards Board

○ The European Union

(1 mark)

28 Which **TWO** of the following are typical of informal groups within an organisation?

☐ Membership is voluntary

☐ Tasks are assigned by management

☐ Communication is open and informal

☐ Members are held accountable to management for their tasks

(2 marks)

29 Some meetings achieve very little because of hindrances.

Sally is learning about these problems and how she can avoid them in her role as chairperson at the next project team meeting.

Following conversations with other people in the business she has come up with four suggestions for making meetings more effective.

Required

Which **TWO** of the above are ways of avoiding participants being unclear about the purpose of the meeting?

☐ Name the person responsible for completing each action point, and assign a completion date

☐ Agree goals in advance

☐ Include all actions required and the assigned dates in the minutes

☐ Prepare a focused agenda and ensure people stick to it

(2 marks)

30 Which **TWO** of the following should be the purposes of an appraisal interview?

☐ To discuss employee performance

☐ To discipline an employee

☐ To agree an employee's salary review

☐ To identify an employee's development needs

(2 marks)

31 Which words correctly complete this statement?

If a government increased its expenditure and reduced levels of taxation, the effect would be to (i)

| (1) ▼ | demand in the economy and to (ii) | (2) ▼ | the size of the Public

Sector Net Cash Requirement.

Pull down list 1
- Raise
- Reduce
- Stimulate

Pull down list 2
- Raise
- Reduce
- Stimulate

(2 marks)

32 Which of the following statements is an example of lateral communication?
- O Communication between middle managers and their first line supervisors
- O Communication between heads of department, who report to the same divisional manager
- O Communication between supervisors and their team members

(1 mark)

33 While out to lunch, you run into a client at the sandwich bar.

In conversation, she tells you that she expects to inherit from a recently deceased uncle, and asks you how she will be affected by inheritance tax, capital gains tax and other matters – which you have not dealt with, in detail, for some years.

Required

Which of the following principles of the ACCA Code of Ethics is raised by this scenario?
- O Professional competence and due care
- O Integrity
- O Professional behaviour
- O Confidentiality

(2 marks)

34 What word correctly completes this definition?

| ▼ | learning is a method in which managers are brought together as a problem-

solving group to discuss a real work issue, and a facilitator helps them to identify how their

interpersonal and problem-solving skills are affecting the process.

Pull down list
- Action
- Behavioural
- Experiential
- Off-the-job

(2 marks)

35 There are a number of different views on ethics within the finance department of TUV Co.

Tina believes that actions should be judged by their outcomes or consequences.

Chris states that there is an unchanging set of ethical principles that always applies.

Will believes that right and wrong are culturally determined

Required

Which view of ethics is given by Will?

O Ethical relativism

O Cognitivism

O Teleological

O Deontological   **(2 marks)**

36 Which of the following words correctly completes the sentence?

Business [▼   ] are a set of moral principles to guide behaviour in business contexts.

Pull down list

• Controls

• Ethics

• Objectives

                                                                             (1 mark)

37 Which **TWO** of the following are best shown using a bar chart?

☐ The nature of activities within an action plan

☐ A sequence of activities within a project

☐ The time required for different activities

☐ Quantitative relationships between activities   **(2 marks)**

38 Emma, John, Pratish and Rekha all work for W Co. Emma ensures that goods are only purchased when they are required. John ensures that goods that are purchased from authorised suppliers. Pratish pays the suppliers' invoices and Rekha evaluates the financial stability of potential suppliers. Three of the members of Q Co work in the purchasing department and one works in the accounting department.

Required

Which member works in the accounting department?

O Emma

O John

O Pratish

O Rekha   **(2 marks)**

39 When an organisation carries out an environmental scan, it analyses which of the following?

O Strengths, weaknesses, opportunities and threats

O Political, economic, social and technological factors

O Strategic options and choice

O Inbound and outbound logistics

                                                                             (2 marks)

BPP
LEARNING
MEDIA

40 Which part of SWOT analysis considers external environmental factors?

   O Strengths and weaknesses

   O Strengths and threats

   O Opportunities and threats

   O Opportunities and weaknesses

(2 marks)

41 The IFAC code is administered by which body?

   O ACCA

   O IESBA

   O FATF

(1 mark)

42 In the context of internal control systems which of the following would be included in the 'control procedures'?

   O Strategies for dealing with significant identified risks

   O Clear definition of authority, responsibility and accountability

   O Detailed policies and procedures for administrative and accounting control

   O Senior management commitment to competence and integrity

(2 marks)

43 Which of the following is likely to pose the *least* number of problems for effective time management?

   O Personal work patterns

   O Meetings

   O The telephone

(1 mark)

44 Which of the following methods of cyber security ensures that the latest software updates are installed on the system when available?

   O Virus protection

   O Patch management

   O Firewalls

   O Access control

(2 marks)

45 Julie and Nick are both on the same salary and grade at P Co.

Julie is the finance director and Nick is the operations director. A new project team has been created to consider an alternative office location for P Co. Julie and Nick are part of this team.

When Julie and Nick communicate with each other, what type of communication is this?

   O Downward

   O Diagonal

   O Lateral

(1 mark)

46 The following qualities are some of those expected of an accountant, but which is a professional quality as opposed to a personal quality?

○ Reliability

○ Respect

○ Timeliness

○ Scepticism

(2 marks)

Section B

ALL SIX questions are compulsory and MUST be attempted

47 (a) Mintzberg defined three categories of managerial role as interpersonal, informational and decisional.

Required

For each of the following managerial roles select the correct category from the above list

Negotiator	▼
Spokesperson	▼
Disseminator	▼
Figurehead	▼
Liaison	▼
Disturbance handler	▼

Pull down list

- Decisional
- Informational
- Interpersonal

(3 marks)

(b) Are the following statements about supervisors true or false?

Supervisors spend all their time on managerial aspects of the job

A supervisor is a filter between managerial and non-managerial staff

Pull down list

- False
- True

(1 mark)

(Total = 4 marks)

___

48 (a) Frank, Gloria, Helen and Ian are discussing how they should structure their newly formed company.

Frank wants a structure which would allow the newly recruited employees to be more flexible. Gloria would prefer a structure where decisions can be made at a local level rather than centrally. Helen wants a structure that will facilitate the recruitment of technical specialists for the business. Ian's preference is for a structure that does not have bureaucratic obstacles that are present in other structures.

Required

Which organisational structure would be preferred by each of the following?

Frank	▼
Gloria	▼
Helen	▼
Ian	▼

Pull down list

- Functional
- Geographic
- Matrix

(2 marks)

(b) Which **TWO** of the following are features of a boundaryless structure?

☐ The employee is a seller of skills

☐ Barriers are removed between the organisation and its suppliers

☐ The organisation only exists electronically

☐ The focus is on the customer

☐ Elimination of bureaucracy

(2 marks)

(Total = 4 marks)

---

49 (a) The Board of Directors of BCD Co discussed corporate governance concepts. The finance director wants to provide financial projections to shareholders which were used as the basis for deciding to proceed with a major overseas investment.

The marketing director has decided not to authorise a proposed advertising campaign which she believes is misleading, despite the other directors pushing for the campaign to go ahead. The HR director, who was responsible for introducing an unsuccessful training programme across the entire business, accepts that he should take the blame for this issue. The chief executive has decided not to proceed with a proposed takeover of a competitor, that would not have increased the value of BCD Co, but would have given the directors higher status.

Required

For each of the above scenarios, select the corporate governance concept being applied by:

The finance director	▼
The marketing director	▼
The HR director	▼
The chief executive	▼

Pull down list

- Integrity
- Judgement
- Responsibility
- Transparency

(2 marks)

(b) Which of the following describes the minimum level of compliance an organisation must have?

○ There is no minimum level

○ Legal obligations only

○ Legal obligations and non-legal regulations

(1 mark)

(c) Managers have a duty of faithful service to an organisation. This is known as their _____.

Which phrase correctly fills in the blank?

[▼]

Pull down list

- Ethical position
- Fiduciary responsibility
- Financial responsibility

(1 mark)

(Total = 4 marks)

---

50 (a) The following are all areas of legal issues that can affect an organisation. For each legal issue, select the appropriate area of law related to it:

Directors' duties	[▼]
Minimum wage	[▼]
Theft	[▼]
Waste disposal	[▼]

Pull down list

- Company law
- Criminal law
- Employment law
- Environmental law

(2 marks)

(b) Are each of the following statements concerning the impact of technology on the role of accountants and auditors true or false?

Cloud accounting reduces the amount of teamwork accountants are involved in	[▼]
Artificial intelligence frees the accountant to work on value-adding services.	[▼]
Data analytics helps the auditor reduce business risks	[▼]
Distributed ledger technology reduces the need for auditors to audit all transactions	[▼]

Pull down list

- False
- True

(2 marks)

(Total = 4 marks)

---

51 (a) The following are qualities that might be found in accounting information.

Select **FOUR** from the list that accounting information should have if it is to be useful.

- ☐ Reliability
- ☐ Irrelevance
- ☐ Electronic
- ☐ Completeness
- ☐ Objectivity
- ☐ Unformatted
- ☐ Incomparability
- ☐ Timeliness

(2 marks)

(b) Match the following finance tasks to the responsible person.

Statutory accounts	▼
Job costing	▼
Taxation	▼

Pull down list

- Financial accountant
- Management accountant

(2 marks)

(Total = 4 marks)

---

52 (a) FGH Co has a culture of informality in most of its communications at lower levels, but communications with and amongst members of the board are typically formal.

Required

In each of the following circumstances select the appropriate method of communication:

Communicating the findings of an external review into investment possibilities to the board	▼
Formal document requiring directors' signatures to be sent to company lawyers	▼
A meeting between sales managers based in geographically distant locations	▼
Letting employees know about a staff meeting to be held in one month's time	▼

Pull down list

- E-mail
- Postal service
- Report
- Video conference

(2 marks)

(b) Which **TWO** of the following are effects on an organisation of its employees being ineffective?

☐ Staff turnover will increase

☐ Deadlines will be missed

☐ Problems are not dealt with as they arise

☐ Customer satisfaction will increase

(2 marks)

(Total = 4 marks)

Answers

DO NOT TURN THIS PAGE UNTIL YOU HAVE
COMPLETED THE MOCK EXAM

Section A

1 The correct answer is: Statement 1 is false and statement 2 is true

Rationale: The key difference between private and public companies is that only public companies can advertise their shares to the general public. Both private and public companies can raise share capital from venture capitalists.

Pitfalls: You had to get your 'private' and 'public' companies the right way round.

2 The correct answer is: The level of complexity in the work is high

Rationale: The organisation has a narrow span of control: this would typically be the case if the work is complex, as it requires closer supervision.

Pitfalls: Remember: narrow span typically means tall organisation; wide span typically means flat organisation.

Ways in: Work through each option. Systematic/routine work would not need such a narrow span of control. With a control span of three in a fairly large organisation, the organisation must be tall...

3 The correct answer is: Creating new products and improving existing ones

Rationale: The other options would be part of the marketing function.

4 The correct answer is: The financial manager

Rationale: The financial manager, among other responsibilities, will decide how much credit should be given to customers.

Pitfalls: The management accountant presents accounting information to support management. The financial accountant reports the results and financial position of a business.

5 *Swimming trips*

4

Badminton sessions

3

Rationale: Utility is greatest at the point where:

$$\frac{\text{Marginal utility of swimming}}{\text{Price of swimming trip}} = \frac{\text{Marginal utility of badminton}}{\text{Price of badminton session}}$$

$$= \frac{60}{3} = \frac{80}{4} = 20$$

= 4 swimming trips and 3 badminton sessions

Note: 4 swimming trips and 3 badminton sessions cost a total of $24 and so are within the $25 budget. Mrs Grey's overall total utility is restricted by her budget, so the total cost of any combination she might wish to choose must be less than $25.

6 The correct answer is: Confidentiality

Rationale: Confidentiality is the immediate ethical issue.

You need the client's authority to disclose the information: you may also need to confirm the identity of the person making the request, and take steps to protect the confidentiality of the information if you send it (ie not using fax or e-mail).

The other ethical principles do not apply here.

7 The correct answer is: Task culture

Rationale: A task culture suits project management structures, with their focus on deliverables (project completion) rather than processes. Role culture suits bureaucratic cultures and power culture suits simple/entrepreneurial structures.

Pitfalls: Just because the organisation is large and well-established, don't immediately jump to the conclusion that it is a bureaucracy (role culture)!

8 The correct answer is: A policy manual

Rationale: Every employee will be expected to have read the areas relevant to their functions and the policy manual should always be readily available for easy reference.

9 The correct answer is: Demonstrating compliance with equal pay legislation

Rationale: Equal pay legislation requires that women be paid equal pay to men for work 'of equal value' (to the organisation): this is established by job evaluation. The others are potential purposes of a performance appraisal. Equal pay is about the value of the job, not the value of the job holder. If you hesitated over evaluating the organisation's recruitment and selection procedures, think of performance appraisal as a way of monitoring whether people really do as well in the job as the selection system predicted they would when they were hired!

10 The correct answer is: Professional body

Rationale: External stakeholder groups – the government, local authorities, pressure groups, the community at large, professional bodies – are likely to have quite diverse objectives.

11 The correct answer is: Helen

Rationale: The Financial Accountant is responsible for activities such as payroll, receivables and payables ledger, credit control, financial accounts and taxation. Jack and Sue would report to the financial accountant. The Treasurer (if there is one) would be responsible for project (investment) appraisal, and his or her priority would be funds management. Joe would report to the treasurer.

Pitfalls: These are essential distinctions: any combination of the tasks and titles could be tested.

12 The correct answers are:

- Managers are responsible for co-ordinating tasks
- Insistence on loyalty to the organisation

Rationale: The correct answers are: Managers are responsible for co-ordinating tasks; insistence on loyalty to the organisation. In contrast, Homer would recognise the other features as typical of an organic system of management.

13 The correct answer is: Compliance

Rationale: Compliance is behaving in such a way as to conform, regardless of underlying commitment or attitude: it applies to organisations as well as individuals! Counter-conformity is rejection of group norms. Internalisation is 'inner' acceptance and ownership of the norms. Identification is a separate idea: it is one of the processes through which norms are reinforced in a group.

14 The correct answer is: Acting as a barrier between the main (executive) board and the external auditors

Rationale: This may sound like an 'independence' benefit, but the key word is 'barrier': the main board needs to take responsibility for the financial statements and be open to question by auditors.

15 The correct answer is: Ensuring that all the subordinate's decisions are confirmed or authorised by the superior

Rationale: There is a fine distinction between making the subordinate accountable and interfering. If the superior doesn't trust the subordinate to make decisions, they shouldn't have delegated at all. The other options should clearly be effective practice.

16 The correct answer is: Deliberate manipulation of depreciation figures is difficult because of its cash flow effects.

Rationale: Depreciation is an expense that doesn't have any cash flow effect, so the figures are easily tampered with: eg understating depreciation to give a healthier net book value. Fraudulently understating expenses will inflate the reported profit figure is clearly true. Selling goods to friends (with a promise of buying them back at a later date) is potentially fraudulent is true because this can be used to create fictitious sales values or manipulate year end results. Employees within or outside the payroll department can perpetrate payroll fraud is true because, for example, any employee can falsify time-sheets, and payroll staff can channel payments to bogus staff accounts.

17 The correct answer is: Criteria (1), (2) and (3)

Rationale: The criteria for team effectiveness are *both* fulfilment of task objectives (which should contribute to organisational objectives) *and* member satisfaction, where that contributes to the ability of the group to fulfil its task (eg in the development of members' skills and abilities).

18 The correct answer is: Extreme sets of assumptions that managers may have about workers

Rationale: Theory X and Y are only managerial assumptions – which then *influence* the kinds of motivational approaches and leadership styles the manager will adopt. They do not describe actual types of people (managers or employees).

Pitfalls: You are often asked to show critical awareness and understanding of theories, so it is worth getting this distinction clear.

19 The correct answer is: Active listening

Rationale: The closest distractor is active listening, as reflecting understanding is one of the ways a listener can be 'active'. (Other ways include questioning, summarising, showing attentive body language, giving feedback and so on.) Rapport-building is the skill of making another person feel at ease with you, and willing to communicate with you.

20 The correct answer is: Dealing in price affected securities

Rationale: This could be insider dealing, if the person dealing was an insider and was using inside information.

21 The correct answer is: Y

Rationale: This is an example of the Y network. Drawing out what is going on may help here.

22 The correct answer is: Appraisal is used as a wrapping up of the unresolved performance issues of the past year, rather than focusing on future improvement and problem-solving

Rationale: This is what Lockett meant by the phrase. Appraisal interviews are subject to interruption or left incomplete is a simple distractor. The other options describe other barriers: 'Appraisal as chat' and 'Appraisal as confrontation'.

23 In the context of work planning, a ⟨project⟩ has a defined beginning and end and is carried out

to meet established goals within cost, schedule and quality objectives.

Rationale: A project is distinguished from routine work because of these characteristics. A contingency plan is a plan for what should be done if changes or problems occur. A strategy is a long-term plan relating to the direction of the firm or business unit.

24 The correct answer is: Restricted access to loan finance

Rationale: Finance may be hard to come by because the financial health of the firm (ability to maintain and pay off loans) is understated. The other options are impacts of fraudulently over-stating results.

Pitfalls: Ensure that you read the question carefully and address understated, not overstated, results.

Ways in: This should have been clear if you worked through each of the options. Once you identified that some of the distractors were overstatement impacts, you would have a good idea what to look for.

25 The correct answer is: A normal good, complementary to X

Rationale: Goods of ostentation have positive PED. Inferior goods have negative IED. Substitutes have positive XED.

26
| Forming |

| Storming |

| Norming |

| Performing |

Rationale: Forming is the tentative 'getting to know each other' stage; storming, the conflict that results as people begin to assert themselves; norming, the 'settling down' stage, as roles, behaviours and working methods are agreed; and performing, 'getting down to work'.

Pitfalls: This can be confusing: make sure you get the terminology right, because it is solid territory for exam questions.

27 The correct answer is: The International Accounting Standards Board

Rationale: The IASB has this as a key objective. The ASB used to issue Financial Reporting Standards in the UK, a role now performed by the FRC. The EU is interested in harmonisation of standards, but does not have global jurisdiction.

Ways in: You should have been tipped off to the international element by the word 'global'. Combine that with 'accounting standards' and you could take an educated guess at the correct answer, if you had to.

28 The correct answers are:

- Membership is voluntary
- Communication is open and informal

Rationale: An organisation can be described as a collection of groups both formal and informal.

Pitfalls: It is important not to underestimate the importance of groups within an organisation. *Elton Mayo* first established this point through the Hawthorne Experiments.

It is also important to remember that there are alliances and power structures that exist within an organisation, other than those documented in an organisational chart.

29 The correct answers are:

- Agree goals in advance

- Prepare a focused agenda and ensure people stick to it

Rationale: Ensuring meeting goals are agreed before the meeting and producing an agenda based around achieving the agreed goals should ensure attendees are fully aware of the meeting purpose.

30 The correct answers are:

- To discuss employee performance

- To identify an employee's development needs

Rationale: There are drawbacks to linking appraisal to salary review, not least that there may not be enough money to reward the employee for their performance.

31 If a government increased its expenditure and reduced levels of taxation, the effect would be to (i)

| stimulate | demand in the economy and to (ii) | raise | the size of the Public Sector Net Cash Requirement.

Rationale: Demand would be raised because firms and households would have more money (after tax) for consumption or saving/investment. The increased expenditure would not be covered by revenue from taxation, so the change would be financed by a higher PSNCR (borrowing mount).

Pitfalls: You have to be able to think through all the permutations of fiscal and monetary policies and their impacts on the economy and (where relevant) business decision-making.

32 The correct answer is: Communication between heads of department, who report to the same divisional manager

Rationale: Lateral communication is between those of equal rank.

33 The correct answer is: Professional competence and due care

Rationale: The principle of due care is that, having accepted an assignment, you have an obligation to carry it out to the best of your ability, in the client's best interests, and within reasonable timescales, with proper regard for the standards expected of you as a professional.

In this scenario, any answer you give on the spot would risk being incomplete, inaccurate or out-of-date, with potentially serious consequences, if the client relies and acts on your reply.

Integrity is honesty, fair dealing and truthfulness; professional behaviour is upholding the reputation of your profession; and confidentiality is not using or disclosing information given to you by employers or clients in the course of your work. (None of these issues applies directly here.)

34 | Action | learning is a method in which managers are brought together as a problem-solving group

to discuss a real work issue, and a facilitator helps them to identify how their interpersonal and

problem-solving skills are affecting the process.

Rationale: Experiential learning is 'learning by doing', usually involving self-managed learning by reflection, planning and adjustment.

Action learning is classed as on-the-job learning, because it involves real work problems and groups. Behavioural and off-the-job are just distractors.

ANSWERS

35 The correct answer is: Ethical relativism

Rationale: This describes Will's view of ethics.

36 Business | ethics | are a set of moral principles to guide behaviour in business contexts.

Rationale: Ethics are 'moral principles': the other options set behavioural guidelines of a different sort.

37 The correct answers are:

- The time required for different activities
- Quantitative relationships between activities

Rationale: Bar charts show data not sequences. They do not explain the nature of an activity.

38 The correct answer is: Pratish

Rationale: Paying suppliers' invoices would be a function of the accounts department, once the purchasing department has authorised the invoices for payment. You may have hesitated over Rekha, but evaluating potential suppliers is a key element in supplier appraisal and selection, not a finance matter. (However, in some companies the finance department would do the supplier appraisal because of their technical skills or knowledge but this is not the norm.)

39 The correct answer is: Political, economic, social and technological factors

Rationale: These are the external factors which impact the business.

40 The correct answer is: Opportunities and threats

Rationale: Strengths and weaknesses are internal.

41 The correct answer is: IESBA

Rationale: The IFAC code is now administered by the IESBA. The ACCA code of ethics is based on the IFAC code. FATF (Financial Action Task Force) promotes policies to combat money laundering.

42 The correct answer is: Detailed policies and procedures for administrative and accounting control

Rationale: The other options relate to the 'control environment' which embraces the overall organisational and cultural context of control. They were highlighted as aspects of a strong control environment in the Turnbull report.

43 The correct answer is: Personal work patterns

Rationale: You can take advantage of personal work patterns, which include times of high energy and focus as well as low. The other options all expose you to the demands of other people, which may be harder to manage.

44 The correct answer is: Patch management

Rationale: Patch management is a cyber security solution in the form of a system procedure. The organisation ensures that the latest software updates are installed on the system when available

45 The correct answer is: Lateral

Rationale: Lateral (or horizontal) communication flows between people of the same rank, in the same section or department or in different sections or departments.

Ways in: Hopefully you would have been able to disregard downward because it suggests communication from superior to subordinate.

46   The correct answer is: Scepticism

Rationale: The professional qualities are: independence, accountability, scepticism and social responsibility.

ANSWERS

Section B

47   (a)

Negotiator	Decisional
Spokesperson	Informational
Disseminator	Informational
Figurehead	Interpersonal
Liaison	Interpersonal
Disturbance handler	Decisional

Negotiator: Negotiation often occurs before a decision is taken.

Spokesperson: The manager provides information on behalf of the organisation to interested parties.

Disseminator: Managers disseminate relevant information to subordinates.

Figurehead: A chief executive spends time representing the company at conferences, dinners etc.

Liaison: Some managers spend a significant amount of time meeting peers rather than their subordinates.

Disturbance handler: A manager has to make decisions when there has been a deviation from the plan.

(b)   Supervisors spend all their time on managerial aspects of the job

> False

A supervisor is a filter between managerial and non-managerial staff

> True

A supervisor spends time doing technical or operational work.

A supervisor is **not** a filter between managerial and non-managerial staff.

48   (a)

Frank	Matrix
Gloria	Geographic
Helen	Functional
Ian	Matrix

A matrix structure encourages flexibility of people.

Local decision-making is a feature of geographic departmentation.

Functional departmentation means that functional specialists can be recruited.

A matrix structure removes bureaucratic obstacles common with taller organisation structures.

The correct answers are:

(b)   • Barriers are removed between the organisation and its suppliers

      • Elimination of bureaucracy

The employee is a seller of skills is a feature of a jobless structure. The organisation only exists electronically is a feature of virtual organisations. The focus is on the customer is a feature of output-focused structure.

49 (a)

The finance director	Transparency
The marketing director	Integrity
The HR director	Responsibility
The chief executive	Judgement

Open and clear disclosure describes transparency. In working life integrity means adhering to principles of professionalism. This demonstrates responsibility. Judgement means making decisions that enhance the prosperity of the organisation.

(b) The correct answer is: Legal obligations only

Fulfilling legal obligations is the minimum standard of behaviour required by an organisation.

(c) Fiduciary responsibility

Managers have a fiduciary interest to act in the best interest of the organisation.

50 (a)

Directors' duties	Company law
Minimum wage	Employment law
Theft	Criminal law
Waste disposal	Environmental law

(b)

Cloud accounting reduces the amount of teamwork accountants are involved in	False
Artificial intelligence frees the accountant to work on value-adding services.	True
Data analytics helps the auditor reduce business risks	False
Distributed ledger technology reduces the need for auditors to audit all transactions	True

51 (a) The correct answers are:

- Reliability
- Completeness
- Objectivity
- Timeliness

Accounting information should be Relevant, Comprehensible, Reliable, Complete, Objective, Timely and Comparable.

(b)

Statutory accounts	Financial accountant
Job costing	Management accountant
Taxation	Financial accountant

Financial accountants are involved in preparing information for users outside the organisation, such as statutory accounts and tax. Management accountants prepare information for use inside an organisation such as job costing.

52 (a)

Communicating the findings of an external review into investment possibilities to the board	Report
Formal document requiring directors' signatures to be sent to company lawyers	Postal service
A meeting between sales managers based in geographically distant locations	Video conference
Letting employees know about a staff meeting to be held in one month's time	E-mail

A report is usually a comprehensive written record, often used for communicating findings to the board.

As a physical signature is required, this needs to be sent by postal service.

A video conference allows geographically distant people to have a visual meeting.

E-mail allows all staff members to be contacted with one communication.

(b) The correct answers are:

- Deadlines will be missed
- Problems are not dealt with as they arise

Staff turnover is not affected by ineffectiveness and customers are more likely to be dissatisfied.

Foundation in Accountancy/ACCA

Business Technology (BT/FBT)

Mock Exam 3

Questions	
Time allowed	2 hours
This exam is divided into two sections: Section A – ALL 46 questions are compulsory and MUST be attempted Section B – ALL SIX questions are compulsory and MUST be attempted	

DO NOT OPEN THIS EXAM UNTIL YOU ARE READY TO START UNDER EXAMINATION CONDITIONS

Section A

ALL 46 questions are compulsory and MUST be attempted

1 Which of the following is another name for an entrepreneurial structure?

  O Matrix structure

  O Flat structure

  O Simple structure

      (1 mark)

2 Stephanie is the typist for Ron, Martin and Josephine. Josephine is the department head and sets Stephanie's work priorities.

Josephine is in a meeting and Martin needs a letter to be typed urgently. Martin orders Stephanie to 'type his work now!'.

Stephanie refuses, saying that Josephine has told her to type a report from Ron, as this is needed for a Board Meeting.

When Josephine returns from her meeting Martin complains and the situation degenerates to a shouting match between Ron and Martin. Josephine reviews the work to be done and tells Stephanie to type Ron's report first, then the minutes of the meeting Josephine has just attended, and then Martin's letter.

She explains to Martin that, although his letter is important, it only needs to catch that evening's post.

Ron's report is needed for a Board meeting in two hours' time and the Board will also need to see the minutes of her meeting. All parties feel happy with the result.

Required

How would you describe Josephine's response to the conflict?

  O Denial

  O Suppression

  O Compromise

  O Dominance

      (2 marks)

3 There are three broad pre-requisites or 'pre-conditions' that must exist in order to make fraud a possibility.

  O Dishonesty, criminality and opportunity.

  O Deception, motivation and opportunity.

  O Dishonesty, motivation and opportunity.

      (1 mark)

4 Are the following statements true or false?

	True	False
Employees who notice fraud or malpractice in a workplace are obliged to reveal their knowledge to external authorities immediately.	O	O
The term given to an employee who reveals fraud or malpractice occurring in a workplace is whistle-blower	O	O

      (2 marks)

5 What elements constitute the purchasing mix?

○ Quantity, quality, product, price.

○ Quantity, quality, discount, delivery.

○ Quantity, quality, price, delivery.   (1 mark)

6 Which **THREE** of the following are the professional qualities expected of an accountant?

☐ Moderation

☐ Social responsibility

☐ Authority

☐ Independence

☐ Scepticism   (2 marks)

7 Which **THREE** of the following personal relationships are likely to constitute a threat to objectivity or the appearance of objectivity?

☐ The audit partner is married to the finance director of an audit client.

☐ A junior member of the audit team plays football with a marketing assistant of a company audited by another office of the firm.

☐ A senior member of the audit team is in a relationship with the financial controller of an audit client.

☐ The financial controller of a company resigned from the company three months ago, is now working for the company's auditors and is working on the audit of the company she previously worked for.

☐ The audit partner attends the annual dinner of the company.   (2 marks)

8 A group of people who are not in the same geographical location, but work together using information and communication technology (ICT) to share data, allocate work and hold meetings is called a _____ team.

Required

Which of the following words most appropriately fills the gap?

○ Multi-skilled

○ Virtual

○ Multi-disciplinary   (1 mark)

9 Which of the following factors would lead to stability of price levels for a product?

○ Supply decisions are based on the prices of an earlier time period.

○ Demand is based on the prices of the present time period.

○ The product has low price elasticities of demand and supply.

○ Output is affected by non-controllable factors such as climate.   (2 marks)

10 Which of the following is an external stakeholder?

○ Supplier

○ Professional body

○ Bank

○ Customer   (2 marks)

11 Which of the following are targets of macroeconomic policy?

	Yes	No
High levels of inflation	○	○
Economic growth	○	○
Zero unemployment	○	○
Balance of payments equilibrium	○	○

(2 marks)

12 What is the name of the fault in the communication process that leads to the loss of the meaning of the message in translation from intention to language or from language to understanding?

○ Noise

○ Redundancy

○ Distortion

○ Physical noise, technical noise and psychological noise.   (2 marks)

13 Accounting Standards (and company law) prescribe that a company should produce _____ to be presented to the _____.

Required

Which two words complete this sentence?

○ Accounts, shareholders

○ Reports, stakeholders

○ Accounts, stakeholders   (1 mark)

14 If a task-force team required to look into a particular short-term problem were set up as a committee, what type of committee would it be?

○ An ad hoc committee

○ An executive committee

○ A standing committee

○ A joint committee   (2 marks)

15 What is a co-operative?

○ A business that works closely with another.

○ A company where ownership is separate from control.

○ A business owned by its workers or customers.

(1 mark)

16 The aim of coaching is to _____ people by providing challenging _____ and _____ in tackling them.

Required

Which words most accurately complete this sentence?

○ Develop; objectives; guidance.

○ Promote; opportunities; guidance.

○ Develop; tasks; guidance.   (1 mark)

BPP
LEARNING
MEDIA

17 What is a 'value activity'?

O   The means by which a firm increases the worth of its products.

O   The processes for which a firm can charge the most money.

O   Actions that promote ethical standards of behaviour.

O   Those work tasks that require large numbers of staff.

(2 marks)

18 What are the main phases of the business cycle?

O   Recession, depression, recovery, boom.

O   Boom, bust, boom, bust.

O   Recession, depression, stagnation, recovery.

(1 mark)

19 Which **TWO** of the following are the names given to the two commonly-adopted approaches to the management of ethics in organisations?

☐   System-based

☐   Integrity based

☐   Inspection-based

☐   Audit based

☐   Compliance based

(2 marks)

20 Which one of the following statements correctly defines corporate governance?

O   Procedures and processes according to which an organisation is directed and controlled.

O   A system that allows for corrective action and penalizing mismanagement.

O   The system that ensures director accountability to shareholders and stakeholders.   **(1 mark)**

21 Willy Hackett has a problem with personal time management. He takes on lots of his manager's work and tries to fit it in with his own. The sheer size of the workload sometimes panics him. He is popular with his staff, though, because he always finds time to talk to them and listen to their problems - which include boredom at work. Sometimes Willy 'just doesn't know where the day has gone'.

Required

Which of the following could Willy benefit from?

O   Delegation only

O   Assertiveness and goal planning

O   Delegation, assertiveness and goal planning

O   Delegation, assertiveness, communication and goal planning   **(2 marks)**

22 Chan, Will and Felipe are employed by an audit firm and conduct the audit of Friendly Faces Co. Felipe is in charge of the audit.

Friendly Faces Co acts as agents for children wanting to work in television. Friendly Faces have offered Felipe's daughter a part in a popular children's television programme.

In return, they want Felipe to sign off this year's audit report without mentioning the serious concerns he has over the solvency of Friendly Faces Co.

Felipe accepts their offer and signs an unqualified audit report.

Chan has found out about the arrangement. Friendly Faces Co have also offered her son a part in the same programme.

Required

What action would you recommend Chan takes?

- ○ Accept the offer but report Felipe to the head of the audit firm anonymously to avoid conflict.
- ○ Refuse the offer and report Felipe to the head of the audit firm.
- ○ Accept the offer and keep quiet.
- ○ Do nothing in order to avoid conflict.

(2 marks)

23 Julie is a valuable member of her team.

She is creative and imaginative and solves difficult problems, although she sometimes ignores details.

Required

Which one of Belbin's team roles does Julie fulfil?

- ○ Specialist
- ○ Completer- finisher
- ○ Team worker
- ○ Plant

(2 marks)

24 An accounting package automatically downloads bank transactions from the bank's system, saving the bookkeeper time entering the transactions manually.

Required

What is this feature of the accounting package an example of?

- ○ Artificial intelligence
- ○ Distributed ledger technology
- ○ Cloud computing
- ○ Automation

(2 marks)

25 Which parties contribute to a 360 degree appraisal?

	Yes	No
Line management	○	○
Colleagues	○	○
The appraisee	○	○
Customers	○	○

(2 marks)

26 When analysing the current situation in a business, a consultant will review the general environment surrounding it.

- ○ Interest rates
- ○ High levels of staff turnover
- ○ New legislation coming into effect in 6 months' time

(1 mark)

27 Assuming best corporate governance practice is applied, who should be responsible for setting directors' remuneration?

○ The chief executive

○ The audit committee

○ Shareholders

○ Independent non-executive directors

(2 marks)

28 Which of the following is an offence related to Money Laundering?

○ Disguising, converting, transferring or removing criminal property.

○ Failure of an engineering company to obtain satisfactory evidence of identity where a transaction is for a small amount.

○ Purchasing stolen goods.

(1 mark)

29 Which **TWO** of the following are part of the role of financial accounting?

☐ Recording transactions in 'books of prime entry'

☐ Preparing budgets and other financial plans

☐ Preparing financial statements for the use of external shareholders

☐ Preparing variance reports

(2 marks)

30 Velma plc is a large car manufacturer that has to regularly source thousands of component parts for input into its range of vehicles. The aim of a joint project between the Finance Director and the IT Director is to reduce the bargaining power of key suppliers and get the best price for the inputs to the business. Several options in terms of the use of IT have been suggested.

Required

Which **TWO** of the following will reduce the bargaining power of suppliers?

☐ An extranet link to allow key suppliers access to future production schedules for Velma plc

☐ A database of all suppliers used by the business to date, with capability to blanket email invitation to tender requests.

☐ Access to an online marketplace set up as a joint venture in conjunction with other large vehicle manufacturers.

☐ Outsourcing the manufacture of whole systems (eg the braking system) to selected suppliers and sharing technical data with the chosen suppliers.

(2 marks)

31 Which of the following statements is true?

(1) An informal organisation exists within every formal organisation.

(2) The objectives of the informal organisation are the same as those of the formal organisation.

(3) A strong, close-knit informal organisation is desirable within the formal organisation this practice?

○ Statement 1 only

○ Statements 1 and 3

○ Statements 2 and 3

○ Statement 3 only

(2 marks)

32 Which of the following groups should look for signs of petty fraud as well as checking work that staff have completed?

○ External auditors

○ Board of Directors

○ Operational managers

○ Audit committee

(2 marks)

33 What type of culture did Handy suggest suits a simple and small organisation run by an entrepreneurial owner or founder?

○ Role

○ Task

○ Power

(1 mark)

34 Are the following statements true or false?

	True	False
Drucker argued that developing people is a management function.	○	○
Drucker argued that the manager of a business has one basic function - economic performance	○	○

(2 marks)

35 Max and Tony run a successful parcel delivery service. By chance Max discovers that Tony has been issuing a large number of invoices for deliveries that have not been made.

When Max investigates further, he discovers that these invoices have been paid, but the funds received by the delivery firm have subsequently been used to pay a company called ABC.

Max discovers ABC is owned by Tony's wife. The payments to ABC were made to pay invoices issued to the parcel delivery company for accounting services provided by ABC. These services have never actually been carried out. Max is suspicious and reports Tony to the police. Eventually Tony is arrested for money laundering.

Required

What phase in the money laundering process has Max's firm been involved in?

○ Placement

○ Layering

○ Integration

○ Failure to disclose

(2 marks)

36 XYZ Ltd has a job vacancy in one of its departments. Sonya Bykemate, the human resources manager, knows that there are people in the company who could do the job if they were promoted to it. There is also a reasonable pool of suitably skilled individuals available in the local area, who are easily reached through the employment agency used by the firm.

Required

Which one of the following is a justification for recruiting externally rather than internally?

○ Reduction of risk

○ Motivation of the existing workforce

○ Time needed for induction

○ Innovation and adaptability

(2 marks)

37 Are the following statements relating to employment protection legislation true or false?

	True	False
Wrongful dismissal relates to the method of dismissal	○	○
Unfair dismissal is dismissal that has breached the contract of employment	○	○

(2 marks)

38 A leader may be distinguished from a manager by lack of dependency on:

○ Personal power

○ Position power

○ Physical power

(1 mark)

39 Which of the following is not an objective of personal development?

○ Providing justification for a promotion.

○ Improving performance in an existing job.

○ Career development.

○ Acquiring transferable skills and competences.

(1 mark)

40 Dan is a very valuable member of staff and so his manager, Lee, wants to make sure that he remains motivated and happy in his job.

Lee knows that Dan has a high desire for success in everything that he does. Lee therefore wants to give Dan appropriate work to fulfil this desire.

Required

Which of the following features would **NOT** help to keep Dan motivated?

○ A degree of personal responsibility

○ Goals that may not be achievable

○ Realistic levels of risk-taking

○ An element of clear feedback

(2 marks)

41 The country of Sportland has recently had a downturn in its economy and is facing a recession.

Many businesses are making large numbers of staff redundant, although all businesses are expected to recover in the long term.

Required

What type of unemployment is this?

○ Frictional

○ Structural

○ Cyclical

(1 mark)

42 Which of the following is most clearly a sign of an ineffective group?

○ Internal disagreement and criticism

○ Competition with other groups

○ Passive acceptance of work decisions.

○ Achievement of individual targets

(2 marks)

43 What does the term diversity mean?

○ A business invests in many different activities in order to reduce risks

○ The business does not discriminate against any groups based on gender or ethnic background

○ The composition of the workforce reflects the population as a whole

○ A policy of fast tracking individuals from minority groups

(2 marks)

44 Which of the following is **NOT** a valid advantages of having accounting standards?

○ They discourage confusing variations in the methods used to prepare accounts

○ They enforce conformity because companies are never allowed to depart from a standard.

○ They are less rigid than enforcing conformity by legislation.

○ They provide a focal point for debate and discussions about accounting practice.

(2 marks)

45 Michael is conducting his appraisal interviews. His philosophy is simple. He tells the subordinate in question how he has been assessed - good and bad - and then gives him or her a chance to put questions, suggest improvement targets, explaining shortcomings, identifying problems.

Required

This approach is known as the:

○ 'tell and sell' method.

○ 'tell and listen' method.

○ 'problem-solving' approach

○ peer rating method.

(2 marks)

46 Which type of control aims to intercept data being transmitted into a system from outside via the internet?

○ Access controls

○ Firewall

○ Data verification controls

(1 mark)

Section B

ALL SIX questions are compulsory and MUST be attempted

47 Here is information about to four companies:

Company W consists mostly of project teams and task forces. The company has no clear leader and performance of the company is judged by results.

Company X is a well-established company with a formal structure. Employees are not particularly ambitious and do not overstep the boundaries of their authority.

Company Y is a company that exists to serve the individuals that make up the company.

Company Z is a small company run by an entrepreneur who makes all of the major business decisions. There are few formal rules across the company.

Required

(a) What type of culture is demonstrated by each company using Harrison and Hany's cultural stereotypes?

Company W	▼
Company X	▼
Company Y	▼
Company Z	▼

Pull down list

- Person culture
- Power culture
- Role culture
- Task culture

(2 marks)

(b) A committee includes the following roles:

- Chair
- Secretary

Required

For each of the following roles, state whether it is the duty of the Chair or the secretary

	Chair	Secretary
Give ruling on disputed points	O	O
Taking notes during a meeting	O	O
Communicating decisions taken in a meeting	O	O
Fixing the date of a meeting	O	O

(2 marks)

(Total = 4 marks)

---

48 (a) Each of the following individuals works for Carberry Co.

Julie takes stationery from the office stationery cupboard home so that she can make notes for a work meeting.

Ken has borrowed money from the office charity collection with the intention of repaying it as soon as possible.

Michael is struggling to meet his deadline for a report for the Chief Executive, so he asks one of his colleagues to assist him.

Nadia has adjusted the three-year cash flow forecasts for the company to increase the chances of obtaining a bank loan.

Required

State whether each individual's behaviour is ethical or unethical.

	Ethical	Unethical
Julie	O	O
Ken	O	O
Nadia	O	O
Michael	O	O

(2 marks)

(b) There are different views about how much external pressures can modify business objectives.

The view that objectives emerge from the differing views of shareholders, managers, employees, customers, suppliers and the public, but they are not all selected or controlled by management is known as the_____.

Which phrase correctly fills the blank above?

O Stakeholder view of company objective

O Framework of rules

O Consensus theory

(2 marks)

(Total = 4 marks)

49   (a) State whether the following statements about internal audit are true or false.

	True	False
All organisations need to have an internal audit department.	O	O
The internal auditor should be independent	O	O
The internal auditor should report to the Finance Director.	O	O
The internal auditor may perform a social audit.	O	O
The internal auditor may review compliance with laws and regulations	O	O
Internal audit will assess the risk management and control culture of an organisation.	O	O

(2 marks)

(b) Do the following statements relate to

- Internal audit
- External audit
- Both internal and external audit

Work relates to the operations of the organisation	▼
Objective of work is to express an opinion on the financial statements	▼

Pull down list

- Both internal and external audit
- External audit
- Internal audit

(2 marks)

(Total = 4 marks)

---

50   Luis, Charlotte, Roy and Jessica all work for QWE Co

Required

(a) For each person, select the appropriate development tool for the situation:

Luis has just completed his first three-month period with QWE Co and is keen to get feedback on his performance level and areas for development.	▼
Charlotte is new to her department and needs an experienced employee to show her how to perform the tasks that she will be expected to do.	▼
Roy has just joined the company, but has ambitions to become a manager at QWE Co and wants to know how he can reach this goal in the long run.	▼
Jessica has just been told she will need to relocate in order to continue working in the marketing department of QWE. She is concerned about several issues arising from this relocation and wants to work through these issues.	▼

Pull down list

- Appraisal
- Coaching
- Counselling
- Mentoring

(2 marks)

(b) Which **TWO** of the following are benefits to an organisation of using counselling?

☐ Identifies future managers

☐ Demonstrates commitment to employees

☐ Establishes learning targets

☐ Determines pay increases

☐ Reduces labour turnover

☐ Provides a role model for employees

(2 marks)

(Total = 4 marks)

51 (a) For each of the following teams, identify the correct stage from Tuckman's model.

Team W has been performing well for some time. It is now concentrating on self-maintenance and the initial task that the team was formed for is beginning to get overlooked.	▼
Team X is fulfilling its objectives, unhindered by difficulties of growth and development.	▼
Team Y consists of members trying to impress their own personality. There is wariness from each team member about introducing new ideas and the objectives of the team are currently unclear.	▼
Team Z is beginning to see agreements about individual requirements and expectations. Procedures are evolving which should bring in methodical working for the team.	▼

Pull down list

- Dorming
- Forming
- Norming
- Performing

(2 marks)

(b) Which **TWO** of the following steps would help to create a team identity?

- ☐ Dealing with conflict within the team openly
- ☐ Creating a separate space, either physical or virtual, for the team
- ☐ Creating a team uniform
- ☐ Encouraging interpersonal relationships within the team
- ☐ Encouraging competition with other groups

(2 marks)

(Total = 4 marks)

---

52 Highgate is a private limited company which is run by the three founders who are John, Oliver and Jemma. The family members also own 80% of the shares and as such control the company as well as running it.

The other 20% of the company is held by private investors who don't have any say in the day-to-day running of the business.

Highgate does not have many customers and is heavily reliant on one main customer (Archway) for a significant percentage of its revenue.

Required

(a) For each of the following, indicate whether they are internal, connected or external stakeholders.

	Stakeholder type
John, Oliver and Jemma	▼
The 20% shareholders	▼
Archway	▼

Pull down list

- Connected stakeholders
- External stakeholder
- Internal stakeholder

(2 marks)

(b) Which **TWO** of the following are advantages of a public sector organisation over a limited company?

☐ Fairness

☐ Accountability

☐ Efficiency

☐ Political interference

☐ No restriction on size

(2 marks)

(Total = 4 marks)

Answers

DO NOT TURN THIS PAGE UNTIL YOU HAVE
COMPLETED THE MOCK EXAM

Section A

1   The correct answer is: Simple structure

    Rationale: Mintzberg described this structure, where the strategic apex exerts a 'pull' to centralise.

2   The correct answer is: Suppression

    Rationale: Josephine has smoothed over the problem to preserve working relationships, which is a suppression response.

    Josephine has responded to the situation and so denial is not the correct answer. You may have hesitated over compromise but Josephine has imposed a solution, she has not bargained or negotiated, so this cannot be the correct solution. Again you may have felt tempted by dominance, but this would lead to lingering resentment and the scenario states that all parties feel happy with the result and so this cannot be the correct answer either.

3   The correct answer is: Dishonesty, motivation and opportunity.

    Rationale: If one or more of them can be eliminated, the risk of fraud is reduced.

4   The correct answers are:

    •   Employees who notice fraud or malpractice in a workplace are obliged to reveal their knowledge to external authorities immediately. - **False**

    •   The term given to an employee who reveals fraud or malpractice occurring in a workplace is whistle-blower - **True**

    Rationale: Employees are not obliged to reveal their suspicions to external authorities. They may risk breaching important codes of ethics such as confidentiality. Alternatively they may feel that informing a senior member of staff would be adequate.

5   The correct answer is: Quantity, quality, price, delivery.

    Rationale: Some of the options include the word 'product', which is part of the marketing mix. Purchasing makes a major contribution to cost and quality management in any business.

6   The correct answers are:

    •   Social responsibility

    •   Independence

    •   Scepticism

    Rationale: Moderation and authority, whilst admirable in many contexts - are not a professional qualities specifically identified as expected of an accountant.

7   The correct answers are:

    •   The audit partner is married to the finance director of an audit client.

    •   A senior member of the audit team is in a relationship with the financial controller of an audit client.

    •   The financial controller of a company resigned from the company three months ago, is now working for the company's auditors and is working on the audit of the company she previously worked for.

    Rationale: The ACCA's Code of Ethics and Conduct sets out that objectivity is threatened or may appear to be threatened as a consequence of a family or other close personal or business relationship. The threat is greater if the individuals concerned are in senior positions at the client or the audit firm. The threat is less where the individuals concerned are not directly involved in the audit or the financial function. A member should not personally take part in the conduct of the audit of a company if he or she has been an officer or employee of the company during the previous two years. Normal social relationships between audit partners and their clients (such as attending the annual dinner) do not necessarily constitute a threat to objectivity.

8   The correct answer is: Virtual

Rationale: Virtual teams and organisations are becoming more common as the potential of ICT is exploited. You should be aware of the extent to which distance is no longer a barrier to team working (or to staff selection, or outsourcing of tasks).

Multi-disciplinary teams bring together individuals from different functions, to pool their skills, experience and knowledge: a virtual team may be multi-disciplinary, but a multi-disciplinary team need not be virtual.

The same applies to multi-skilled teams (which bring together individuals, each of whom can switch flexibly between tasks) and project teams (formed to complete a particular project).

9   The correct answer is: Demand is based on the prices of the present time period.

Rationale: Price instability can be caused by problems on the supply side such as high prices in a previous period. Non-controllable factors influencing supply means there is an uncertain level of supply which will cause price fluctuations. Low price elasticity of demand and supply create price instability as small changes in the level of demand or supply lead to significant price changes.

10   The correct answer is: Professional body

Rationale: External stakeholder groups – the government, local authorities, pressure groups, the community at large, professional bodies – are likely to have quite diverse objectives.

11   The correct answers are:

- High levels of inflation - **No**
- Economic growth - **Yes**
- Zero unemployment - **No**
- Balance of payments equilibrium - **Yes**

Rationale: Macro-economic policy objectives relate to managing economic growth, inflation, unemployment and the balance of payments.

The macroeconomic policy is to achieve full employment, meaning unemployment is low (not zero) and involuntary unemployment is short-term.

Low, stable inflation is a macroeconomic policy target.

12   The correct answer is: Distortion

Rationale: Noise is the other main type of communication problem.

Noise usually takes the form of distractions and interferences in the environment in which communication takes place, affecting the clarity, accuracy or even arrival of the message.

Redundancy is a useful principle to apply to communication. If you use more than one channel of communication, even if the message fails to get through on one means, it may still arrive on another.

Feedback is the response that indicates to the sender that his message has (or has not) been received, properly interpreted and understood.

13   The correct answer is: Accounts, shareholders

Rationale: There are usually detailed regulations on what the accounts must contain and this enables shareholders to assess how well the directors (or management board) have run the company.

14 The correct answer is: An ad hoc committee

Rationale: An ad hoc committee is a fact-finding or special committee which achieves its specified purpose, reports and then disbands - like a task-force team.

An executive committee has powers to govern or administer.

A standing committee is formed for a particular purpose, but on a permanent basis, with routine business to perform at regular meetings.

A joint committee is not - as it may sound - simply an interdisciplinary team: it is a body formed to co-ordinate the activities of two or more committees.

15 The correct answer is: A business owned by its workers or customers.

Rationale: In many large commercial organisations, ownership is separate from control, but they are not cooperatives. A business that works closely with another is not a cooperative.

16 The correct answer is: Develop; tasks; guidance.

Rationale: Coaching is an approach whereby a trainee is put under the guidance of an experienced employee who shows the trainee how to perform tasks.

17 The correct answer is: The means by which a firm increases the worth of its products.

Activities incur costs, and, in combination with other activities, provide a product or service which earns revenue.

18 The correct answer is: Recession, depression, recovery, boom.

Rationale: Business cycles or trade cycles are the continual sequence of rapid growth in national income, followed by a slowdown in growth and then a fall in national income.

19 The correct answers are:

- Integrity based
- Compliance based

Rationale: A compliance-based approach is primarily designed to ensure that the company acts within the letter of the law and that violations are prevented, detected and punished.

20 The correct answer is: Procedures and processes according to which an organisation is directed and controlled.

Rationale: All the other options are aspects of corporate governance, but not a complete definition.

21 The correct answer is: Delegation, assertiveness, communication and goal planning

Rationale: Willy needs to delegate because he is overloaded, and his subordinates are bored. He needs assertiveness to say 'no', where appropriate, to his subordinates and even to his boss. He also needs to practise goal-planning to break down his workload and to prioritise and schedule his tasks.

You may have paused with the thought that Willy's communication skills and inclinations are, if anything, too good. However, they are not: he wastes time on communication. Learning to read faster, to write more concise reports and to sort out essential from non-essential communications also come into this area.

22 The correct answer is: Refuse the offer and report Felipe to the head of the audit firm.

Accepting the offer and keeping quiet is dishonest. Accepting the offer and then reporting Felipe anonymously shows a lack of integrity. Doing nothing in order to avoid conflict may be understandable but shows a lack of professional behaviour.

23 The correct answer is: Plant

Other characteristics of the plant include being unorthodox and becoming too preoccupied to communicate effectively.

24 The correct answer is: Automation

Automation is where systems perform repetitive and routine tasks. Booking bank transactions automatically is an example of this.

Artificial intelligence implies that the system learns from data and is therefore able to assist a human operator make business decisions.

Distributed ledger technology, also referred to as blockchain, is where several organisations or individuals share an agreed record of events. In this case, the record of events is only the banks record - there are no other parties that have the right to update the records.

Cloud computing refers to computer software or hardware resources that are accessed via the internet. The accounting package might well be a cloud based system, but that is not mentioned in the question.

25 The correct answers are:
   - Line management - **Yes**
   - Colleagues - **Yes**
   - The appraisee - **Yes**
   - Customers - **Yes**

Rationale: The 360 degree appraisal is a technique that involves feedback being obtained from various different sources who come into contact with the appraisee.

This ensures a much more thorough and comprehensive assessment than would be possible with a straightforward line management appraisal.

26 The correct answer is: High levels of staff turnover

This will be examined in the internal position audit of the company rather than the environmental analysis which looks at matters external to the company.

27 The correct answer is: Independent non-executive directors

Independent non-executive directors should form the remuneration committee who should set directors' remuneration.

28 The correct answer is: Disguising, converting, transferring or removing criminal property.

Purchasing stolen goods is not an offence linked to money laundering.

Failure of an engineering company to obtain satisfactory evidence of identity where a transaction is for a small amount is not an offence linked to money laundering. **Membership is voluntary; Communication is open and informal.**

29 The correct answers are:
   - Recording transactions in 'books of prime entry'
   - Preparing financial statements for the use of external shareholders

Rationale: Financial accounting is concerned with preparing financial statements for external shareholders. It starts with the recording on transactions in the books of prime entry, includes categorising those transactions appropriately, and on the basis of this, preparing financial statements.

Budgets and variance reports are used by internal management and are therefore part of the role of the management accountant.

30 The correct answers are:

- A database of all suppliers used by the business to date, with capability to blanket email invitation to tender requests.
- Access to an online marketplace set up as a joint venture in conjunction with other large vehicle manufacturers.

Both of these options should mean that Velma plc has access to a large number of suppliers who will then have to compete on price & terms to win each contract.

To discuss employee performance; To identify an employee's development needs.

Rationale: There are drawbacks to linking appraisal to salary review, not least that there may not be enough money to reward the employee for their performance.

31 The correct answer is: Statement 1 only

Note that formal and informal organisations are NOT mutually exclusive. The informal organisation is the network of informal inter-personal and inter-group relationships that exists within every organisation.

This is likely to have its own priorities and even objectives, though they may not be easily apparent or consistent over time and across the breadth of the informal organisation. These objectives and priorities may or may not be the same as those of the formal organisation.

Statement 3 requires some thought: a strong, close-knit informal organisation can improve morale and communication within the formal organisation, but can also divert energy and loyalty from it. Also, if the objectives of the informal organisation are not aligned with those of the formal, there is danger of serious conflict. **Stimulate, Raise**

32 The correct answer is: Operational managers

Operational managers should be alert for signs of petty fraud, as well as checking the work staff have done and also being aware of what staff are doing.

33 The correct answer is: Power

Rationale: The power culture is based around personalities, flexibility and informality; this is most appropriate to simple organisations.

34 The correct answers are:

- Drucker argued that developing people is a management function. - **True**
- Drucker argued that the manager of a business has one basic function - economic performance - **True**

Drucker emphasised the economic objectives of managers in business but he also grouped the work of managers into five categories including:

- Setting objectives
- Organising the work
- Motivating employees
- Measurement
- Developing people

35 The correct answer is: Layering

Max's firm has been involved in the transfer of monies from business to business to conceal the original source.

36 The correct answer is: Innovation and adaptability

The great advantage of external recruitment is in bringing 'new blood' and a fresh viewpoint to potentially 'stale' situations : therefore innovation and adaptability is the correct answer.

Straightforward enough, once you've worked out the relevance and implications of the four options. There are pressures to promote from within, from the familiarity of the promotee: reduction of risk - he is a 'known quantity' to the organisation, unlike the external recruit, with whom it will be risking possible disappointment or incompatibility. Promotion of insiders is also visible proof of the organisation's willingness to develop its employees' careers, which can enhance motivation and avoid some resentments. Promotees will not have to be instructed, coached, 'broken-in' and otherwise 'socialised' into the methods, norms, politics, culture and personal relationships of the organisation to the extent that an outsider will.

37 The correct answers are:
    • Wrongful dismissal relates to the method of dismissal - **True**
    • Unfair dismissal is dismissal that has breached the contract of employment - **False**

Dismissal that has breached the contract of employment is wrongful dismissal not unfair dismissal.

38 The correct answer is: Position power

The only valuable definitions of leadership, as distinguished from management, stress its capacity to secure from others more than mere compliance with the requirements imposed by organisational authority. A leader is therefore someone who does not have to depend on position power alone.

39 The correct answer is: Providing justification for a promotion.

Personal development implies a wide range of activities. A personal development plan is a clear developmental action plan for an individual which incorporates a wide set of developmental opportunities, including formal training.

40 The correct answer is: Goals that may not be achievable

Goals that present a huge challenge will not achieve the manager's wish to keep Dan motivated: they are more likely to oppress and worry him. Dan's manager should give him moderately difficult tasks and goals that present a challenge and an opportunity to display ability.

41 The correct answer is: Cyclical

This is cyclical unemployment. During decline and recession years, the demand for output and jobs falls, and unemployment rises to a high level.

When the economy picks up again, demand for jobs picks up again as well. This is why it is cyclical unemployment.

42 The correct answer is: Passive acceptance of work decisions.

Members of an effectively functioning group will take an active interest in decisions affecting their work, rather than passively accepting them.

Internal disagreement and criticism can constitute healthy communication within the group in that they will encourage compromise and agreement, rather than having decisions and opinions forced upon the group members

Competition with other groups brings the group closer together as the members work towards a common goal in competing with other groups perceived as a threat or an enemy.

43 The correct answer is: The composition of the workforce reflects the population as a whole

A business invests in many different activities in order to reduce risks is an example of diversification.

Non discrimination is likely to be part of diversity, but diversity goes further than non-discrimination.

A policy of fast tracking individuals from minority backgrounds may help to achieve a more diverse mix on employees - however, the organisation could be accused of "positive discrimination".

44 The correct answer is: They enforce conformity because companies are never allowed to depart from a standard.

It is not true that companies can never depart from a standard. In rare cases, it may be necessary to depart from a standard in order to show a true and fair view.

45 The correct answer is: 'tell and listen' method.

Three types of approach to appraisal interviews are identified by Maier. Michael's approach is 'tell and listen' method. It's a fairly participative approach, with the assessor taking on the dual role of critic and counsellor, and does not assume that the sole key to performance improvement is in the employee himself:

'Problem-solving' approach is a step further in this direction, where the assessor abandons the role of critic altogether. Discussion is centred not on the assessment but on the employee's work problems, which are worked through together with the assessor/counsellor.

'Tell and sell' method is the more one-sided approach. The manager tells the subordinate how he's been assessed, and then tries to 'sell' (gain acceptance of) the evaluation and the improvement plan.

Peer rating is where an individual is assessed and counselled by colleagues of the same level in the organisation hierarchy, rather than by his superiors, not the case here.

46 The correct answer is: Firewall

This is a system that monitors incoming and outgoing network traffic. a network.

Section B

47 (a)

Company W	Task culture
Company X	Role culture
Company Y	Person culture
Company Z	Power culture

(b) The correct answers are:

- Give ruling on disputed points - **Chair**
- Taking notes during a meeting - **Secretary**
- Communicating decisions taken in a meeting - **Secretary**
- Fixing the date of a meeting - **Secretary**

48 (a) The correct answers are:

- Julie - **Ethical**
- Ken - **Unethical**
- Nadia - **Unethical**
- Michael - **Ethical**

(b) The correct answer is: Consensus theory

With the stakeholder view, management does select or control all the objectives.

49 (a) The correct answers are:

- All organisations need to have an internal audit department. - **False**
- The internal auditor should be independent - **True**
- The internal auditor should report to the Finance Director. - **False**
- The internal auditor may perform a social audit. - **True**
- The internal auditor may review compliance with laws and regulations - **True**
- Internal audit will assess the risk management and control culture of an organisation. - **True**

(b)

Work relates to the operations of the organisation	Internal audit
Objective of work is to express an opinion on the financial statements	External audit

50 (a)

Luis has just completed his first three-month period with QWE Co and is keen to get feedback on his performance level and areas for development.	Appraisal
Charlotte is new to her department and needs an experienced employee to show her how to perform the tasks that she will be expected to do.	Coaching
Roy has just joined the company, but has ambitions to become a manager at QWE Co and wants to know how he can reach this goal in the long run.	Mentoring

Jessica has just been told she will need to relocate in order to continue working in the marketing department of QWE. She is concerned about several issues arising from this relocation and wants to work through these issues.	Counselling

Justification:

- Luis wants feedback and development points, which are part of an appraisal process.
- Charlotte will benefit from coaching where an experienced employee will guide her through the tasks.
- Roy is looking for a long-term mentoring programme.
- The aim of counselling is to help a person work through a problem.

(b) The correct answers are:

- Demonstrates commitment to employees
- Reduces labour turnover

Counselling mostly shows care for employees, which can reduce labour turnover and absenteeism.

51 (a)

Team W has been performing well for some time. It is now concentrating on self-maintenance and the initial task that the team was formed for is beginning to get overlooked.	Dorming
Team X is fulfilling its objectives, unhindered by difficulties of growth and development.	Performing
Team Y consists of members trying to impress their own personality. There is wariness from each team member about introducing new ideas and the objectives of the team are currently unclear.	Forming
Team Z is beginning to see agreements about individual requirements and expectations. Procedures are evolving which should bring in methodical working for the team.	Norming

The other options would all help to create team solidarity.

(b) The correct answers are:

- Creating a separate space, either physical or virtual, for the team
- Creating a team uniform

The other options would all help to create team solidarity.

52 (a)

	Stakeholder type
John, Oliver and Jemma	Internal stakeholder
The 20% shareholders	Connected stakeholders
Archway	Connected stakeholders

Explanation

- John, Oliver and Jemima: Shareholders who are also management are internal stakeholders.
- The 20% shareholders: Shareholders who have no say in running the company are connected stakeholders.

- Archway: Customers are connected stakeholders.

(b) The correct answers are:

- Fairness
- Efficiency

Accountability and Political interference are disadvantages of public sector organisations. No restriction on size is an advantage of a limited company.

Tell us what you think

Got comments or feedback on this book? Let us know.
Use your QR code reader:

Or, visit:
https://bppgroup.fra1.qualtrics.com/jfe/form/SV_cuphESF344D68Mm